The Hitchhiker's Guide to Computer Games

Author: Dennis Michael Heine

Index

Chapter 1: The Birth of Computer Gaming

The world of computer gaming began in the 1950s and 60s with simple programs on massive mainframe computers. The earliest games were basic simulations, but they set the stage for what was to come. **Let's explore this fascinating beginning** of an industry that would grow beyond anyone's wildest expectations.

The Dawn of Computer Games

In the 1950s, the idea of playing games on computers was a novel concept. These early programs were created by computer scientists who saw the potential for simple entertainment. Let's see how it all began.

The first computer game is commonly accepted to be 'Tennis for Two.'

'Tennis for Two' holds a significant place in gaming history as one of the earliest known computer games. Developed in 1958, this pioneering game introduced thc idea of interactive entertainment on computers. It simulated a simple tennis match viewed from the side, displaying the movement of a "ball" on a two-dimensional court with players controlling the game's trajectory.

Although the graphics were basic, especially by today's standards, 'Tennis for Two' captured the imagination of its audience and demonstrated the potential of video game technology. This game is credited not only for its innovative concept but also for planting the seeds for future video gaming milestones.

Created in 1958 by physicist William Higinbotham to entertain visitors at Brookhaven National Laboratory.

William Higinbotham, a physicist at Brookhaven National Laboratory, developed 'Tennis for Two' as a clever exhibition piece during the lab's annual public visitors' day. The primary aim was to create an engaging demonstration that showcased the scientific capabilities of computer technology in a friendly and accessible way.

Higinbotham's background in science and his curiosity about nuclear energy applications inspired him to leverage his expertise to bring something unique to the audience. Surprisingly, this impromptu creation left an indelible mark on electronic entertainment history, going beyond its initial intent and becoming a cornerstone for future interactive technologies.

The game ran on an analog computer and used an oscilloscope for the display.

'Tennis for Two' was technologically innovative for its time, operating on an analog computer compared to the digital systems used today. Specifically, it utilized an analog Donner Model 30 computer, which calculated the ball's trajectory based on player input. The game's output was displayed on an oscilloscope, reflecting the technological constraints and ingenuity of the era.

This setup leveraged the oscilloscope’s ability to depict moving graphics, showcasing a rudimentary tennis court and ball in motion. Despite these technological limitations, the experience was interactive and immersive, highlighting early creativity in the gaming industry.

'Tennis for Two' wasn't made for commercial purposes, but rather as a demonstration of technology.

The creation of 'Tennis for Two' served a specific demonstration purpose, deviating from the commercial intentions typical of later video games. During the late 1950s, commercializing such technology was not yet conceivable. Instead, the game was a tool to engage scientific minds and the public audience in a fresh and entertaining way.

Higinbotham never patented or commercially marketed his creation, reflecting its non-commercial intent. Instead, 'Tennis for Two' demonstrated how technology could be molded to provide joy and engagement, foundational principles that would later underpin the gaming industry.

It set a precedent for using computers for entertainment, paving the way for future developments.

By employing a computer for the sole purpose of entertainment, 'Tennis for Two' set a transformative precedent that would echo throughout subsequent decades. It challenged the perception of computers being purely functional devices, instead showcasing their leisure potential.

This initiative laid the groundwork for future development in the video game industry. As technology advanced, the seeds planted by 'Tennis for Two' grew into a vibrant industry. This innovation fostered an environment where computers became not only tools of logic and calculation but also facilitators of creativity and fun.

Spacewar! The First Major Breakthrough

In 1962, a group of students at the Massachusetts Institute of Technology (MIT) created a game that would become a cornerstone of computer gaming. This section dives into the significance of Spacewar!.

Spacewar! was developed by Steve Russell and his team on a PDP-1 mainframe computer.

Spacewar! was conceived and brought into existence in 1962 by Steve Russell, along with his inventive team at the Massachusetts Institute of Technology (MIT). This game was developed on a PDP-1 (Programmed Data Processor-1), which was one of the earliest mainframe computers available at that time. The PDP-1 was known for its interactive capabilities, which made it an attractive platform for Russell's pioneering project. His efforts were supported by fellow enthusiasts, including Martin Graetz and Wayne Wiitanen, who contributed to programming and design ideas. This collaborative project was pivotal, as it resulted in one of the first computer games with real-time graphics and interactive gameplay, elements that laid the groundwork for future game development.

It was a two-player game where each player controlled a spaceship, trying to destroy the other.

At its core, Spacewar! was a thrilling two-player game that required strategic maneuvering and precise shooting. Each player controlled a spaceship, engaged in a combat scenario with the primary objective of destroying the opponent's ship. The spaceships were depicted as simplistic graphical representations but provided a challenging experience through the game's underlying physics engine. This involved simulating gravity from a central star, around which the spaceships orbited. Players had to skillfully navigate their ships, avoiding gravitational pulls and obstacles, while simultaneously engaging in combat with their adversary. This direct player-versus-player interaction made Spacewar! an engaging and compctitive endeavor, setting the stage for multiplayer gaming in the future.

Spacewar! introduced many elements common in modern games, like real-time graphics and user interaction.

Spacewar! was revolutionary in its introduction of features that are now fundamental in modern gaming. The implementation of real-time graphics allowed players to experience a dynamic and immersive play environment, simulating an active and responsive outer space battleground. This incorporation of real-time feedback and interaction transcended the era's typical batch processing tasks seen in computers. Additionally, Spacewar! allowed players to interact directly with the game through input devices—early forms of game controllers—enhancing the player's engagement and control. These features laid essential groundwork, influencing the design and functionality of countless future games, and showcasing the potential of computers as interactive entertainment systems.

The game was distributed to other institutions with PDP-1 computers, spreading its influence.

Following its development at MIT, Spacewar! rapidly spread as a fascinating display of technological prowess. As other institutions acquired PDP-1 computers, Steve Russell and his team made the code freely available, allowing duplication and adjustments by other enthusiasts. This open distribution approach meant that Spacewar! could be experienced elsewhere, contributing significantly to its adoption and cultural impact. Institutions such as Stanford University embraced and modified the game, reinforcing its reputation and reach within academic circles. This early example of software distribution and collaboration underscored the nascent idea of sharing digital creations across networks, highlighting community-driven development long before the rise of the internet and open-source movements.

Spacewar! is often regarded as the first influential computer game to gain a following.

Spacewar! is widely acknowledged as a trailblazing force within the realm of computer gaming, gaining a dedicated following and influencing future game development. With its captivating gameplay and interactive elements, it commanded the attention of students and researchers, sparking interest and passion in computer science and entertainment technology. The game's ability to garner a following was showcased by its continued presence and popularity at institutions equipped with suitable hardware. Spacewar!'s development and subsequent spread marked a significant milestone, demonstrating not only technical innovation but also the burgeoning potential for computing technology as a medium for complex and engaging entertainment. This recognition has cemented its status as a foundational game in the history of computer gaming.

The Pioneer Influence of Early Games

These early games were more than just small curiosities; they laid the groundwork for future innovators. Let's consider how these pioneers influenced computer gaming history.

Early games served as a testbed for programming and innovation in human-computer interaction.

In the infancy of computer gaming, early games such as *OXO* and *Tennis for Two* were not just simple pastimes; they were a fertile ground for developing programming skills and experimenting with human-computer interaction (HCI). As programmers crafted these games, they encountered and addressed numerous challenges in interfacing with hardware, optimizing software efficiency, and inventing new ways for humans to interact with machines.

These technological and philosophical obstacles spurred innovation, leading to advancements that resonated beyond the realm of gaming, influencing fields like artificial intelligence and computer graphics. Each iteration of early games honed the expertise of those involved, progressively elevating the complexity and capabilities of computer systems. Through these trials, early gaming established a feedback loop of experimentation and learning that remains a cornerstone of game development today.

They inspired future generations of developers, showing what was possible with emerging technology.

The pioneering efforts in early computer games ignited the imaginations of future developers. By proving that simple programs could enthrall and engage, these games provided a glimpse into the potential of digital entertainment. Young programmers of the 1960s and 70s looked to these early works as proof that the gaming experience could intersect with emerging technology to produce profound results.

Employing primitive graphics and rudimentary interfaces, these games encouraged subsequent developers to dream bigger and push technological boundaries further. Their ability to captivate despite technological limitations sowed the seeds of a burgeoning industry, inspiring a continuum of innovation that would evolve into the multifaceted gaming experiences we cherish today. Over time, these foundational games would be revisited, serving as both a nostalgic homage and a blueprint for creativity and innovation.

Some game features, like player control and scoring, became standard in the industry.

As the first wave of computer games emerged, they inadvertently established conventions that would become staples across the gaming industry. The concepts of player control and scoring were among the first to crystallize. For example, games like *Spacewar!* allowed user input to influence the game state, introducing interactive elements that distinguished them from passive entertainment forms like films or books.

Scoring systems added a competitive dimension, compelling players to strive for improvement and mastery. Such mechanics not only provided instant feedback but also extended the longevity and replayability of games. These standards have endured, forming a crucial element of video game design. By laying this foundation, early games equipped future developers with a toolkit to craft engaging and challenging experiences.

These simple games encouraged experimentation, which is still a vital part of the gaming industry.

Experimentation has been a driving force in gaming since its inception, with early games serving as both laboratory and canvas for creative and technical exploration. Developers in the nascent stages of computer gaming were not burdened by commercial expectations, allowing the freedom to experiment with game mechanics, narratives, and technology.

This spirit of experimentation forged an environment where trial and error were not only accepted but encouraged. It paved the way for unique concepts to be tested and implemented, which enabled the diversity of genres and experiences available in gaming today. By nurturing a culture that values innovation and creativity, these early games set an enduring precedent that remains integral to game development and design.

They demonstrated an appetite for interactive entertainment that would later fuel the gaming revolution.

The early computer games tapped into a latent demand for interactive entertainment, revealing a public enthusiasm that would ultimately propel the gaming revolution. As early as the 1960s, audiences showed a keen interest in experiences that allowed them to participate in narratives rather than merely observe them.

This appetite provided a business case for expanding the scope of gaming beyond academia and research laboratories, prompting entrepreneurs and companies to invest in further development. The early games' ability to captivate players set a precedent for more sophisticated and immersive entertainment experiences. As gaming technology and design evolved, this demand snowballed, transforming gaming into a global industry and cultural phenomenon that continues to expand and captivate audiences worldwide.

The Role of Academic Institutions

Academic settings played a critical role in the early days of gaming, offering resources and fertile ground for experimentation. Here’s how educational institutions contributed to gaming history.

Universities provided access to expensive mainframe computers, crucial for developing early games.

In the nascency of computer gaming, mainframe computers were not only a marvel of technology but an expensive asset well beyond the reach of hobbyists. Universities were among the few institutions that possessed these powerful machines, providing a fertile environment for innovation and experimentation. These colossal computers, often the size of entire rooms, were housed in research labs at academic institutions.

Students and researchers were granted the unique opportunity to experiment with these machines outside of their originally intended purposes. The presence of mainframe computers at universities such as MIT enabled students to explore their interests in computing and gaming. Without the access provided by these institutions, many early games might have never been developed, delaying the emergence of a vibrant gaming culture.

MIT and Stanford were among the key players in fostering early computer game development.

Massachusetts Institute of Technology (MIT) and Stanford University were pivotal in the early stages of computer game creation. At MIT, the creation of "Spacewar!" in 1962 marked one of the first known digital computer games. This game was developed by a group of students and researchers who wanted to optimize the capabilities of the PDP-1, an innovative computer for its time.

Similarly, at Stanford, the arrival of the ARPANET (the precursor to the internet) facilitated groundbreaking developments in computing. The university became a hub for passionate programmers and developers who employed computers for entertainment and experimentation. The momentum from these key institutions established a foundation for the evolution of gaming and tech culture that continues to influence the industry today.

These institutions became hotbeds of innovation, where students used computers for both research and fun.

Academic institutions transformed into thriving epicenters of innovation, whcre the lines between research and recreational computing often blurred. Students capitalized on the freedom to experiment with computing resources, pushing the boundaries of what these machines could achieve. For many, the experience provided by these institutions was a gateway to marrying academic research with creative pursuits.

The playful side of computing became increasingly appealing, leading to the development of interactive programs that evolved into early computer games. The spirit of exploration and discovery at these universities fueled both technological advancements and the growth of a community passionate about computers and gaming. This intersection of curiosity, creativity, and technology set the stage for future game development.

Open sharing of software in academic networks helped spread game developments across the globe.

A distinct ethos emerged within these academic circles: the open sharing of software. Universities fostered collaborative environments that encouraged sharing, leading to the distribution of code and ideas through educational networks. This culture of openness was instrumental in disseminating early game creations and innovations beyond mere local boundaries.

The networked academic communities allowed games and software tools to reach other institutions and development enthusiasts globally. This connectedness accelerated the pace of technological progress, with each campus contributing to a collective patchwork of knowledge and creativity. The foundational practice of sharing developments freely helped cement the idea that collaboration could propel the budding world of computer gaming.

The collaboration among students and researchers led to rapid technological advancements.

Within the collaborative environments of academic institutions, students and researchers worked side by side, fueling an unprecedented rate of technological progress. The open exchange of ideas and technical know-how among academic peers enabled complex problem-solving and innovation in the gaming sector. These collaborations were critical in advancing both software development and computing hardware.

The synergy among students and faculty members laid the groundwork for several seminal developments in gaming technology. By pooling skills and intellectual resources, early collaborators pushed the boundaries of what was deemed possible, setting milestones that would guide future developments in computer gaming. This tradition of collaborative effort is arguably one of the most potent forces that shaped the technological landscape of the gaming industry in its formative years.

Chapter 2: A Brief History of Pixels

Before Fortnite and Call of Duty took over, there was a magical era when **pixels** were the size of your thumbnail, and loving them was as much about using your imagination as it was about the game itself. Welcome to the start of our retro-gaming journey, where it all began with simple lines and a bouncing ball. Get ready to travel back to the days when graphics were measured in bits, and every game felt like a new adventure.

The Birth of Arcade Games

Welcome to the flashing lights and buzzing sounds of arcade games, where it all began! Let's look at how a clunky cabinet became every kid's favorite hangout spot.

Pong set the ball rolling in 1972, marking the start of the arcade craze.

In 1972, a simple game called **Pong** bounced its way onto the scene and forever changed the landscape of digital entertainment. Created by the legendary Atari, Pong was a basic tennis simulation consisting of two paddles and a ball. Despite its simplicity, it captured the imagination of players everywhere, laying the groundwork for the arcade revolution.

Pong's brilliance lay in its straightforward yet addictive gameplay. It didn't require players to spend hours learning complex rules or mastering intricate controls. Instead, it presented a fun challenge that anyone could pick up and play. This accessibility made it an instant hit and gave rise to the arcade game phenomenon, inspiring countless other games in its wake.

Atari, the company behind Pong, became a household name almost overnight.

Atari, co-founded by the innovative Nolan Bushnell, quickly became synonymous with video games in the 1970s. Following the smashing success of Pong, Atari positioned itself as a pioneering force in the burgeoning gaming industry. The company's ability to marry technology with entertainment appealed to a broad audience, turning arcades into popular social venues filled with eager players.

Its impact was such that Atari became more than just a brand; it was a cultural icon. Families gathered around Atari machines in malls, pizza parlors, and arcades across the country. This rapid rise to fame helped solidify video games as a viable form of entertainment, setting thc stage for future generations of gaming innovation.

Pac-Man's debut in 1980 introduced a blobby yellow hero who chomped his way into our hearts.

When **Pac-Man** was introduced by Namco in 1980, it wasn't just a game—it was a cultural phenomenon. Unlike the shooter games that dominated the era, Pac-Man offered players a new type of challenge: navigating mazes and devouring pellets while avoiding colorful, pesky ghosts.

The game’s protagonist, a lovable yellow circle with a never-ending appetite, quickly became a worldwide icon. PacMan's engaging gameplay and charming design turned it into an arcade favorite, attracting both seasoned players and newcomers. Its influence spread beyond the arcade, spawning merchandise, animations, and a fanbase that continues to celebrate its legacy today.

Space Invaders sparked the concept of high scores, turning friendly competition into fierce battles.

Space Invaders, released by Taito in 1978, shifted the landscape of gaming with its innovative introduction of high scores. This arcade shooter game not only challenged players to fend off waves of descending aliens but also encouraged them to surpass each other's scores, igniting a competitive spirit among gamers.

The concept of recording high scores added a new dimension to gaming, transforming mere playtime into intense sessions of bragging rights. Friends became rivals as they tried to outdo one another, spending countless quarters in the pursuit of virtual glory. This emphasis on competition became a staple in future games, creating a gaming culture that thrives to this day.

Arcades became social hubs for gamers before the era of online multiplayer.

Long before the rise of **online multiplayer**, arcades served as vibrant social hubs where gamers gathered to share their passion. These bustling venues were filled with the sounds of digital excitement, hosting an array of games that catered to diverse tastes and skill levels.

Arcades offered more than just entertainment; they provided a communal experience where players could meet, challenge, and learn from each other. Friendships were formed over shared high scores and strategy discussions, making arcades a crucial aspect of early gaming culture. This sense of community remains a cherished memory for many veteran gamers today.

These early games focused on simple, addictive gameplay that kept quarters flowing into machines.

In their heyday, arcade games capitalized on the very essence of gaming: **simplicity and addictiveness**. With straightforward mechanics and immediate appeal, these games were designed to hook players from the first moment they dropped a quarter into the machine.

The allure of beating personal bests or reaching new high scores kept players coming back for more, ensuring a steady stream of currency into the coin slots. This focus on gameplay over graphics made these early games timeless, proving that sometimes less truly is more. Even today, their charm and challenge continue to captivate new audiences, showcasing the enduring power of classic game design.

Home Consoles: Bringing the Arcade Experience Home

Remember when home consoles were the ultimate birthday wish? Let's explore how living rooms turned into digital playgrounds.

The Magnavox Odyssey, launched in 1972, kicked off home gaming, even if it looked like a toaster.

The **Magnavox Odyssey** holds the honor of being the world's first commercial home video game console. Despite its rather peculiar design resembling a kitchen appliance, this groundbreaking device brought the arcade into the comfort of living rooms worldwide. Created by Ralph H. Baer, often referred to as the "Father of Video Games," the Odyssey allowed players to enjoy simple but novel video games at home.

With its color overlays and controller paddles, the Odyssey didn't just introduce the concept of console gaming; it laid out a framework for all future systems. While the games were rudimentary by today's standards, featuring simple dots and lines, the excitement they generated was palpable. The Odyssey may have been a visual oddity, but it marked the genesis of a revolution, igniting imaginations and setting the stage for decades of home gaming evolution.

Atari 2600, released in 1977, popularized cartridges and brought bowling alleys home.

When the Atari 2600, initially called the *Atari VCS*, hit the market in 1977, it didn't just offer players a single game but a library they could build from an array of revolutionary cartridges. Suddenly, bowling, space adventures, and endless hours of fun were attainable without leaving home. The 2600's colorful graphics and engaging gameplay turned the console into an instant hit.

The introduction of interchangeable cartridges was a game changer. Gamers no longer had to be content with built-in games, as each new cartridge opened the door to a fresh universe. Packed with memorable titles like Space Invaders and Pitfall!, the Atari 2600 captivated millions and cemented its legacy as the entertainment centerpiece of the late '70s and early '80s—a true bowling alley in your living room.

The simplicity of connecting to a TV was a big deal back then—no HDMI required!

Back in the day when high-definition wasn't even a pipe dream, connecting a console to your TV was a straightforward affair. With no need for **HDMI cables**, resolutions, or complex setups, gaming was a plug-and-play experience. The magic lay in simple RF switches and coaxial cables that snaked into the back panels of boxy televisions, transforming them into windows to pixelated wonderlands.

This simplicity was a luxury that made video gaming accessible to the average household. Parents esteemed it for its ease, while kids cherished the immediate jump into games without a hitch. In the days of analog signals, even a bit of static was just part of the charm. It was an era defined by less complexity, amplifying the joy of pure, undistracted gaming playtime.

Nintendo's NES shook up the 1985 holiday season and gave us gaming legends like Mario.

The 1985 launch of the **Nintendo Entertainment System (NES)** was more than just a console debut—it was a cultural phenomenon. Seizing the spotlight during the holiday season, the NES pulled video gaming out of the shadowy downturn of the early '80s. It introduced the world to now-iconic franchises and characters, with *Super Mario Bros.* at the forefront.

With groundbreaking graphics and unforgettable music, the NES raised the bar for home entertainment. On-screen adventures were complemented by engaging narratives, a novel concept at the time. As Mario leapt over goombas and Bowser's castles, he also bounded into the hearts of millions, leading the charge for Nintendo's illustrious future in console gaming. The NES wasn't just a system; it was a beacon that heralded the new era of gaming bliss.

Sega joined the console race with the Genesis, known for 'blast processing' (or just fast games).

In 1989, **Sega** launched itself into the frenzy of the console wars with the Genesis, touting the ubiquitous (and infamous) marketing term "blast processing." While the actual impact of this technology was more myth than reality, the Genesis did deliver speedy and fluid gaming experiences, stealing the limelight with its fast-paced action titles.

Housing classic games like Sonic the Hedgehog, the Genesis garnered attention with its sleek design and a library that showcased vividly animated graphics actively rivaling Nintendo's offerings. Its success wasn't just through hardware. Sega's aggressive marketing and memorable commercials struck a chord with players eager for something edgy and new. The Genesis placed Sega as a formidable competitor, spurring an intense rivalry that defined an era. **These consoles laid the groundwork for future gaming generations with controllers and ports.**

The evolution of console gaming was not just about games; it was intrinsically tied to the design and functionality of **controllers and ports**. During this golden age, innovations in input devices transformed the way players engaged with their consoles. The Atari 2600's joystick, the NES's gamepad, and the complex button layouts of later systems like the Genesis set standards still recognized today.

Connectivity options saw notable advancements too, with ports evolving from simple connectors on CRT televisions to multi-functional interfaces supporting expansions and peripherals. Each technological leap facilitated more immersive and versatile gaming experiences. These early developments shaped ergonomic considerations and the creative possibilities of modern systems, laying a solid foundation that future generations of consoles would build upon into the expansive landscapes of gaming we enjoy today.

The Pixel Revolution

Ah, pixels! Tiny squares made of magic and dreams. Come along as we see how they evolved from jagged blobs to charming artwork.

Early games featured simple graphics but used pixels to create recognizable shapes.

In the early days of video gaming, simplicity was king. Developers worked with limited technology and had to make every pixel count. It's astonishing how they managed to create recognizable shapes with mere blocks of color. Despite jagged edges and low resolution, players could instantly identify paddle-like objects in **Pong** or chomp down on ghosts in *Pac-Man*.

These early graphical representations were the result of clever use of pixels, allowing the human brain to fill in the gaps and complete the image. Even basic shapes could convey familiarity, making these games beloved classics. This minimalist approach encouraged players to engage their imagination, bridging the gap between the game world and the pixels that formed it.

8-bit graphics were the sweet spot for blending creativity with technology limits.

The 8-bit era was a magical time in gaming history, a perfect balance between creative expression and technological constraints. With improved processing power, developers could craft more detailed visuals, yet they still had to think outside the box. The limitations of 8-bit graphics demanded creativity, and it was this necessity that sparked innovation.

Games like **Super Mario Bros.** and *The Legend of Zelda* showed how vibrant worlds and iconic characters could emerge from blocky pixels. The 8-bit palette was restrictive, yet developers leveraged it to its fullest, resulting in energetic environments that felt alive. This era demonstrated that when creativity meets constraint, magic happens.

Color palettes were humble, often just a handful of colors, yet they painted magical worlds.

In the early days of gaming, color was a luxury, and developers had to work with limited color palettes. With only a handful of hues, game designers painted their worlds in imaginative ways. These humble beginnings laid the foundation for the vibrant digital landscapes we see today.

Games like **Donkey Kong** and *Galaga* used a small set of colors to great effect, leveraging contrast and variation to simulate depth and style. The result was a unique charm that invited players to explore and experience these virtual worlds. This resourcefulness proved that even a few colors could make a game unforgettable.

Sprites—those little moving characters—became animated icons of gaming culture.

Sprites were the lifeblood of early video games, those charming little characters that roamed across our screens. Despite their pixelated appearance, sprites brought games to life, adding movement and personality. These tiny heroes and villains became the face of gaming culture, recognizable to players around the globe.

From **Link** in *The Legend of Zelda* to *Pac-Man* himself, sprites were more than mere pixels; they were cultural icons. These characters demonstrated the power of animation, showing how a few frames of movement could convey a world of emotion and action. Sprites remind us of the magic that can be achieved with limited resources and boundless creativity.

Game designers used pixel art cleverly to convey emotions and storytelling.

Pixel art in early video games was more than just a technical achievement; it was a storytelling vehicle. Game designers cleverly used pixel arrangements to convey emotions, create atmospheres, and drive narratives. The challenge was in suggesting complex themes and emotions with limited visual tools.

Despite this, titles like **Final Fantasy** and *Chrono Trigger* demonstrated how pixel art could evoke deep stories and rich emotions. Facial expressions, mood settings, and even plot twists were depicted with just a few colors and pixels.

These games showed that storytelling transcends graphical fidelity, relying instead on imagination and creativity.

Nowadays, 'retro style' is trendy, with pixel art celebrated for its nostalgic charm.

Fast forward to the present, and pixel art has enjoyed a renaissance. Once seen as a necessity of limitation, it is now revered for its nostalgic charm and artistic expression. Modern developers embrace the retro style to evoke nostalgia and pay homage to gaming's golden era.

Games like **Shovel Knight** and *Stardew Valley* are a testament to pixel art's enduring legacy. They use the simplicity of pixel graphics to craft engaging, memorable experiences that harken back to a simpler time. This resurgence highlights how vintage aesthetics can still capture the hearts of gamers, proving that classic never goes out of style.

Game Over? The Crash of 1983

What's that? Our beloved industry hit a rough patch? Sure, it wasn't all high scores and easy wins. Let's explore the crash of 1983.

An overload of poor-quality games, anyone rcmember E.T. for the Atari?

Ah, the infamous **E.T. the Extra-Terrestrial** for the Atari 2600—often dubbed the game that nearly destroyed an industry. Released in a rush to capitalize on the movie's success, this game became synonymous with the downfall of the video game market in 1983. Poor gameplay mechanics and confusing objectives left players frustrated, resulting in a memorable flop.

While E.T. might have been one of the most notable failures, it wasn't alone. The market was flooded with hastily developed, low-quality games as companies scrambled to cash in on the video game boom. Gamers, expecting quality entertainment, were sorely disappointed and soon turned away. The story of E.T. buried in a New Mexico landfill became an industry legend, a stark reminder of what can happen when businesses prioritize quick profits over quality.

Oversaturated market with too many consoles vying for the living room space.

The early 1980s saw an explosion of home video game consoles. Companies like Atari, Coleco, and Mattel all pushed to dominate living rooms across America. This overabundance led to consumer confusion as different systems offered varying games, often without any clear advantage over one another.

With no clear market leader, families were overwhelmed by choices—blame it on having more consoles than you could shake a joystick at. The lack of standout quality and differentiation between platforms further pushed consumers away. In trying to appeal to everyone, these companies struggled to connect with anyone, contributing to the market's overall decline.

Retailers lost faith and heavily discounted consoles, creating a downward spiral.

As game sales plummeted, retailers found themselves with stocks of unsold merchandise. Store shelves, once proudly bearing the latest video game hardware, were now filled with outdated technology no one wanted. In a desperate attempt to recoup losses, retailers slashed prices, further devaluing the brand perception of these consoles.

This practice marked the beginning of a vicious cycle: reduced prices led to further devalued perception, making potential buyers even more wary. A once booming industry saw its products treated as clearance items, effectively pulling the rug out from under its own feet.

Consumers got fed up with shovelware—sorry, generic bad games.

Imagine being promised thrilling adventures and instead receiving countless games that offered little more than recycled ideas and broken mechanics. Known as *shovelware*, these low-quality games filled store shelves and quickly wore thin on consumer patience.

Without quality control, eager gamers were left with a sour taste and a distrust of new titles. Companies that flooded the market with undistinguished products underestimated their audience's expectations, proving that quantity never trumps quality. This glut of uninspired content contributed significantly to the industry's economic nosedive.

Many companies, even big names, closed their doors during this harsh time.

The crash of 1983 wasn't just a setback; it was an earthquake that rattled the very foundation of the gaming industry. Once profitable companies faced financial ruin as market demand evaporated. Major players like Atari, which had been synonymous with home gaming, were left reeling.

This period saw the demise of numerous businesses, big and small. Even industry veterans struggled to weather the storm. The landscape of gaming was irreversibly altered, and the economic impact rippled through the entire tech industry for years to come.

This crash paved the way for stalwart Nintendo to lead the industry's revival.

In the wake of this crash, hope emerged from an unlikely source—Japan's Nintendo. By introducing the Nintendo Entertainment System (NES) in 1985, Nintendo revived the industry with a model that focused on quality games and innovative technology.

Nintendo's strategy emphasized strict quality control and memorable experiences. By requiring third-party developers to adhere to high standards, Nintendo regained consumer trust and helped forge a path to recovery. The NES ushered in a new era of gaming, setting the stage for the multibillion-dollar industry we enjoy today.

Chapter 3: Arcade Fever - Quarters, Cabinets, and Chaos

Imagine a time when kids fervently collected quarters, not for candy, but to fuel their obsession with arcade games. Get ready to hear the clink of coins and the beep-boop of arcade machines as we explore the **golden age** of arcades and the neon-lit sanctuaries they created for gamers young and old.

The Rise of the Arcade Phenomenon

Before the internet was a thing and console wars gripped living rooms, arcades were the undisputed kings of gaming entertainment. Let's look at how it all started.

Arcades became the social hubs of the '80s, where kids and adults gathered to play the latest games.

In the 1980s, a trip to the local arcade was more than just a gaming session—it was a social event. Arcades evolved into dynamic community centers where gamers of all ages came together. Youngsters eagerly anticipated the weekend, clutching their quarters like treasure, ready to conquer high scores.

These gaming meccas featured a kaleidoscope of screens and enticing sounds, inviting novices and experts alike to try their hand at the latest titles. Friendships were forged over dazzling displays and competitive duels, while rivalry added an edge and buzz to the air. In a pre-internet age, arcades offered a unique meeting place that fostered a shared culture and camaraderie among players.

Games like Pong and Space Invaders set the stage for the arcade boom, attracting players with their simple, addictive gameplay.

The arcade boom of the late '70s and early '80s was launched by groundbreaking games like **Pong** and **Space Invaders**. These games captivated audiences with their straightforward yet engaging gameplay, paving the way for more sophisticated offerings.

Pong, with its minimalist design, invited players to enjoy its easy-to-grasp mechanics, while *Space Invaders* upped the ante with its immersive alien invasion storyline. Both became instant classics, driving legions of fans to flood arcades in search of the next big thrill. The addictive nature of these games was a key factor in their success, as players continuously returned for just one more round, pushing themselves to master strategies and achieve legendary high scores.

With catchy tunes and flashy lights, arcades were designed to draw in gamers like moths to a neon flame.

Arcades were a sensory experience like no other. Imagine being drawn into these electrifying dens of digital excitement, where the air was filled with the rhythmic bleeps of machines vying for your attention. The vibrant glow of cabinet screens and enticing marquees beckoned players to immerse themselves in the action.

The ambient music and soundtracks, expertly composed to match each game's theme, heightened the overall atmosphere. This carefully orchestrated combination of sights and sounds created an irresistible allure. Arcades were consciously designed to captivate visitors, ensuring that once you entered, the kaleidoscope of lights and melodies would keep you coming back for more. These elements provided an escape from reality, a place where gamers could lose themselves in pixelated adventures and neon-lit wizardry.

The arcade scene not only fueled gaming culture but also pushed technological advancements in game design and computer graphics.

Beyond being hotspots of entertainment, arcades were catalysts for major technological innovations. Game developers, driven by the fierce competition to create the next big hit, constantly pushed the boundaries of what was possible in game design and graphics.

This era witnessed the advent of increasingly sophisticated graphics and creative designs. Technological advancements made it possible to craft more intricate and colorful game environments, captivating players with vivid worlds and complex gameplay mechanics. The push for innovation in arcades also laid the groundwork for future home consoles and influenced the broader tech landscape.

The intense technical arms race within the arcade industry fostered the rapid evolution of gaming technology, shaping the tools and techniques that continue to influence modern game development. In many ways, the lasting legacy of the arcade scene is its vital role in laying the foundation for today's advanced gaming experiences.

The Thrill of Competition

Besides just playing for fun, arcades were all about bragging rights and who could get the highest score. Let's dive into the world of arcade rivalry.

Leaderboard rankings became a badge of honor, with players constantly trying to top each other's high scores.

During the golden age of arcades, the quest for the top spot on the leaderboard was no trivial matter. Players dedicated countless hours and quarters mastering their reflexes, memorizing patterns, and perfecting their strategies. This focus often turned arcades into arenas of silent competition, where a spot on the leaderboard was akin to having your name in lights. It was a time when each player's initials became as recognizable as their face, holding a near mythical status within local gaming circles.

The leaderboard wasn't just a way to keep track of scores; it was a social contract of bragging rights. Players engaged in friendly—and sometimes not-so-friendly—rivalries as they vied for greatness over their peers. The allure of seeing one's initials rise to the top spurred some to become local legends. Achieving a high score turned players into arcade celebrities, idolized by both those desperate to dethrone them and newbies eager to learn from their mastery.

Games like Pac-Man offered endless challenges that kept players coming back, hungry to beat their last record.

Ah, Pac-Man, the cheerful yellow circle that gobbled its way into the hearts of millions! This game, with its deceptively simple premise, became an obsession for many players. The labyrinthine mazes seemed to taunt players with the promise of reachable mastery, yet kept them coming back with just enough struggle to keep it compelling. For gamers, Pac-Man was more than a game—it was a mental workout and a test of perseverance.

The challenges in Pac-Man escalated quickly, with the ghosts—Blinky, Pinky, Inky, and Clyde—becoming relentless adversaries. Each session was an unpredictable rollercoaster, as players sought not only to outmaneuver the ghosts but to amass as many points as possible before meeting a grim end. The simplicity of the game belied its depth, and each new quarter dropped into the machine was not just the cost of a new game, but a ticket to another shot at arcade glory.

Arcade tournaments and competitions emerged, adding another layer to the competitive spirit.

The arcade scene blossomed with the rise of organized tournaments, introducing a new dimension of excitement and rivalry. These events attracted waves of players eager to prove their mettle on a grander stage. Among the flickering neon lights and the smell of freshly popped popcorn, participants battled it out in frenzied bouts of skill and timing.

The stakes were more than just high scores; they were about being crowned the best in the arcade circuit.

Competitions added much-needed fanfare to gaming, transforming players into performers. Crowds gathered to watch, cheer, and even comfort those knocked out early. Tournaments could stretch long into the night, becoming intense marathons of endurance and concentration. But beyond the shouts and the fervor, these competitions carved out a space where champions weren't just playing games—they were making history.

The social aspect of gaming in arcades fostered a sense of community among players, often leading to lifelong friendships.

Arcades were more than just a collection of machines; they were bustling hubs of social interaction. These spaces, filled with the gleeful noise of electronic beeps and laughter, became unique ecosystems where friendships flourished. Amid the shared struggles over joystick controls and enthusiastic cries of victory, players formed bonds that transcended the games themselves.

It wasn’t uncommon for strangers to become fast friends while huddled around the glow of a particularly challenging game. Tips and tricks were exchanged like secrets over battles; camaraderie came naturally in this competitive yet friendly environment. There was always someone around with a story about their latest victory or their most memorable defeat. These connections often lasted far beyond the arcade's closing time, turning casual encounters into lifelong camaraderie, proving that sometimes the best games are played in friendship.

Iconic Games That Defined an Era

Every arcade had its stars—games that kept people lining up with quarters in hand. Here's a closer look at the classics that left a lasting impact.

Space Invaders marked a turning point in the gaming industry, inspiring countless clones and successor games.

The release of **Space Invaders** in 1978 was nothing short of a revolution for the gaming world. Created by Tomohiro Nishikado, this deceptively simple game became an obsession, capturing imaginations across the globe as players furiously button-mashed to fend off descending waves of aliens. Its appeal wasn't just about shooting space invaders; it was an experience of escalating tension, where each alien eliminated upped the ante, quickening the march of the relentless enemy.

The lasting impact of Space Invaders can't be overstated. It inspired an avalanche of imitators and set a template for what video games could achieve. Arcade owners couldn't get enough of it, and the game reportedly caused a temporary shortage of 100-yen coins in Japan. Not a bad problem to have! This widespread acclaim cemented Space Invaders as a trailblazer, proving that video games were not just a passing fad but an enduring medium ripe for innovation and artistic expression.

Pac-Man was not just a game but a cultural phenomenon, with an instantly recognizable character and theme tune.

Pac-Man, released in 1980, gobbled up more than just dots—it consumed the world, propelling itself to iconic status. Created by Toru Iwatani, this arcade smash hit flipped the scrappy, aggressive narratives of contemporary games on their head by focusing on non-violent fun. The main character, an ever-hungry, yellow circle, became a superstar, and its simple but catchy theme tune echoed across arcades worldwide.

The genius of Pac-Man lay in its universal appeal. From its maze-chase gameplay to the relentless pursuit of escaping ghosts and clearing levels, Pac-Man hooked players of all ages. Its success was a catalyst for a tidal wave of merchandise, cartoons, and even a hit single, "Pac-Man Fever." More than just a game, Pac-Man became a symbol of the early '80s, embodying the arcade culture at its peak and proving that a game character could be as beloved as any comic book hero.

Donkey Kong introduced players to Mario, who would become one of gaming's most enduring icons.

In 1981, **Donkey Kong** took the gaming world by storm, not just with its engaging gameplay but by introducing a character who would become synonymous with video games themselves—*Mario*. Conceived by Shigeru Miyamoto, the game was a departure from the typical shooter genre, placing players in a vibrant, platform-jumping quest to rescue the damsel in distress.

Mario's debut was under the alias "Jumpman," a nod to his springy athleticism. Armed only with a legendary stash of courage, players navigated steel girders, dodged barrels hurled by the titular gorilla, and faced all sorts of perils. The game's innovation lay in its structure, offering multiple levels, which was rare at the time. Donkey Kong didn't just churn out quarters—it forged a legacy. Mario's journey continued beyond the arcade, laying the foundations for what would evolve into the beloved Super Mario franchise.

The simplicity and addictive nature of games like Frogger and Galaga make them timeless favorites.

Some games transcend time, and **Frogger** and **Galaga** are prime examples, capturing hearts with their straightforward yet thrilling gameplay. Frogger, released by Konami in 1981, tasked players with navigating a frog across a busy highway and treacherous river. Its charm lay in its apparent simplicity, hiding a world of strategic depth, where timing was everything and lives could be lost in a heartbeat.

Meanwhile, *Galaga*, released the same year, took the space shooter genre to new heights. Building upon the foundations of its predecessor Galaxian, Galaga introduced player power-ups and intricate enemy patterns that kept gamers rooted to their screens. Both games were as addictive as they were challenging, ensuring players returned time and again to master their mechanics. Their enduring appeal attests to their brilliance, echoing the timeless allure of skillful simplicity over flashy complexity. Even decades later, these games continue to jet-set into the hearts of new generations craving the thrill of the chase.

The Technological Marvels Inside the Cabinets

Arcade cabinets were more than just wooden boxes; they were home to the technological wonders of their time. Let's peek under the hood.

Arcade hardware was designed to deliver the best possible graphics and sound for each game, long before similar capabilities reached home systems.

Back in the dazzling era of arcades, hardware developers were like the mad scientists of gaming. With each game, they were driven by the singular mission: blow minds with graphics and sound. These cabinets packed customdesigned components that made your home TV blush with envy. Imagine animation so smooth, it's like butter on a frying pan!

Arcade machines boasted vibrant displays and stereo sound that echoed throughout the room, creating an immersive experience light years ahead of its time. Even if your home TV could only manage two shades of grey, arcades were already delivering the rainbow. Both sights and sounds reached levels that felt akin to stepping inside a pulsating, electronic wonderland.

Developers experimented with new technologies, like vector graphics and three-dimensional gameplay, pushing the boundaries of innovation.

Arcade developers weren't content with just pixels on a screen; they were gaming Da Vincis always seeking the next innovation. Enter vector graphics—a revolutionary tech that traded chunky pixels for crisp lines, making games like *Asteroids* and *Tempest* pop with clarity unparalleled by traditional displays.

While vector graphics was one frontier, some brave developers dared to venture into the mystical realm of 3D. They created simulations that hinted at the digital possibilities of future gaming epochs. This relentless pursuit of innovation turned arcades into bustling hubs of ingenuity, where the only limit was the developers' imagination—or perhaps how many quarters one could cram into a pocket.

Each game was typically housed in a unique cabinet design, adding to the aesthetic appeal and draw in arcades.

Imagine stepping into an arcade—a symphony of flashing lights and a gallery of intricate cabinet designs, each screaming for your attention. Unlike the plain black boxes we know from home consoles, arcade machines were decked out like carnival attractions, each a vivid work of art dedicated to its game.

Cabinet designs became a critical part of the arcade experience. From the sleek, sci-fi allure of *Space Invaders* to the playful, exuberant appearance of *Pac-Man*, these machines beckoned players like sirens in a sea of neon. So, next time you see a nostalgic gamer with misty eyes, they're probably dreaming of a time when games were as much about the looks as they were about the high scores.

Mechanical elements, like joysticks and buttons, were crafted to withstand the intense use from the hordes of enthusiastic players.

Arcades were the stomping grounds for passionate gamers, and their wear and tear made it clear: buttons and joysticks had to be built like tanks. These parts could take a pounding, sustaining frantic attempts to dodge alien ships or gobble all the pellets before ghosts closed in.

More than mere tools, these mechanical elements were extensions of the player's willpower, seamlessly translating human decisions into digital actions. Engineers meticulously designed each component to hold up against countless hours of play, delivering a tactile feedback that both thrilled and soothed the frenzied gamer. It's safe to say, if those buttons could talk, they'd have tales of glory and defeat aplenty.

The Decline of the Arcade Era

All good things must come to an end, and arcades were no exception. Let's explore why their dominance faded in the gaming world.

The rise of home consoles offered gamers the chance to enjoy complex games from the comfort of their own homes.

The allure of gaming at home became irresistible with the ascent of home consoles in the early 80s. Gamers no longer needed a pocketful of quarters to enjoy their favorite pastime. Systems like the Atari 2600 brought the thrill of the arcade right to living rooms across the globe. With games such as *Space Invaders* and *Pac-Man* available on these new devices, players had access to endless gaming sessions without the frantic hunt for spare change.

Beyond the economic convenience, home consoles offered a sense of ownership and progression. Players could pick up a game and continue their adventure at their own pace. This shift not only transformed gaming into a more personal experience but also challenged the arcades' dominance. As home consoles became increasingly powerful, the temptation to swap the boisterous arcade atmosphere for the comfort of one's couch grew, compelling players to embrace home gaming as the ultimate entertainment option.

The improvement of PC games provided even more options and flexibility for gamers, drawing them away from the arcades.

In parallel with the rise of home consoles, personal computers began showcasing their potential as formidable gaming platforms. As technology advanced, so too did the sophistication and genre diversity of PC games. Titles such as *Ultima* and *King's Quest* offered immersive narratives and complex gameplay mechanics that were often unmatched by arcade games.

PCs provided a level of customization and flexibility that was simply unavailable in arcades. Players could tweak settings, explore mods, and even engage in the emerging world of multiplayer gaming via local networks. This adaptability made PC gaming appealing not just for casual gamers but also for those seeking deeper, more customizable experiences. As a result, many players favored PCs as their go-to gaming platform, leaving arcades searching for relevance in this rapidly evolving gaming landscape.

Economic factors, such as higher costs of maintaining arcade operations, made it harder for arcades to stay profitable.

Running an arcade wasn't just about installing a few machines and flicking on the power. It involved significant overheads: rent for prime real estate, maintenance for the heavy-use machines, and a steady influx of new titles to keep players' interest alive. As arcade games became more intricate, the machines themselves became more expensive to produce and maintain.

Furthermore, economic shifts meant that disposable income wasn't as readily available for families. In a climate where pinching pennies became a necessity, the cost of an arcade visit could no longer compete with the one-time investment of a console or PC game. Arcades that once buzzed with activity found themselves struggling to cover these escalating costs, leading many to close their doors or transform into hybrid entertainment centers, offering other forms of amusement like laser tag or mini-golf.

Despite the decline, arcades remain a cherished part of gaming nostalgia and continue to influence game design today.

While the arcade era may have faded, its legacy is anything but forgotten. Modern gamers and developers alike hold a fondness for the simplicity and purity of those early experiences, and this nostalgia permeates contemporary game design. Many developers pay homage to arcade classics, embedding retro aesthetics and mechanics into new creations to recapture some of that vintage magic.

Moreover, the resurgence of "barcades"—venues combining the social element of a bar with the classic charm of arcade cabinets—illustrates how these pixelated pioneers still enchant us. The chaotic hum of the arcade laid the groundwork for multiplayer experiences and competitive gaming scenes that thrive today. In paying tribute to this past, the gaming community ensures that arcades, while no longer dominant, remain an indelible part of gaming's vibrant tapestry.

Chapter 4: The Home Console Rebellion

Why head to the arcade when you can have the thrill right in your living room? This chapter takes you through the game-changing entrance of home consoles like the Atari and NES. Learn how these gray boxes of wonder redefined playtime forever.

Welcome to the Home Console Revolution

In an age when bold colors ruled and pixels were king, home consoles stepped up to challenge the arcade giants.

Let's dive into the living rooms of the 80s and see what all the fuss was about.

A new battleground: With arcade games dominating the scene, the arrival of home consoles set off a gaming revolution at home.

Picture this: a world where games were only found at neon-lit arcades, demanding quarters like greedy trolls at a bridge. Then suddenly, amid a cacophony of synthesizers and power ballads, emerged the humble home console—a plastic gateway to infinite worlds. These machines transformed homes into new arenas, where joysticks ruled and family members were divided in epic clashes.

Previously dominated by noisy arcades, gaming found a new frontier in the living rooms of the 80s. No longer confined to a designated location outside the home, gaming became an everyday indulgence, accessible and personal. Home consoles seized the spotlight, snatching it away from the arcades and ushering players into a realm of private digital adventures.

Odd-looking boxes: These consoles might look like toasters with weird antennas, but they promised endless hours of fun.

At first glance, early consoles resembled strange kitchen appliances—quirky, boxy devices with knobs and switches that looked more at home near a microwave than a TV. Yet, beneath their odd exteriors, they packed worlds of imagination and discovery. The consoles had more in common with a sci-fi contraption than a serious entertainment device.

Despite their unusual appearance, these consoles delivered on their promise—providing a portal to universes where pixels danced and adventure awaited. The intrigue only grew once the power switch was flipped, casting players into electronic dreams. These quirky devices became household staples, each with its distinctive charm, fueling countless hours of joy.

Affordable entertainment: Bringing arcade fun home meant saving that pocket change for a rainy day.

Imagine waving goodbye to the relentless clatter of arcade coins cascading into machines. Home consoles cleverly offered a cost-effective alternative to the weekly arcade pilgrimage. Families could now enjoy entertainment without the financial strain of feeding quarters into endless games.

The appeal of affordable gaming was irresistible. Kids were no longer tethered to the whims of their piggy banks. Instead, they conquered digital landscapes without constantly pleading for more change. Home consoles democratized play, turning a luxury into a commonly shared experience, and gamers embraced it with open arms—and heavier wallets.

First in line: The mighty Atari kicked off this home-bound quest, sparking a craze among gamers around the world.

If gaming consoles were a rock band, Atari would be its breakout star. This pioneering device landed in homes with the swagger of a rock legend, setting off a frenzy that captivated players on a global scale. Atari's shiny promise of home entertainment transformed casual players into devoted fans.

By introducing its iconic line of games—like the beloved Pong—Atari not only popularized home consoles but also built the foundation for an entire industry. It was a sensation, an emblem of the gaming renaissance that enticed a legion of fans. Atari's venture into the living room was not just a commercial success; it was a cultural milestone.

Beyond four walls: Home consoles helped gaming expand beyond arcades, making it a part of everyday life.

Home consoles demolished the boundary that confined games to arcades, allowing the gaming phenomenon to spill over into households everywhere. No longer limited to coin-op cubicles, gaming became an integral part of daily life, transforming living rooms into new stages for grand adventures.

This shift marked a cultural evolution—transforming electronic entertainment from a communal pastime into a personal, yet shared, experience. Home consoles allowed families to bond, friends to compete, and individuals to explore virtual worlds at their leisure. As consoles found their place in homes, one thing was clear: gaming was here to stay.

Atari: The Game Changer

Meet the Atari 2600, the magical gadget that planted itself under countless TVs and played a starring role in gaming history.

Simple yet striking: The Atari 2600 made graphics look like a dream, even if they were just colorful blocks.

The Atari 2600, also affectionately known as the VCS (Video Computer System), was a marvel of its time, turning simple pixelated graphics into captivating adventures for players of all ages. Despite consisting of basic shapes and blocks, these graphics had an unparalleled charm that sparked the imagination.

Games like "Adventure" transformed a few pixels into epic quests, proving that visual fidelity wasn't the sole driver of immersive gameplay. The creativity behind these simple graphics inspired future generations to explore the endless possibilities within the gaming landscape.

Each colorful square and rectangle on the screen was a dynamic element in the storytelling, providing just enough detail to allow players to insert their own imagination into the experience. In many ways, the Atari's visuals laid the foundation for what we today consider the artistic dimension of video gaming.

Joystick wonders: Let's not forget those iconic joysticks that defined a whole new era of thumb exercises.

Before ergonomic controllers became the norm, there was the iconic Atari joystick—a single stick with a red button, yet full of infinite possibilities. It was simplicity that led to a revolution; the humble joystick offered an intuitive interface that made control more direct and engaging.

The design, despite its Spartan appearance, encouraged movement and coordination. Players mastered the art of deft thumb maneuvers, launching spaceships, chomping dots, and dodging aliens with newfound agility.

These joysticks paved the way for the tactile, interactive experiences we seek today. They taught players to interact beyond pressing buttons, fostering a skill-based engagement that was both challenging and rewarding. Those joysticks might have been primitive, but they laid the groundwork for the evolution of game controllers.

Game cartridges aplenty: Rediscover the joy of inserting a cartridge and getting lost in a world of pixels.

Long before digital downloads took over, there was the satisfying *click* of an Atari cartridge slipping into its slot. This ritualistic experience, of physically inserting a game into the console, held a special magic that digital media simply can't replicate.

Each cartridge promised a new adventure or challenge, with titles ranging from "Pitfall" to "Centipede," each offering a distinct world of blocks and bytes. Players eagerly anticipated the moment these worlds would burst to life on their screens, transforming living rooms into arcades.

These cartridges also symbolized the beginning of video game collections, as players could build tangible libraries of their favorite titles. Sharing games with friends introduced a social element, enhancing the communal experience of early gaming culture.

Pop culture icon: Atari wasn't just a gaming console - it was a cultural phenomenon with a lasting impact.

The Atari 2600 wasn't merely a gaming device; it became a symbol of the burgeoning home entertainment revolution. Its presence marked a shift in how people approached leisure time, bringing the thrills of the arcade into the confines of the family home.

More than just a console, Atari infiltrated different aspects of popular culture—it was featured in movies, TV shows, and even music, symbolizing the cutting-edge technology of the era. This iconic status extended beyond gamers; it captured the attention of the general public, embedding itself in the cultural lexicon of the time.

Atari's influence stretched far and wide, from the aspiring developers it inspired to the gaming lounges and competitions it helped foster. Its legacy is felt today, as modern consoles pay homage with retro revivals and reboots.

Unending innovation: Atari set the stage for future consoles, laying the groundwork for the digital adventures ahead.

Atari's impact on the gaming industry extends beyond entertainment; it paved the path for future technological advancements in home consoles. The Atari 2600 introduced key concepts, such as interchangeable media and backward compatibility, that would drive innovation in the years to come.

The system's architecture, designed to be versatile and expandable, encouraged developers to push boundaries and explore new gameplay mechanics. This forward-thinking approach sowed the seeds of creativity that would bloom in the form of the intricate games we enjoy today.

As technology evolved, so did the ideas incubated by Atari's presence. It inspired an ongoing quest for improvement, enhancement, and expansion, which continues to define the industry, making it a timeless reminder of the power of innovation.

Rise of the NES: Nintendo's Power Play

With the gaming world holding its breath, Nintendo dropped the NES bombshell, and it was hard to recover from this gaming brilliance.

Plumber power: Mario jumped in with the Nintendo Entertainment System, redefining gaming with charm and choice.

When the Nintendo Entertainment System (NES) was launched, it brought with it a certain red-hatted, mustachioed plumber who quickly became a household name. Mario was more than just a character; he was the face of a revolution in gaming. With his debut in *Super Mario Bros.*, players were introduced to a game that combined whimsical charm with strategic choice, laying the groundwork for what would become the hallmark of Nintendo's game design philosophy.

What made Mario's adventures especially compelling was their ability to offer both simplicity and depth. Players could navigate straightforward levels or explore hidden secrets, depending on their play style. This dual approach appealed to both new gamers and seasoned players seeking a richer experience. The NES and Mario duo didn't just redefine what a video game hero could be; they redefined what gaming itself could achieve, leaving a legacy that continues to influence game design today.

A library of magic: NES didn't hold back with its vast collection of games - from saving princesses to shooting ducks, it had it all.

The NES was a veritable treasure chest filled with game cartridges that spanned every conceivable genre. Whether you were venturing out to rescue Princess Toadstool from Bowser's clutches or honing your shooting skills with the Zapper in *Duck Hunt*, the sheer variety of experiences was staggering. The NES offered more than just gaming; it offered entire worlds to explore and conquer.

This extensive library showcased Nintendo's commitment to delivering not just quantity, but quality. Each title, from *The Legend of Zelda* with its epic quests to *Metroid* and its groundbreaking non-linear gameplay, demonstrated the diverse storytelling and interactive potential of video games. Such a broad selection ensured there was something for everyone, making gaming an inclusive and universally appealing pastime.

Gameplay like no other: Gamers were hooked with unforgettable gameplay, sparking a long-lasting love affair with the brand.

One of the NES's greatest triumphs lay in its innovative and engaging gameplay mechanics. From the pitch-perfect platforming of *Super Mario Bros.* to the nerve-wracking intensity of *Castlevania*, the console provided experiences that kept players coming back for more. These games introduced tight controls and imaginative design that made every session a memorable adventure.

It wasn't just about playing; it was about immersion in wonderfully crafted worlds that invited exploration and experimentation. The NES succeeded in making each game a unique journey, filled with twists, turns, and excitement. For many, these experiences formed the bedrock of lifelong gaming enthusiasm, solidifying Nintendo's position as an industry leader and trendsetter.

Changing the game: Nintendo flipped the script on how consoles worked, giving gamers more control and fun.

Nintendo didn't just enter the console market; they transformed it. The NES was more than a mere gaming device; it was a technological marvel that altered perceptions of home entertainment. With its user-friendly design and interactive interface, it placed power and control directly into players' hands.

Innovations like interchangeable cartridges and the iconic D-pad controller revolutionized how games were played and perceived. No longer were players passively consuming content; they were active participants, making decisions that influenced outcomes. This approach laid the groundwork for future advancements in gaming, emphasizing player agency and interaction as core elements of the experience.

Influence that lasted: With NES, Nintendo charted the future, shaping the gaming landscape in ways that echo even today.

The legacy of the NES extends far beyond its lifespan, with its influence permeating every corner of modern gaming. It wasn't just a console; it was a cultural phenomenon that inspired countless developers and set standards still revered in the industry. Many of today's game design principles, like intuitive controls and level design, owe their existence to the groundwork laid by the NES.

Perhaps its most enduring contribution is the importance of storytelling and character development within games. By infusing heart and imagination into every title, Nintendo showed that games could be as impactful and meaningful as any other form of media. The NES's impact is still felt today, echoing in the vibrant, dynamic gaming landscape we enjoy, underscoring Nintendo's revolutionary role in shaping the world of gaming.

Battles in the Living Room: Console Wars

As home consoles gained ground, battles erupted—not in games, but between the companies themselves. Let's check out how the great console wars unfolded.

Competition heats up: Once-a-fun novelty, now a serious battlefield for console supremacy.

In the late 20th century, the quaint pastime of gaming underwent a monumental shift. Once merely a whimsical diversion, video games became a high-stakes arena for technological one-upmanship. Home consoles like the Atari 2600 and the Nintendo Entertainment System (NES) transformed living rooms into battlegrounds for this burgeoning digital arena.

As technology advanced, the stakes grew higher, pushing companies into fierce competition. Every new console release was not just a product launch, but a declaration of war. Competing companies scrambled to outdo each other in graphics, gameplay, and sheer creative genius, driving a sort of digital arms race. This competition didn't just refine technology; it defined a generation of gamers who eagerly awaited the next innovation.

Taking sides: Gamers picked their champions, leading to fierce loyalty between Atari and Nintendo fans.

With the console market heating up, gamers were faced with a choice: which brand to pledge their allegiance to? Atari or Nintendo? This decision went beyond mere preference; it became a defining part of one's identity. Kids on playgrounds, friends in living rooms—they all boasted about the superiority of their chosen console.

The rivalry was palpable, with intense debates often echoing through classrooms and community spaces alike. Loyalists defended their brands with zeal, citing superior game libraries, innovative controllers, or exclusive titles as evidence of their console's reign. These allegiances weren’t just a matter of convenience; they fostered communities and forged lasting friendships, bound by shared enthusiasm and backing their chosen champions with unwavering devotion.

The secret weapon: Each console offered unique perks, making decisions tough for buyers with only one TV to spare.

Choosing a console was akin to picking the perfect secret weapon, each equipped with its own unique set of perks. The Atari 2600, for instance, was lauded for its variety of games while the NES dazzled with superior graphics and immersive storytelling. Understanding these differences was crucial for those making a purchase.

Households, often with only one television, faced the challenging decision of selecting a system that everyone could enjoy. This choice was further complicated by the exclusives each console offered, making every decision an insightful evaluation of each machine's capabilities. Features like graphics, sound quality, and control interfaces were scrutinized intensely. Ultimately, this made the choosing process both a thrilling and daunting experience, as each option presented compelling advantages.

Games galore: Every new release was a weapon in these battles, drawing lines between brands and their growing fanbases.

Each new game release during the console wars was akin to launching a new offensive in an ongoing campaign.

Studios produced titles that would become legends in their own right, from the strategic depth of "The Legend of Zelda" to the frenetic action of "Space Invaders." These games became exclusive armaments in the larger battle for dominance.

The competition spurred companies to invest in more creative and innovative games, each release eagerly anticipated by their loyal fans. The virtual treasures each console provided became potent symbols of their brand's strengths. The gaming catalogues of these consoles became their strongest marketing tools, drawing clear lines in the sand between brand loyalists and capturing new fans who were drawn like moths to these digital flames.

Forever friends or foes: The rivalries sparked during those early days created a legacy that continues with fever today.

The heated rivalries of the past have left a lasting legacy in the gaming world. Gamers who grew up during these battles often carry fond memories and nostalgic loyalties into the modern era. The contest between consoles, once merely a commercial venture, evolved into an integral part of gaming culture.

These early rivalries laid the groundwork for the vibrant, competitive landscape of today's gaming industry. The echoes of these battles are felt with every new console generation, each promising players a new era of gaming excellence. Whether reliving past skirmishes or engaging with new ones, gamers carry the spirit of these early contests forward, ensuring that the legacy of these home console battles remains ever-present, their embers never fully extinguished.

Chapter 5: The Role-Playing Renaissance

Scroll through pixels and polygons and into a world of magical quests and epic fantasies. Be part of the **role-playing** revolution with titles like *The Legend of Zelda* and *Final Fantasy*, which crafted complex stories and enchanted gamers to lead double lives.

The Birth of Role-Playing Games

Let's hit the rewind button and see how role-playing games took their baby steps in the gaming universe.

Back in the day, tabletop RPGs were the real deal, inspiring future digital adventures.

Before you could save the galaxy with a gamepad, adventurers gathered around tables, rolling dice and crafting epic stories in the world of tabletop **Role-Playing Games** (RPGs). Games like *Dungeons & Dragons* offered intricate worlds and character development, serving as a sandbox for creativity. These sessions fueled the imaginations of developers who dreamt of bringing such experiences to computer screens.

Tabletop RPGs were the innovators of the narrative and character-driven gameplay that would soon become the hallmark of electronic RPGs. With pen and paper, players shaped storylines that inspired programmers to think beyond the joystick, leading to digital role-playing adventures that mirrored their analog ancestors. This analog to digital transition laid the groundwork for gaming's most sweeping epics, from quests to save princesses to journeys through magical realms.

The first digital RPGs were all about stats and imagination, with text and numbers doing a dance on your screen.

The early digital RPGs might seem a bit primitive by today's standards, but their charm lay in their reliance on player imagination and a bunch of statistics. Titles like *The Bard's Tale* transcended mere pixels, offering a digital playhouse of numbers where your actions affected a cascade of outcomes. Instead of cutting-edge graphics, you got an exercise in creativity with walls of text and strategy tables.

Exploring these games felt like deciphering a tome where every stat boost and equipment upgrade told a story richer than mere visuals could convey. Players became adept at imagining realms through a smattering of pixels and descriptive prose. Though simple, these games forged deep connections, inviting players to greater adventures in a brave new digital world.

Some early RPGs were more like digital dungeons, where getting lost was half the fun!

If you think getting lost in a dungeon crawl was just a mistake, think again! There was a unique thrill in navigating the digital labyrinths of early RPGs, where losing your way could lead to unexpected discoveries. Games like *Wizardry* thrust players into sprawling mazes, demanding mapping and spatial awareness in a pre-GPS era.

Armed with graph paper and a fierce determination, players would trace these intricate worlds, their imagination filling in the gaps left by the monochrome screens. Every turn offered a potential surprise, spawning real tension as virtual reality began just beyond the next corridor. For many, solving these labyrinths felt like a rite of passage into the elite club of RPG aficionados.

Fueled by fantasy books, these games let players escape reality and save make-believe worlds.

Inspired by the fantastical escapades within novels like *The Lord of the Rings*, early RPGs opened portals for players to become heroes. These games quickly became mini escape pods from daily life, offering adventures crafted not with swords, but with keys and command lines. The quest was simple: save worlds envisioned through nothing more than your home's cardboard box TV screen.

The mix of literary allusion and gaming innovation gave birth to titles rich in lore and legend, allowing players to become the protagonists of their own sagas. Whether battling dragons or negotiating with aliens, gamers hungered for the chance to step beyond the mundane. Early RPGs offered cherished glimpses of the extraordinary, rewarding players with entire realms of mystical possibility and unlimited imagination.

The Zelda Phenomenon

Grab your virtual sword and shield! It's time to explore how Zelda changed the gaming landscape forever.

***The Legend of Zelda* was like a choose-your-own-adventure book, but with pixels.**

Imagine opening a book where each page offers limitless possibilities and unexpected twists. *The Legend of Zelda* delivered this exhilarating experience but with the immersive twist of a video game. It blended narrative freedom with interactive gameplay, allowing players to steer their own paths. The game's non-linear structure was revolutionary, providing players with the autonomy to decide their adventure's direction.

This open-ended format was groundbreaking, offering an unprecedented level of player choice in a time when most games were strictly linear. With each new decision, a different part of the game's world unfolded, making every player's journey unique. It was a digital playground where curiosity and strategy coalesced, setting new standards for player engagement and narrative depth in video gaming.

With a map in hand, players got their first taste of open-world gaming, minus the GPS help.

Before the days when GPS directed our every move, *The Legend of Zelda* handed players a simple 8-bit map and said, "Off you go, adventurer!" This game introduced what many consider the genesis of the open-world genre. Players took on the daunting task of exploring a vast, interconnected world with only their wits and a rudimentary guide to lead them.

Without the luxury of modern navigation aids, exploration required real attention and memorization. This open-world experience encouraged players to think creatively, solve problems, and dive into every nook and cranny of the digital landscape. It gave a sense of accomplishment and discovery that resonated deeply, influencing countless titles that followed in the open-world gaming tradition.

Memorable music from *Zelda* made it even more magical and nostalgic.

Music has the uncanny ability to evoke emotion, and in *The Legend of Zelda*, Koji Kondo's compositions did just that. The iconic overworld theme, with its adventurous and triumphant melodies, became synonymous with the feeling of exploration and wonder. This music not only complemented the game's magical atmosphere but also became an integral part of its identity.

Decades later, these enchanting tunes still resonate with players, triggering nostalgia and transporting them back to those early days of adventure. The themes were simple yet powerful, cementing *Zelda*'s status in video game history as some of the most memorable soundscapes ever created. The music of *Zelda* showed that soundtracks could elevate a game from mere pixels to an emotionally engaging experience.

The game introduced puzzles that made you feel like a genius... right after feeling lost for hours.

One hallmark of *The Legend of Zelda* was its clever integration of puzzles that could both perplex and delight. These challenges were not just obstacles but intricate parts of the adventure, requiring players to think critically and explore thoroughly. The initial bewilderment of navigating labyrinthine dungeons would eventually give way to the euphoria of solving a puzzle, triggering a rush of accomplishment.

Whether it was deciphering cryptic clues or discovering hidden passages, each solved puzzle offered a satisfying 'aha' moment. This duality of feeling lost and then elated amplified the players' immersion and engagement, creating a dynamic gameplay loop. It was a masterclass in game design, teaching players patience and perseverance, rewarding them with the ultimate triumph of intellect and will.

Final Fantasy's Lasting Legacy

Who knew that having the word 'Final' in the title would lead to countless sequels and a gaming institution?

The first *Final Fantasy* wasn't supposed to be the last, but maybe it should have been 'First Fantasy' instead.

The creation of the original *Final Fantasy* was nothing short of a miracle, born from the desperation of a company on the brink of collapse. Hironobu Sakaguchi, the game's creator, envisioned it as Square's last-ditch effort, hence the "Final" in its title. Ironically, it led not to an end, but to a beginning of an enduring franchise. Naming it "First Fantasy" might have been more fitting, although lacking the dramatic flair brought by its eventual success.

The game showcased a perfect blend of risk-taking innovation and nostalgic homage to tabletop RPGs. From humble beginnings, *Final Fantasy* tapped into the imagination of players worldwide, laying the groundwork for a perpetual series filled with magic, myth, and legend. This initial release was a critical moment in gaming history, turning an anticipated curtain call into a never-ending encore.

Turn-based combat in *Final Fantasy* made every battle feel like a chess match, but with more explosions.

The turn-based combat in *Final Fantasy* was revolutionary for its time, bringing a strategic depth that electrified players. Battles required careful planning, much like a chess game, but with an added flair of fantastical abilities.

Think of it as chess, but instead of moving pawns, players wielded lightning spells and swung oversized swords.

This approach to combat emphasized tactics over timing, allowing players to pause and ponder each move. It was about anticipating enemy actions, understanding character strengths, and unleashing apocalyptic attacks when the time was right. Explosions, flamboyant magic, and epic confrontations filled these strategic skirmishes, keeping players on the edge of their seats and their fingers on the controller buttons.

Rich storytelling and character development gave players an emotional roller coaster ride.

One of *Final Fantasy*'s enduring contributions to gaming is its detailed storytelling and emotional character arcs. Players were not just mindlessly slashing through dungeons; they were diving into narratives that could rival epic novels. Characters weren't just pixelated heroes; they were complex individuals with dreams, flaws, and personal quests.

The games tackled themes of love, bravery, sacrifice, and betrayal, creating stories that resonated with players on multiple levels. Characters evolved not just in power but in personality, allowing players to form strong, lasting connections. Each plot twist and emotional high and low was orchestrated to grip the heartstrings, making these adventures unforgettable chapters in gaming history.

Each sequel managed to keep exploring new worlds and ideas, proving you can never have too many Final Fantasies.

With each release, *Final Fantasy* continually redefined itself, exploring new realms and innovative ideas. Each sequel was a reinvention rather than a continuation, bringing fresh settings, characters, and game mechanics. The series's creativity served as proof that there could never be too many Final Fantasies to satisfy the insatiable appetite of its fanbase.

From steampunk-infused cities to high-tech metropolises, the worlds of *Final Fantasy* varied as much as the stories they held. This flexibility allowed the franchise to stay fresh, captivating veterans and newcomers alike. It's this willingness to experiment and evolve that has kept the series relevant and beloved across generations, cementing its legendary status in the annals of gaming history.

The Magic of Interactive Storytelling

Let's chat about how RPGs turned mere gaming sessions into epic tales where players became heroes.

Branching narratives in RPGs meant you weren't just watching a movie; you were directing your own saga.

Role-playing games, particularly during the renaissance of the genre, transformed passive gaming experiences into interactive epic tales. No longer confined to linear storylines, players could make decisions that branched into a multitude of pathways, leading to diverse outcomes. This innovation allowed players to wield the narrative wand themselves. Imagine Frodo deciding to keep the One Ring or Luke choosing the dark side — such possibilities became integral to the gaming experience.

This level of interactivity gave rise to a new dimension of storytelling, where gamers weren't just spectators but active participants in their journey. Each choice felt significant, creating a personalized adventure as unique as the player themselves. These stories, shaped by actions and decisions at every crossroad, turned traditional gaming into a personalized, unfolding narrative. Stray from the path, and you might find a hidden treasure, or, whoops—a fearsome dragon!

Non-playable characters (NPCs) in RPGs made worlds feel alive, even if some just repeated the same lines.

Non-playable characters are the unsung heroes of role-playing games. They populate the digital landscapes with merchants, villagers, and reluctant quest-givers, turning otherwise barren environments into bustling hubs of activity. Each NPC contributes a glimpse into the larger world, adding to the tapestry of the game's lore. Sure, some of these folks had the vocabulary of a miffed parrot, repeating the same line ad nauseam, but they played their part.

Even those NPCs who seemed stuck in a loop added layers of realism and immersion. They provided crucial information, comedic relief, and sometimes a well-needed side quest or two to pad out the adventure. Those quirky lines they muttered became part of the culture, injecting humor and nostalgia as players remembered their repetitive yet somehow charming dialogue. NPCs, simply put, made fantastical worlds feel richly inhabited.

Saving your game wasn't just smart; it was essential, unless you liked redoing hours of questing.

In the realm of role-playing games, the ability to save your progress was nothing short of a lifeline. While seasoned gamers can recount the heartache of losing hours to an unexpected power cut or vicious boss battle, saving became a hallmark of smarter gameplay. It stood as the great equalizer, offering a checkpoint for knights-in-training before daring to slay another digitally-rendered dragon.

Saving wasn't just a mere convenience; it allowed for experimentation without hefty consequences. Want to see what happens if you insult the king or attempt to pull off that sneaky heist? No problem at all — just save first! This feature transformed worlds of potential punishment into delightful playgrounds for both strategic and occasionally reckless gaming. Remember: a hero is only as good as their last save.

Experiencing different outcomes based on your choices taught players that every action had consequences, just like in real life.

RPGs taught valuable life lessons through the lens of virtual consequence and reward. Much like a choose-your-ownadventure book but with even greater implications, the choices made could ripple across the game's landscape affecting allies, outcomes, and even the endgame itself. Your seemingly simple decision to save a townsperson from a burning building might later net you a crucial ally or a powerful item to aid your quest.

This feature was not just about adapting gameplay to personal styles, but also reinforcing a mirror of real-life wisdom: actions have consequences. Bearing the responsibility for one's decisions — whether leading to triumphs or catastrophes — was a groundbreaking realization within the gaming community. Players learned to strategize, weigh moral decisions, and appreciate the weight of their choices, adding layers of depth to their adventures.

Technical Advancements in RPGs

From clunky mechanics to smooth gameplay, RPGs have come a long way in tech innovation.

Graphics evolved from squares and triangles into detailed worlds you wanted to explore for days.

Ah, the pixel art days, when characters were charmingly boxy and landscapes resembled a toddler's doodle. Early RPG graphics were simple yet groundbreaking, setting the scene for adventures that captured our imaginations. Over time, these squares and triangles transformed, becoming lush and intricate terrains you could practically get lost in—if only your parents would let you play just a bit longer.

The evolution of graphics hardware allowed RPGs to create detailed, expansive worlds. Sprites transformed into polygons, then into fully rendered 3D models, giving players locales so captivating they deserved postcards. These changes not only enhanced visual storytelling but also deepened player immersion. Instead of just hitting a button, you felt like you were truly swinging that sword in a lush, pixel-perfect forest!

Improved soundtracks and voice acting made games feel like blockbuster movies, not just pastimes.

Remember when your character's best dialogue was a strategically placed exclamation mark? Thankfully, those days are (mostly) behind us. As technology evolved, so did the sound component of RPGs. Soundtracks grew from monotone beeps into full symphonic scores that could make John Williams nod in approval. Now, you could finally rescue that princess with a whole orchestra cheering you on!

Voice acting added another level of depth, transforming characters from silent protagonists into voices worth listening to—both heroic and otherwise. NPCs no longer muttered the same tired phrases on repeat; they were alive, vibrant, and interactive, enhancing your game with storytelling worthy of a silver screen debut.

Better AI meant enemies were smarter, or at least less predictable in their cluelessness.

Wow, the days when opponents moved in robotic patterns or barely noticed you while you walked around them endlessly! Thankfully, RPG AI has evolved beyond the IQ of a potted plant. Technical leaps allowed enemies to employ creative strategies, react to player actions, and provide a challenge that felt rewarding rather than repetitive.

Improved AI empowered adversaries with personal grudges who wouldn't just roll over when poked. Each encounter became a dance of strategy—dodging spell-casting wizards who actually aimed where you were going, not where you were. While some might argue that AI still plays “hard to get… right,” the improvements made battles less about patterns and more about cunning.

Expansive maps became the norm, transforming RPGs into epic journeys rather than quick quests.

Remember when "open world" meant a slightly bigger screen? Early RPGs often consisted of limited pathways and contained environments. The advent of advanced game engines blew those doors wide open, creating sprawling landscapes players could roam freely. The horizon wasn't just a line of pixels; it was out there, calling you to explore.

These expansive worlds provided more than just geographical freedom—they offered endless quests, hidden lore, and countless collectible goodies for the die-hard completionists. Extensive maps transformed RPGs into journeys of discovery, with every hilltop promising new vistas and hidden secrets, making it easy to forget the concept of a "quick gaming session."

Chapter 6: Multiplayer Madness - Friends, Foes, and Fun

Time to gather your friends (and your worst enemies) for some couch co-op chaos. Discover how multiplayer gaming turned from a competitive sport to a cherished group activity, where losing was (almost) as fun as winning.

The Birth of Multiplayer - Arcade Beginnings

Long before online matches, multiplayer gaming was all about friendly rivalry in the arcade corner. Let's look at how this all began.

Arcades were the earliest multiplayer platforms where players went head-to-head on classic machines.

In the early days of video gaming, **arcades** were the ultimate battlegrounds. These vibrant venues, often filled with flashing lights and electronic bleeps, served as the first true multiplayer platforms. Players from all walks of life would flock to arcades to test their skills, eagerly awaiting their turn on classic machines.

The competitive nature was palpable as players *went head-to-head*, striving not only for high scores but for the sheer satisfaction of besting their peers. Arcade culture thrived on this face-to-face interaction, which set the stage for the social aspect of gaming that we cherish today. It was in these dimly lit rooms that the essence of multiplayer gaming was born.

Games like Pong and Spacewar! were pioneers of multiplayer gaming, featuring direct player competition.

Pong and *Spacewar!*, two trailblazers of the gaming world, introduced the concept of multiplayer gaming to the masses. *Pong*, with its simple two-paddle, one-ball concept, became an instant classic, inviting players on either side to compete in a game of electronic table tennis.

Spacewar!, on the other hand, offered a more experimental approach, with two players commanding spacecrafts in a battle for survival. These games established the blueprint for direct player competition, demonstrating that multiplayer wasn't just about scoring points, but about creating a thrilling contest that kept players coming back for more.

Social interaction in arcades was as important as the games themselves, creating a vibrant community.

The arcade was not just about games; it was a **social hub** where friendships were forged and rivalries kindled. The bustling atmosphere allowed gamers to bond over shared victories and crushing defeats, transforming solitary gaming into a shared experience.

Whether it was the camaraderie developed over arcade machines or the banter exchanged in the heat of competition, the social interactions were pivotal. These interactions helped build a sense of community among gamers, making arcades a place where friendships flourished as much as high scores.

The introduction of two-player modes laid the groundwork for cooperative gaming experiences.

As multiplayer evolved, **two-player modes** began to emerge, paving the way for cooperative play. These modes allowed players to join forces, strategizing and collaborating rather than merely competing. This shift expanded the gaming experience, enabling players to share the thrill of victory and the agony of defeat.

By shifting from head-to-head contests to cooperative gameplay, gamers learned the value of teamwork, communication, and shared goals. This evolution was crucial in broadening the scope of gaming, setting the stage for the cooperative adventures that many enjoy today.

Multiplayer arcade cabinets became the cornerstone for friendly competitions and local tournaments.

Arcade cabinets featuring multiplayer capabilities quickly became the heart of local competitions. Friendly rivalries were kindled in front of these machines, as players aimed to outscore one another and earn a coveted spot on the high-score board.

Not only did these cabinets provide endless entertainment, but they also sparked the formation of local tournaments. These events gathered aspiring champions and spectators alike, turning gaming into a spectator sport long before esports became a global phenomenon. The excitement and energy of these gatherings left a lasting impression on the gaming culture.

Home Consoles - Bringing Friends Together

As gaming moved into the home, couch co-op rose in popularity. Here's how consoles reshaped multiplayer fun.

Home consoles enabled multiplayer gaming without the need to visit arcades, fostering more frequent gatherings.

Once a purely arcade-bound experience, multiplayer gaming took a giant leap towards accessibility with the advent of home consoles. Gone were the days when players needed to pocket a roll of quarters and trek to the nearest arcade to enjoy a round of their favorite games. Instead, the living room became the new battleground for friends determined to prove their superiority.

By bringing the arcade experience home, consoles such as the Atari 2600 and later systems allowed gamers to host regular get-togethers. These gaming marathons turned casual gaming sessions into regular social events, sparking a new era of interactive entertainment where anyone could join the fun from the comfort of their own couch. The convenience of home gaming fueled an upsurge in frequent gatherings, changing how and where we connected with friends through gaming.

Two-player games like Frogger and Mario Bros. made family game night a regular event.

Home consoles introduced a new dynamic to family game nights, with many systems capitalizing on the popularity of two-player games. Titles like *Frogger* and *Mario Bros.* created opportunities for players of all ages to join in the fun, often turning an ordinary evening into a competitive showdown.

Instead of just a family viewing of a TV show, these games allowed for interactive participation, pulling family members of all generations into their pixelated worlds. The thrill of outmaneuvering frogs across traffic lanes or stomping koopas together made these experiences memorable. Whether it was siblings, parents, or even grandparents taking up the controllers, these games democratized gaming and cemented it as a beloved household pastime.

Consoles like the NES and Sega Genesis introduced third and fourth controllers, expanding the multiplayer experience.

The evolution of home consoles didn't stop at two players. Systems like the NES and Sega Genesis expanded multiplayer capabilities by introducing support for additional controllers. This innovation was a game-changer, literally, as it allowed more participants to get involved in the action.

With up to four players able to compete simultaneously, gaming nights could become group spectacles filled with laughter and good-natured trash talk. Titles like *Super Bomberman* and *Gauntlet* became the go-to party games, transforming a quiet night at home into a raucous affair.

Multiplayer gaming evolved beyond a duel into a full-fledged melee, scaling up the excitement and the chaos.

Split-screen modes allowed multiple players to share the same gaming experience directly on one TV.

Split-screen gaming brought a new dimension to local multiplayer sessions. Instead of taking turns, players could engage in simultaneous adventures, racing against each other in *Super Off-Road* or battling it out in *GoldenEye 007*.

This format was an innovation that aligned perfectly with the camaraderie of couch co-op play. Sharing the same TV, friends could react to each other's strategies in real time—not to mention engage in a bit of harmless screen-peeking. Split-screen fostered both teamwork and rivalry, making every match feel personal and every victory that much sweeter.

Friendly rivalry was enhanced through in-home tournaments and long gaming sessions with friends.

Multiplayer gaming wasn't just about playing together; it was about thriving on the competitive spirit it whipped up. The introduction of home consoles paved the way for in-home tournaments where participants would face off for bragging rights—or, in some families, even chores-free weeks.

Long gaming marathons, often stretching into the wee hours, became the norm as friends and family gathered to participate in endless rounds of *Street Fighter II* or *Tetris*. These competitions were the breeding ground for friendly rivalries, where losing was often as fun as winning, provided there was a good match to be had.

The Magic of Couch Co-op and Competitive Play

The living room became a battlefield and a cooperative playground, forever changing how we played together.

Couch co-op games fostered teamwork as friends and family joined forces to complete challenging missions.

Remember the days when solving a puzzle in a game meant calling your siblings or friends over to the couch? Couch co-op games transformed living rooms into mission control centers, with players teaming up to overcome obstacles that one could not conquer alone. From the pixelated quests of *Gauntlet* to the adventurous expeditions in *Contra*, these games encouraged creative problem-solving and collaboration.

Players learned to divide tasks effectively—one keeping the enemies at bay while another solved a tricky puzzle. The shared victory, whether it was completing a level or defeating a formidable boss, reinforced bonds and left lasting memories. Few experiences could match the jubilation of high-fiving a friend after a particularly hair-raising mission.

Competitive spirit thrived in games like Street Fighter II and Mortal Kombat, where friendships were tested.

For those who preferred a bit of friendly rivalry, games like *Street Fighter II* and *Mortal Kombat* offered the perfect arena. Competitive matches became the highlight of gatherings, as players honed their skills to deliver devastating combos and claim bragging rights. The trash talk was fierce, the victories sweeter, as players aimed to be the undisputed champion of the living room.

For those on the losing end, the sting of defeat often sparked motivation to improve. Players would practice different characters, seeking new skills to counter their rival's tactics. These games didn't just test reflexes and skill; they also required quick thinking and adaptability, adding layers to the competitive experience.

Multiplayer gaming encouraged social interaction, making it a shared activity with laughter and friendly banter.

Whether it was a thrilling victory or a humorous in-game blunder, multiplayer gaming created endless opportunities for social interaction. The constant chatter, laughter, and playful jabs enhanced the experience, transforming it from a solitary activity into a vibrant social event.

The living room became a hub for lively discussions as friends debated strategies or recounted legendary victories and comical defeats. With everyone competing or cooperating in these games, there was never a dull moment. The shared gaming adventures provided stories that were recounted for years, often with much embellishment and joy.

The balance between cooperation and competition drove many of the best gameplay experiences.

Many vintage games struck a masterful balance between cooperation and competition, crafting experiences that were both engaging and unpredictable. Titles like *Double Dragon* allowed players to work together throughout most of the game, only to face off against each other for the coveted high score or final victory. This blend of camaraderie and rivalry kept players hooked for hours.

Finding the perfect equilibrium between aiding a teammate and outperforming an opponent was integral to enjoying these games. This push and pull created dynamic gameplay where strategies could shift suddenly based on the players' decisions or unexpected game events, keeping everyone on their toes and ensuring each gaming session was unique.

Unexpected alliances and rivalries formed, adding layers to the gaming experience.

One of the most exciting aspects of multiplayer games was the formation of unexpected alliances and rivalries. Friends might suddenly find themselves at odds in a competitive game, while previous foes could team up for a common cause in co-op challenges. These unpredictable shifts in allegiance added a delightful twist to gaming sessions.

Games became more than just challenges of skill; they were also arenas of diplomacy and strategy. Deciding who to trust and ally with or when to strike out on your own added depth to the experience. These dynamics ensured that each gaming session was a unique narrative with its stories of camaraderie and cunning.

LAN Parties and Arcade Nostalgia

Before high-speed internet gaming, LAN parties and arcades were the ultimate hangout spots. Let's take a nostalgic stroll down memory lane.

LAN parties offered a unique experience, transforming basements into battlegrounds for massive multiplayer events.

Before the rise of online gaming, LAN parties were an innovator in multiplayer experiences, offering gamers something truly unique. Imagine transforming an ordinary basement into a buzzing battleground where just a fridge full of snacks stood between contenders and victory. Participants would haul massive PCs around like prized possessions, ready to conquer in games like Unreal Tournament.

The electricity in the air as players battled in real-time, right there in the same room, created an atmosphere unparalleled by today's standards. Many nostalgic gamers fondly recall shouting across the room to relay strategies or celebrate point-winning moments. It was an immersive experience that built camaraderie and intense competition among friends, leaving behind a legacy of unforgettable moments.

The logistical feat of setting up LAN parties became half of the fun, with cables and clunky PCs everywhere.

Setting up for a LAN party was an event in itself; it required considerable planning and execution that turned into part of the enjoyable chaos. Tangles of Ethernet cables sprawling across the room complemented the sound of old modems struggling to keep up with the blistering pace of gameplay.

Players would transform dining tables and coffee tables into operational gaming hubs. Assembling this intricate setup required ingenuity akin to building an elaborate fortress. The massive CRT monitors that ensured eye strain and clunky CPUs that were literal towers of power added to the spectacle. The logistical madness was not a deterrent but rather a catalyst for excitement, and brought everyone together in anticipation of the gaming fun ahead.

Arcades offered nostalgic fun, becoming both a gaming venue and a social hub.

Arcades were the epicenter of gaming culture, charmingly drenched in neon light and buzzing with the rhythmic sound of digital bleep bloops. For many gamers, arcades were not just places to play, but venues where friends could meet, share stories, and experience the joy of gaming side by side. It was where high scores became the stuff of legends, and bragging rights were earned the hard way.

These dens of digital delight were often filled with rows of cabinets inviting players to test their skills, making even failures feel like a win thanks to the communal atmosphere. The journey to the arcade itself felt like an adventure. In essence, they provided an early glimpse of gaming as a social activity, setting the foundation for the communitycentric experiences we see in gaming today.

Both LAN and arcade environments provided opportunities for real-world interactions and friendships beyond gaming.

Beyond the glow of pixels and the thrill of play, LAN parties and arcades were instrumental in forging friendships that extended beyond the realm of gaming. These environments fostered genuine human interaction where real-world connections thrived amidst the digital mayhem. Players shared not only spaces but stories, laughter, and sometimes, intense rivalries that became lifelong friendships.

The intimate nature of these experiences was unrivaled; the laughter, high-fives, and occasional good-natured jeering added layers of human touch. It was these interactions that laid the seeds for today's online communities, reminding us that gaming has always been greater when shared with others, regardless of the medium.

LAN parties popularized games like Counter-Strike and Warcraft, expanding multiplayer genres.

LAN parties were crucial in the rise to fame of many iconic games, cementing them as milestones in multiplayer gaming. Titles like Counter-Strike and Warcraft II sprang out of these gatherings, as LAN environments offered the perfect setting for spontaneous strategy and exhilarating matches. Players explored maps and honed tactics, pushing these games to new heights of popularity.

The success of these games at LAN events showcased the immense potential of multiplayer genres, inspiring countless developers to explore similar paths. As a result, LAN parties did not just host gaming — they became incubators for genre evolution, cultivating a generation of titles that paved the way for the competitive esports culture we know today.

The Transition to Online Multiplayer

When the internet took over, it revolutionized multiplayer gaming, connecting players globally. Here's how the shift happened.

The rise of online multiplayer brought gamers together from across the globe in real-time battles and collaborations.

As the digital landscape expanded, online multiplayer games became the virtual equivalent of inviting the whole neighborhood over for a gaming marathon. No longer constrained by geography, players could now compete or collaborate with others halfway across the globe. *Street Fighter* bouts were no longer confined to crowded hotel lobbies at comic conventions, and daring raids in *World of Warcraft* required teamwork with virtual warriors from faroff lands.

This real-time connectivity revolutionized the way gamers approached challenges. Strategies evolved, reflecting the diverse thoughts and creative solutions of a global player base. Late-night skirmishes weren't just battles of skill but cultures, fostering a unique camaraderie among players who reveled in the thrill of real-time interaction, overcoming language barriers with the universal language of gaming.

Platforms like Xbox Live and PlayStation Network redefined multiplayer, making it more accessible and structured.

The launch of Xbox Live and PlayStation Network marked a seismic shift in the gaming world, offering structured platforms for players to connect, compete, and celebrate victories. These network services turned every console into a doorway to global adventures, eliminating the need for tangled LAN cables or close-knit friend groups huddled around a single screen.

With user-friendly interfaces, built-in matchmaking, and seamless integration, these platforms democratized online gaming, making it accessible to enthusiasts of all skill levels. They ensured even novice players could venture into the competitive arena with matchmaking systems that facilitated fair competition, level by level. It was like turning on your console and having the whole world online, ready to play, right at your fingertips.

Internet gaming communities grew, offering forums and social spaces for players to discuss strategies and form teams.

With the dawn of online gaming came a surge in virtual communities and forums where players could swap strategies, share triumphs, and forge friendships. These digital realms quickly became bustling marketplaces for ideas, with forums acting as town halls where cliques of gamers would gather to debate the merits of different strategies.

Platforms like Steam, Reddit, and Discord became digital watering holes, where gamers could boast about high scores, book gaming sessions, and even trade in-game goods like digital entrepreneurs. They also provided breeding grounds for organized gaming teams, decks of cards now replaced with avatars and team names, as unknowns revolutionized the scene by building alliances in preparation for online campaigns and tournaments.

Online gaming created opportunities for competitive eSports, turning multiplayer battles into professional sports.

As online multiplayer flourished, a new era of competition dawned, birthing the phenomenon of eSports. What started as friendly online skirmishes evolved into high-stakes tournaments where digital gladiators vied for fame and fortune. Multiplayer battles transformed from casual fun to professional careers, as talented gamers became celebrities in their own right.

Games like *Dota 2* and *League of Legends* spearheaded this revolution, with tournaments offering prize pools that rivaled traditional sports events. Players trained rigorously, spectators filled arenas, and millions tuned in to thrilling broadcasts. It was a realm where strategy was king, reflexes were honed to perfection, and victory could launch careers into the virtual stratosphere.

The shift online didn't eliminate couch co-op but added another layer of global competitiveness to multiplayer gaming.

Contrary to popular belief, the rise of online gaming didn't sound the death knell for cozy nights of couch co-op. It simply added another dimension to the multiplayer experience. While online gaming offered global connections, couch co-op retained its cherished role as the ultimate test of friendship and patience.

Games like *Overcooked* and *Moving Out* have kept local multiplayer alive and kicking, with their commitment to sowing delightful chaos in living rooms worldwide. The magic of sharing a screen remains, while online connectivity brings forth another layer of competition, giving players a full palette of multiplayer interaction to choose from, be it digital diplomacy or direct, in-your-face challenges.

Chapter 7: The Enduring Legacy - Where Are They Now?

What happened to our pixelated pals? Are they nestled in a cozy digital retirement home, or still alive and kicking? Discover the incredible impact these vintage games have had on modern gaming and pop culture, and why their legacy is anything but game over.

The Magic of Pixel Art

Pixel art might seem like ancient history, but it's had a serious glow-up over the years. What started as a necessity due to technological limits is now a celebrated art form.

From necessity to nostalgia, pixel art is now a popular design choice in indie games, reminding us why simple visuals are still cool.

Once upon a time, pixel art was all that game developers had to work with, crafting worlds limited by technology but rich with creativity. In today's world, what was born out of necessity has transformed into a cherished aesthetic. Indie game developers have embraced pixel art, not only as a nod to the past but also as a way to stand out in a crowded market. This love for the simpler graphics of yore is not merely about retro appeal; it's a testament to how effective visuals can evoke powerful emotions and tell compelling stories. The enduring popularity of pixel art proves that detail isn't always king—sometimes, simplicity rules.

Games like Stardew Valley and Celeste borrow heavily from classic pixel styles, turning simplicity into a rich experience.

Titles like *Stardew Valley* and *Celeste* have redefined what pixelated graphics can achieve, weaving simple visuals into evocative storytelling and tightly crafted gameplay. These games borrow heavily from the classic pixel styles of the 8-bit and 16-bit eras, infusing them with modern gameplay mechanics and narratives that captivate players. They transform simplicity into richness by marrying minimalistic art with expressive details, creating environments that feel both nostalgic and fresh. This blending of old-school charm with innovative design speaks to the enduring strength of pixel art: its ability to engage players with a look that's both straightforward and deeply immersive.

Pixel art's rise in pop culture is epic, showing up not just in games but in fashion and art galleries too.

Vintage is always in style.

The influence of pixel art has spilled over from the digital realm into broader pop culture, cementing its place in fashion, décor, and art galleries worldwide. From pixelated clothing prints to gallery exhibits showcasing the artistry of this minimalist style, pixel art has proven its versatility and staying power. It's embraced in everything from quirky T-shirts to high-end art pieces, suggesting that while technology has advanced, the charm of pixelated visuals never goes out of style. This cultural phenomenon highlights the timeless appeal of vintage aesthetics, showing that what is old can continuously inspire new interpretations in various creative domains.

The love for pixel art is a testament to how something 'old-school' can stay forever young in the digital age.

Pixel art's timeless appeal lies in its paradox of old-school roots with a perpetually youthful spirit. Despite the rapid advancements in graphics technology, pixel art continues to thrive, beloved by new and returning fans alike. It serves as a comforting reminder that, amidst constantly evolving tech, some things remain constant and captivating. This enduring appreciation showcases the ability of vintage styles to adapt and resonate across generations. The art form celebrates the past while maintaining relevance, proving that sometimes, the most 'old-school' concepts are those that stay forever young, continually refreshed by each new wave of admiration.

Characters That Time Forgot (Or Did They?)

Remember the likes of Frogger and Q*Bert? These digital buddies aren't just sitting in the gaming attic collecting dust. Here's how they continue to level up in today's world.

Frogger has hopped his way back into the spotlight with modern remakes and even a TV game show—what a leap!

Frogger, once just a frog with the audacious goal of safely crossing a busy road, has become a classic symbol of the golden age of video games. His unique charm has resulted in numerous modern remakes, each infusing fresh graphics while retaining the core gameplay that made it a hit. But that's not all—Frogger has indeed leaped beyond the digital world.

In recent years, the amphibious star found a new stage in the form of a TV game show. Aptly named "Frogger," this show, airing on NBC, reimagines the classic game into a larger-than-life obstacle course. Contestants experience firsthand what it's like to navigate through a real-world version of Frogger's challenging environment. It's a testament to Frogger's ongoing relevance and appeal, reminding us that some games, no matter how old, never truly fade away. Leap after leap, Frogger keeps hopping into new territories, proving he's not just a relic of the past but a vibrant part of today's entertainment landscape.

Q*Bert may not be the buzz of new releases, but he's found new life in cameos in blockbuster movies like Wreck-It Ralph.

Q*Bert, the quirky, cube-hopping character, might not headline new video game titles nowadays, but he remains a beloved face thanks to his cameo appearances in films. Most notably, Q*Bert bounced back into public consciousness thanks to Disney's "Wreck-It Ralph." In this animation, he finds himself as a nostalgic character who interacts with modern gaming icons, providing a fun homage to gaming's earlier days.

His appearance in "Wreck-It Ralph" not only tickled the nostalgia of older fans but introduced him to a younger audience who may have never encountered the oddball character in his original gaming format. It's fascinating how cinematic cameos have given Q*Bert a second wind, showing that even the most obscure characters can leap into new roles and delight audiences across different media. So while he might not be the star of new game titles, Q*Bert's iconic status remains intact, thanks to these creative revivals on the big screen.

Even Pong has its moments, inspiring minimalist design approaches in current mobile games.

Pong, the granddaddy of arcade games, has an enduring legacy that continues to shape modern gaming design. Its simple paddles-and-ball gameplay has influenced countless minimalist mobile games. By reducing complexity and focusing on engaging gameplay mechanics, Pong paved the way for the success of streamlined game designs on today's mobile platforms.

Contemporary titles like "Atomas" and "Threes!" carry Pong's minimalist torch, proving that less can indeed be more. The straightforward yet addictive nature of Pong serves as a blueprint, demonstrating how elegance and simplicity can captivate players. Despite the technological advancements of the gaming industry, the core principles established by Pong remain valuable, influencing designers to create experiences that prioritize fun over flash. It's a minimalistic marvel that proves a minimalist game need not be complex to be engaging, genuinely continuing Pong's legacy in pixel-perfect ways.

The charm of these characters continues to echo in their spiritual successors, ensuring they never really left.

The legacy of these vintage characters extends far beyond their original games through what we affectionately term as their spiritual successors. Many modern video games retain the essence of these classics through homage and inspiration. For instance, the endless runner genre recalls the relentless pace of Frogger, while unique design elements in puzzle games nod to Q*Bert's iconic hopping style.

The charm these characters brought to the gaming world can still be felt in titles that prioritize clever mechanics and charming quirks. These newer games may not bear the exact names of their precursors, but the influence is unmistakable. Developers often draw from the simple yet captivating strategies of old hits, reinforcing that these characters and their games have left indelible footprints on the DNA of modern game design. Indeed, they've never truly disappeared. Instead, they've evolved and multiplied their presence through countless successful successors, echoing their pixelated charm across generations.

Soundtracks from a Bygone Era

Those 8-bit tunes that buzzed through our childhood are more than just audio nostalgia—they're now the focus of live concerts and remixes.

8-bit and chiptune music has rocketed out of the past into music festivals, blending old sounds with new technology.

The infectious beep-boop of 8-bit and chiptune music isn't just reserved for retro video game enthusiasts anymore. Today, these nostalgic sounds are headlining music festivals worldwide, proving that the charming simplicity of yesteryear's game music has far-reaching appeal. In a curious blend of old and new, artists utilize modern technology to remix and elevate these tracks, creating a unique aural experience that bridges generations. Imagine dancing to the familiar melodies of classic games, only now they're accompanied by pulsing synths and fresh beats. It's not just a flashback; it's a forward-looking celebration of one of gaming's most enduring elements. Vintage video game music has found a new audience, showing that what was once considered digital background noise is now center stage in a musical renaissance.

Legendary soundtracks from games like Super Mario Bros. are being celebrated in orchestral concerts worldwide.

Ah, the iconic overworld theme from Super Mario Bros.—a tune so recognizable it's practically a household anthem. But these days, you might actually hear it reverberating through grand concert halls rather than the cozy confines of your living room. Orchestral performances dedicated to classic video game soundtracks have become a global phenomenon, with maestros transforming pixel-era bleeps into sweeping symphonic productions. The thrilling crescendo of an orchestral version of the Mario theme not only rekindles fond memories for veteran gamers but also introduces younger audiences to these compositions in a grandiose setting. These concerts are a testament to how video game music has transcended its original purpose, earning a well-deserved spot in the world of classical music presentations.

Remixes of classic game soundtracks have surged in popularity, breathing new life into tracks we all loved.

Remember jamming to the bassline of Mega Man's level themes or vibing to the adrenaline-pumping rhythms of Sonic the Hedgehog? These iconic tracks have been given a new lease on life through modern remixes that explode with creativity. Artists and DJs are reimagining these beloved tunes, infusing them with elements of techno, dubstep, and even lo-fi beats. This surge in remix culture not only showcases the lasting appeal of these melodies but also demonstrates their adaptability to contemporary musical landscapes. With digital platforms making such remixes easily accessible, these updated tracks have become a staple for both nostalgic gamers and music lovers seeking something fresh yet familiar.

Gamers find comfort in the simplicity and charm of these melodies, proving that good tunes never die.

There's an undeniable warmth that comes with the plucky simplicity of vintage game soundtracks. For many, these tunes are akin to old friends, offering a comforting familiarity amidst the fast-paced buzz of modern gaming. Each melody, whether it's the jaunty notes of Tetris or the haunting harmonics of Zelda, holds a special place in the hearts of players, evoking cherished memories of "just one more level" nights. The endurance of these melodies is a testament to the idea that music doesn't need to be complex to be impactful. Instead, the charm lies in their catchy refrains and how they effortlessly evoke a sense of nostalgia that continues to resonate across generations. It's proof that truly good tunes never fade; they merely evolve, continuing to bring joy in their simplicity.

Game Mechanics: Old is New Again

Why fix what isn't broken? Many of today's games still use mechanics pioneered by those early titles. Power-ups, side-scrolling, and level-ups—let's hit the replay button on these timeless treasures.

Platformers like Super Mario Bros. laid the groundwork for countless games, making side-scrolling an eternal favorite.

Imagine a world without *Super Mario Bros.*; the gaming universe would indeed look fundamentally different. The magic of side-scrolling, first popularized by this iconic platformer, has become a timeless staple in game design. It's the bread and butter of navigating characters through environments, dodging obstacles, and collecting treasures.

This mechanic isn't just about moving from left to right; it's about creating a journey filled with secrets, challenges, and exploration. It provides simplicity, yet allows for complexity in terms of level design and player engagement. Even today, side-scrolling games are celebrated for their ability to offer both casual fun and hardcore challenges, ensuring these mechanics continue to captivate gamers across generations.

The concept of power-ups is alive and kicking, driving players to keep exploring and experimenting.

Who can forget the first time they grabbed a mushroom in *Super Mario Bros.* and felt the thrill of Mario leveling up with newfound abilities? Power-ups have since become an integral part of gaming lore, igniting the imagination of players as they seek out these quirky enhancements.

These mechanics invite players to roam far and wide, rewarding their curiosity with boosts in power, speed, or even aesthetics. This ancient concept persists as a vital element in today's games, encouraging players to experiment, adapt, and replay. Whether it's a strength-augmenting potion or a temporary invincibility star, power-ups add layers of strategy and excitement, keeping players perpetually engaged.

Real-life escape room concepts mirror early adventure games, where solving puzzles is key to survival.

Before escape rooms challenged groups to think outside the box, early adventure games like *Zork* and *King's Quest* laid the groundwork for puzzle-solving escapades. These games were more than just entertainment; they were cerebral playgrounds where logic, creativity, and patience were crucial for success.

Today's escape rooms owe much to these digital predecessors, with intricate puzzles, clues, and narrative twists that echo the challenges of yesteryear. While players may no longer need to type "open door" or "light lamp," the satisfaction derived from cracking a cunning conundrum remains timeless. These concepts highlight the lasting appeal of games that stimulate both the mind and the imagination.

The legacy of these mechanics lives on, inspiring modern developers to keep creativity and challenge at the forefront.

In the world of video gaming, mechanics from the past remain very much part of the present. Today's developers stand on the shoulders of giants, borrowing, refining, and sometimes reinventing the principles of those early game design pioneers. Their influence encourages a continual exploration of creativity, ensuring that games not only entertain but challenge players intellectually and emotionally.

By implementing and adapting these vintage mechanics, developers connect generations of gamers, proving that old ideas can still provide fresh experiences. The legacy lives on in every challenging side quest, every cleverly hidden power-up, and every head-scratching puzzle, ensuring that these treasured gaming traditions remain ever relevant in a rapidly evolving digital landscape.

Collectors and Communities: Vintage Love

For some, vintage gaming is more than just nostalgia—it's a full-blown hobby. These communities and collectors keep the spirit of classic gaming alive and thriving.

Retro gaming conventions bring people together to celebrate their love for the classics, from old consoles to arcade cabinets.

Retro gaming conventions are vibrant gatherings where enthusiasts unite to indulge in their shared passion for vintage games. These events showcase an array of nostalgic delights, from the clunky arcade cabinets that once dominated local arcades to the beloved consoles that graced living rooms in the 80s and 90s.

Aside from the visual feast of retro hardware, these conventions often feature spirited gaming competitions, allowing attendees to pit their skills against fellow aficionados. Whether it's a Pac-Man high-score battle or a

Tetris showdown, the competitive spirit is alive and well. Beyond gaming, these conventions offer panels, workshops, and meet-andgreets with industry veterans, providing insights into the development of classic games and consoles.

Ultimately, these conventions are more than just a trip down memory lane—they are a celebration of gaming history, fostering connections among people across generations who share a love for pixels and old-school soundtracks.

Collector's markets for vintage games and consoles are booming, with rare items fetching impressive sums.

The value of vintage video games has skyrocketed, turning collector's markets into bustling hubs of activity where nostalgia meets commerce. Rare games and consoles are highly sought after, with collectors willing to pay eyepopping sums for these digital relics.

Marketplaces, both online and at dedicated trade shows, are filled with enthusiasts hunting for that elusive cartridge or system to complete their collection. Some games have sold for thousands, notably those in mint condition or still in original packaging. The allure of owning a piece of gaming history is irresistible to many, fueling bidding wars that rival the intensity of an arcade brawl.

The booming collector's market not only reflects the growing appreciation for vintage games but reinforces their value as cultural artifacts. It’s a testament to how much these once-simple creations have influenced the gaming landscape and continue to capture the hearts (and wallets) of passionate gamers worldwide.

Online communities allow gamers to share their vintage finds and discuss the impact of these gems on modern gaming.

The digital age has revolutionized how vintage gaming enthusiasts connect, with online communities serving as bustling forums for discussion, trading, and sharing of retro treasures. Through various platforms, gamers from all corners of the globe can showcase their latest finds, exchange tips on preservation, or simply revel in nostalgia.

These virtual spaces often host lively debates about the influence of games like *Super Mario Bros.* and *Chrono Trigger* on today's gaming giants. Images and videos circulate regularly, sparking conversations about graphical innovations, storyline depth, and gameplay mechanics that many modern games owe to their predecessors.

By nurturing these communities, vintage gaming enthusiasts not only keep the history alive but also ensure that the legacy of these pioneering games is appreciated and understood in the context of contemporary gaming culture. It's a digital archaeology site where every pixel tells a story.

The passion of collectors not only preserves the past but sets the stage for how we remember it moving forward.

Vintage game collectors play a crucial role in preserving the rich history of gaming. Their dedication to curating and maintaining collections of old games, consoles, and memorabilia ensures that these artifacts are not forgotten, but instead celebrated as quintessential chapters of video game history.

This passion goes beyond mere accumulation; it involves meticulous efforts to understand, document, and present the stories behind these items. Collectors often become unofficial archivists, creating detailed catalogs that provide invaluable resources for historians, developers, and curious gamers alike.

By safeguarding the past, collectors shape how future generations will recall and learn from it. As gaming technology continues to evolve at a breakneck pace, the work of these enthusiasts forms the foundation of our collective memory, reminding us of the humble beginnings and incredible achievements that continue to influence the industry today.

Chapter 8: Spacewar! - The First Real Game

Spacewar! is often regarded as the first true computer game. Developed in 1962 by a group of MIT students, it was a fundamental step forward. With its interactive features and competitive play, **Spacewar!** would influence countless games to follow.

Origins of Spacewar!

The creation of *Spacewar!* marked a pivotal moment in computer gaming history. This section explores its beginnings.

Developed in 1962 by MIT students, *Spacewar!* was one of the first digital computer games.

Spacewar! was conceived and developed by a group of talented MIT students in 1962, marking the dawn of digital computer gaming. At the time, computers were massive machines used primarily for academic and business purposes, significantly limited by their size and capability. Despite these constraints, the ambitious students saw the opportunity to explore interactive digital entertainment.

Using the PDP-1 computer, *Spacewar!* was a pioneering effort that laid the groundwork for future developments in gaming. As one of the first examples of a real-time interactive computer game, it captivated the imaginations of those who experienced it, turning the concept of a "game" into something more dynamic and engaging. The game's development was a testament to the inventiveness and curiosity prevalent at MIT during that era.

Steve Russell led the project, inspired by science fiction and the capabilities of the PDP-1 computer.

Steve Russell emerged as the leading figure in the development of *Spacewar!*, channeling his love for science fiction into creating a revolutionary gaming experience. Books, like E.E. "Doc" Smith’s "Lensman" series, heavily influenced Russell's vision. His admiration for these adventurous tales of space combat inspired him to bring a similar universe to life on the PDP-1.

This computer, notable for being one of the first systems designed for interactive computing, provided the perfect platform to realize such a vision. Its groundbreaking graphical capabilities allowed Russell and his team to step beyond the constraints of textual output, enabling them to visualize battles in outer space. This transformation from imagination to visualization was a significant leap in computer game development at the time.

The initial concept involved two spaceships fighting in the gravity well of a star.

The core concept of *Spacewar!* focused on two competing spaceships locked in a battle amidst the gravitational pull of a star. This setup introduced innovative gaming mechanics, including maneuvering strategies and resource management.

The star's gravity not only added a realistic element of physics to the game but also created strategic depth.

Players had to carefully navigate their ships, avoid collisions with the star while simultaneously trying to outwit their opponents. This blend of action and strategy set the stage for future game design, emphasizing interactive environments and player choices as crucial elements of the gaming experience. The concept of positional and tactical play has heavily influenced countless games over the following decades.

It was created to showcase the computational power of the PDP-1 and to experiment with graphical computing.

The PDP-1 computer had unique capabilities that *Spacewar!* aimed to highlight. Its interactive nature and ability to manage graphical output were groundbreaking features that intrigued the MIT developers. By creating *Spacewar!*, they not only illustrated the PDP-1's potential beyond traditional computation but also pushed the boundaries of what graphical computing could achieve.

This experimentation with graphics and real-time interactivity allowed the team to explore what was technologically possible. Their work demonstrated that computers could serve an artistic and entertaining purpose, which was a novel idea for the time. The influence of their exploration is evident in how computers are used today across various creative fields, extending well beyond the realm of gaming.

Game Mechanics and Features

Understanding the mechanics of *Spacewar!* sheds light on its innovative features.

Players controlled spacecraft equipped with limited fuel and ammunition.

In *Spacewar!*, players were tasked with piloting agile spacecraft that were not only nimble in their movements but also limited by finite resources. Each ship came equipped with a set amount of fuel, which was crucial for maneuverability and avoiding enemy fire. This constraint forced players to plan their moves carefully, balancing between offense and conservation.

The ammunition limitation added another layer of strategy, as players had to aim and fire with precision to ensure they could disable their opponent before running out of shots. Such dynamics created a tense gaming environment where resource management was just as important as tactical skill. Players had to anticipate their opponent's maneuvers, decide when to engage in combat, and know when it would be more prudent to retreat.

The game featured real-time control, a novelty for its time.

Unlike many contemporary computer programs, which were predominantly batch-processed and turn-based, *Spacewar!* broke new ground by incorporating real-time gameplay. This meant players could interact dynamically with the game world, making instantaneous decisions that directly affected the outcome.

The real-time control allowed for intense dogfights as players weaved through space, avoiding projectiles and seeking advantageous positions. This level of immersion was unprecedented, as it placed players directly in the piloting seat of their spacecraft. As players responded to onscreen actions without delay, it demonstrated the potential of computers to simulate engaging, responsive environments—a concept that became foundational in future game design.

A distinctive feature was the gravitational pull exerted by the central star in the playfield.

The central star in *Spacewar!*, affectionately referred to as "The Sun," wasn't merely a visual set piece; it played an integral role in gameplay. This celestial body exerted a gravitational pull, constantly drawing nearby objects inward, including the players' spacecraft. This feature added complexity and depth, requiring players to navigate with precision.

Skilled players learned to use the star's gravity to their advantage, slingshotting around it to gain speed or positioning an opponent into its fatal pull. The gravitational dynamics introduced a challenging environment that demanded both foresight and reflexes. This element of play established a physics-based interaction that enriched player experience, laying groundwork for future space-themed titles that capitalized on realistic mechanics.

Utilizing a hyperspace function allowed for strategic gameplay maneuvers.

A particularly innovative feature in *Spacewar!* was the hyperspace function, a last-resort tool for players in dire situations. By engaging hyperspace, a player's spacecraft would randomly teleport to an unknown location on the playfield, offering a potential escape from immediate danger or a chance to re-engage from a different angle.

However, using hyperspace came with inherent risks—players could reappear in a worse location, possibly near the central star or directly in an enemy's line of fire. This feature required thoughtful consideration and was best employed as a calculated gamble rather than a first response. The introduction of such mechanics in the game design encouraged players to weigh risks and rewards continuously, resulting in dynamic and unpredictable combat scenarios.

Impact on Future Games

Spacewar! set the stage for future developments in gaming. This section looks at its lasting effects.

Influenced the development of arcade games, leading to titles like *Asteroids* and *Galaga*.

The innovations present in *Spacewar!* laid foundational elements for future arcade games. Its core mechanics, focusing on rapid player interaction and real-time emphases, directly inspired the action-packed nature of arcade hits such as *Asteroids* and *Galaga*.

Introduced the concept of multiplayer gaming, paving the way for competitive video games.

Spacewar! was pioneering in introducing multiplayer elements, allowing two players to compete in real time. This was a novel concept that highlighted the potential of video games as social and competitive platforms.

The multiplayer component not only made for entertaining play but also laid the groundwork for future competitive games. As more sophisticated titles emerged, such as *Pong* and *Street Fighter*, they expanded on this dynamic, ultimately contributing significantly to the development of today's online multiplayer experiences.

Illustrated the potential for engaging graphics and interactive gameplay in electronic entertainment.

Despite the technological constraints of the early 1960s, *Spacewar!* showcased how engaging graphics and interactive gameplay could captivate players. Its visual presentation, though primitive by today's standards, was groundbreaking at the time, illustrating how computer graphics could be leveraged to enhance gaming experiences.

The interactive elements introduced by *Spacewar!*, such as ship controls and strategic actions, demonstrated early on how interactivity could transform user engagement in electronic entertainment, setting the stage for complex game designs in the future.

Fostered a community of hobbyists and developers interested in creating new game experiences.

Spacewar! not only influenced future games but also catalyzed a community of enthusiasts dedicated to exploring the possibilities of digital gaming. Its creation inspired a new wave of hobbyists and developers who were eager to push the boundaries of what games could achieve.

This burgeoning community laid the foundation for a collaborative environment, promoting innovation and the exchange of ideas. As a result, *Spacewar!* helped foster a spirit of experimentation and creativity that would remain vigourous in the game development industry for decades to come.

Technical Aspects of Spacewar!

The technical challenges and solutions in *Spacewar!* were pioneering for its time.

Programmed on the PDP-1, which boasted an impressive 200,000 operations per second.

The PDP-1 (Programmed Data Processor-1) was a pioneering computer that played a pivotal role in the development of *Spacewar!*. Introduced in 1959 by Digital Equipment Corporation, it was one of the first minicomputers, compact enough to be accessible for academic and research use. Boasting an impressive 200,000 operations per second, the PDP-1 provided the computational capability needed for real-time gameplay, which was a remarkable feat for its era. This processing power allowed the game to manage continuous interaction between players, process inputs, and render visual updates, establishing a foundation for future interactive media.

The PDP-1's design encouraged user programming and experimentation, which made it an ideal platform for creating
Spacewar!. With a powerful central processing unit for the time, developers could push the boundaries of what was possible, crafting an interactive experience that inspired the computer gaming industry for decades to come.

Utilized vector graphics for its visual display, a cutting-edge choice then.

Spacewar! made pioneering use of vector graphics to display its captivating space combat. Unlike the raster graphics that dominate modern computing, vector graphics used mathematical equations to render images with smooth lines and curves. This choice was cutting-edge for the 1960s and allowed for clear and dynamic visuals despite the limited graphical capabilities of the time.

By employing vector graphics, developers could effectively simulate a spacecraft's movement in a visually appealing manner. This approach also reduced the computational load on the PDP-1, as vector displays can portray large objects without extensive pixel data. As a result, *Spacewar!'s* visual effects, such as the floating stars and missile tracks, were both efficient and engaging, setting a standard for future graphical innovations.

Code was open-source, encouraging modifications and enhancements by other programmers.

The open-source nature of *Spacewar!* played a crucial role in its historical impact on the gaming industry. The game's code was freely distributed among academic and research communities, inviting programmers to modify and enhance it. This openness fostered a spirit of collaboration and innovation, as developers could build on the original design to explore new ideas and techniques.

This communal development process not only enriched *Spacewar!*'s gameplay but also paved the way for a culture of sharing and learning that is central to open-source projects today. By inspiring a generation of computer enthusiasts, *Spacewar!* helped establish the foundation for programming communities and the open-source movement, which remain vital to software development in the present day.

Innovative use of real-time interaction was a precursor to modern game development.

Spacewar! was groundbreaking in its use of real-time interaction, a concept now fundamental to gaming. The game's design allowed two players to control their spaceships simultaneously, reacting to each other's actions in a continuous flow. This was a significant departure from turn-based gameplay, demanding quick reflexes and strategic thinking.

This focus on real-time dynamics laid the groundwork for the interactive experiences we enjoy in modern games. The immediate responsiveness of *Spacewar!* foreshadowed the fast-paced, fluid gameplay that would become a hallmark of video games. The game's emphasis on real-time player engagement has influenced countless genres, from actionadventure to multiplayer online games, demonstrating its enduring legacy in game development.

Chapter 9: Pong - The Original Arcade Hit

The release of **Pong** in 1972 marked the beginning of the arcade gaming era. This simple yet highly addictive game captivated players in bars and arcades, setting off a craze that would last for decades.

Origins of Pong

Pong wasn't created in a corporate lab. Its origins are, in fact, quite humble and fascinating.

Pong was developed by Atari, founded by Nolan Bushnell and Ted Dabney.

Atari, the brainchild of Nolan Bushnell and Ted Dabney, was founded with the vision of making gaming accessible and fun for everyone. The company was officially established in 1972, right when the video game industry was starting to find its footing. Bushnell and Dabney's initiative quickly turned into a catalyst for innovation in the emerging arcade scene. **Pong**, their breakthrough creation, was Atari's first major product and set the stage for the company's success.

Pong's development marked the beginning of Atari's significant influence on the gaming world. It wasn't just the simplicity of the game that made it a hit, but the strategic foresight of its founders to bring video gaming into mainstream entertainment. Bushnell's insightful leadership and Dabney's technical prowess formed a dynamic partnership, one that would propel Atari to become a giant in the gaming industry.

The idea for Pong was inspired by an earlier game called 'Tennis for Two' developed in 1958.

The concept of Pong drew inspiration from a much earlier game, *Tennis for Two*, which was developed by physicist William Higinbotham in 1958. Unlike Pong, which was designed as a commercial arcade game, Tennis for Two was a simple demonstration built to entertain visitors at a national lab open house. The game depicted a simplified tennis match viewed from the side and used an oscilloscope as a screen.

Though Tennis for Two's technology was rudimentary, it laid foundational ideas that would later influence the creation of Pong. This historical connection highlights how innovative ideas, even those that begin as mere curiosities, can evolve into worldwide phenomena. The idea sparked by Tennis for Two helped transform Pong not only into a compelling game but also into a cultural icon.

Atari's goal was to create a simple game that could be played by anyone.

Atari set out to develop a game that was straightforward and enjoyable, ensuring that it appealed to a broad audience. This philosophy stemmed from the understanding that gaming should be inclusive, allowing anyone, regardless of age or gaming experience, to join in the fun. Pong's design epitomized this approach, featuring intuitive controls and clear objectives.

The beauty of Pong lay in its elegance and ease of play—just two paddles and a bouncing ball. With its minimalistic approach, Pong invited people who had never encountered video games to engage with its dynamic and competitive gameplay. It's this simplicity that made Pong a huge hit in bars and arcades, catching on rapidly among diverse groups of players.

Pong was initially crafted as a training exercise for a young engineer named Allan Alcorn.

When a young employee named Allan Alcorn joined Atari, Nolan Bushnell tasked him with a training exercise to design an electronic ping-pong game. Despite being a mere exercise, Alcorn poured his creativity and skill into the project, ultimately creating what became Pong. His resourcefulness and fresh outlook were pivotal in shaping the game's development.

Alcorn's iteration of the game, initially intended simply to hone his engineering skills, exceeded all expectations. His successful execution of the task demonstrated his increasing proficiency while also giving birth to one of gaming's first major hits. This story underscores the often-unpredictable pathways to success in the tech world, where even small projects can lead to revolutionary outcomes.

The game was housed in a simple wooden cabinet, emphasizing its humble beginnings.

Pong's initial presentation further reflected its unassuming origins; it was encased in a modest wooden cabinet that stood in stark contrast to the flashy designs common among arcade machines today. This simple housing was emblematic of the early 1970s arcade culture, where functionality was frequently prioritized over aesthetics.

The straightforward design of Pong's cabinet aligned perfectly with the game's uncomplicated nature. It was not the external flashiness that drew in players but the addictive gameplay that Pong offered. The use of a wooden cabinet was not just a practical choice but also a testament to its origins during a time of technological experimentation and innovation, paving the way for future generations of arcade machines.

Gameplay Dynamics

Despite its simplicity, Pong's gameplay was compelling and ushered in a new era in gaming.

Pong is a two-dimensional table tennis simulation.

Pong, the game that revolutionized the arcade scene, is a straightforward yet ingenious simulation of table tennis. It was inspired by tennis and table tennis, capturing their essence in a digital form. The game's top-down 2D view is both simplistic and charming, allowing players to easily grasp the core mechanics.

Despite its minimalistic approach, Pong embodies the concept of "easy to learn, hard to master." The clean lines and basic design bring focus to the gameplay, making the interaction between players and the ball the star of the game. This aspect of Pong contributed to its massive appeal, as it could be enjoyed without needing sophisticated graphics or complex storylines.

The game involves two in-game paddles and a ball.

At the heart of Pong are its two paddles and a bouncing ball, which represent the essence of its gameplay. The paddles are controlled by opposite players, vertically moving on either side of the screen with the ball bouncing back and forth across the center line. This setup creates a dynamic, competitive environment where precision and anticipation are key.

The simplicity of using just three fundamental elements – paddles, a ball, and the linear pathway of the ball – creates a minimalist yet highly engaging experience. This stripped-down approach to game design was influential in demonstrating that compelling gameplay doesn't require intricate elements but rather a solid foundational concept.

Players control the paddles, trying to hit the ball back and forth.

In Pong, players engage in an interactive battle of wits and reflexes, controlling their paddles to keep the ball in play. The main challenge lies in predicting the ball's trajectory and positioning the paddle accordingly to maintain the rally. This requires quick thinking and fast reflexes, especially as the ball speeds up over time.

The mechanics create a competitive atmosphere that encourages players to develop strategic approaches, considering angles and the opponent's weaknesses. The simplicity of the controls allowed for a low barrier to entry, making Pong accessible to a wide audience, yet retaining depth that rewarded skillful play, ensuring longevity and appeal.

The objective is to score points by getting the ball past the opponent's paddle.

The primary goal in Pong is straightforward: outmaneuver your opponent and score points by getting the ball past their paddle. Each player must remain vigilant, controlling their area while applying pressure to force mistakes. Scoring points requires precision and sometimes involves trick shots or angles that the opponent has trouble defending against.

Each successful score is not just a point but a triumph of strategy and dexterity. With this simple scoring system, players are continuously motivated to improve their skills, focusing on both offensive and defensive tactics. The scorekeeping adds an exciting level of competition, transforming simple gameplay into a battle of prowess.

The game increases in difficulty as players improve, which keeps it challenging and engaging.

As players become more proficient at Pong, the gameplay naturally scales in difficulty. The ball gradually increases in speed, demanding quicker reaction times and more precise control of the paddle. This escalation ensures that even seasoned players remain challenged and engaged, as the margin for error becomes smaller.

The increase in difficulty is subtle yet effective, providing a sense of growth and progression for players. This aspect of Pong was innovative for its time, as it encouraged repeated playthroughs, each session offering a new opportunity to test and hone skills. The increasing challenge remains one of the key reasons for Pong's enduring popularity and success.

Pong's Commercial Success

Pong was not just a game; it was a commercial phenomenon.

The first coin-operated Pong machine was installed at Andy Capp's Tavern in Sunnyvale, California.

The journey to Pong's monumental success began humbly at Andy Capp's Tavern in Sunnyvale, California. This local watering hole became the birthplace of the arcade gaming revolution when the first coin-operated Pong machine was installed in 1972. Conceived by Nolan Bushnell and Ted Dabney, founding figures of Atari, Pong provided eager patrons with interactive entertainment that was both novel and captivating.

Designed as a simple tennis simulation, Pong's gameplay was easy to grasp yet addictive enough to keep players engaged. The machine's installation at the tavern offered valuable insight into public interest and responsiveness. Almost overnight, the pong machine became a highlight at

Andy Capp's, quickly drawing attention from manufacturers and potential arcade operators alike.

Pong quickly became a hit, leading to a demand for more machines.

Following its initial success at Andy Capp's Tavern, Pong rapidly turned into a seismic hit, capturing the imagination of the public and industry insiders. The game's simplicity and engaging gameplay led to enthusiastic word-of-mouth promotion, as players lined up to experience the novel joy of electronic gaming. Observing this excitement, Atari faced an unprecedented demand for more Pong machines, compelling the company to ramp up production swiftly.

This overwhelming interest marked a paradigm shift in entertainment venues, where standalone arcades and bars sought to enhance their offerings with gaming machines. Pong's instant popularity underscored the immense potential of electronic games, ushering in a new era where video gaming would become an integral part of popular culture.

By the end of 1974, Atari had sold over 8,000 Pong machines.

In just a few years, Pong solidified its status as a commercial juggernaut, with Atari selling over 8,000 units by the end of 1974. This success was a testament to the game's wide appeal and the burgeoning interest in video games as a form of entertainment. Atari's ability to scale production so effectively underscored the inherent demand that Pong had uncovered.

The sheer number of machines sold demonstrated the viability of video games as a profitable business venture. Establishments across the country clamored to house these machines, recognizing their appeal in attracting customers. Pong set the stage for Atari's future endeavors and established a template for future arcade successes. **The success of Pong inspired a wave of similar games and clones.**

Pong's sweeping success naturally attracted attention from other aspiring game developers leading to a tsunami of similar games and outright clones. These imitations emerged as both a tribute and a testament to Pong's pervasive influence. Numerous companies sprouted, striving to capitalize on the Pong phenomenon by producing their versions, each with slightly different twists on the original gameplay.

This flood of Pong-like games contributed to a rapidly expanding market, fueling the nascent video game industry. While some clones were direct copies, others sought innovation, ultimately contributing to a diverse and rich gaming ecosystem. Pong's legacy thus transcended its own commercial success by instigating an entire genre that laid the foundation for future gaming innovations.

Pong's popularity marked the start of the arcade golden age.

The unprecedented success of Pong served as the catalyst for what is now recognized as the Golden Age of Arcades. This era, spanning the late 1970s to the mid-1980s, witnessed the proliferation of arcade gaming as an integral part of entertainment culture. Pong opened the doors for a myriad of classics that would follow in its footsteps, each contributing to the rich tapestry of video game history.

As arcades became regular urban fixtures, they turned into social hubs where people gathered to test their skills and enjoy shared experiences. Pong's legacy lived on through successive generations of games, helping to establish the arcade as a cultural institution. This period of rapid innovation and popular engagement remains a formative chapter in the history of electronic entertainment.

Cultural Impact

Pong's influence on culture and society was profound and far-reaching.

Pong introduced the concept of video games to mainstream culture.

Pong was not just a game; it was a cultural phenomenon that introduced millions to the concept of video gaming. Before Pong, the notion of interactive digital entertainment was largely unexplored. Pong's simple, engaging gameplay provided players with an entirely new form of amusement that was straightforward but highly captivating.

By bringing this innovative form of entertainment to a wider audience, Pong helped blur the lines between traditional and digital leisure activities. Its success showed the world that digital devices were not merely suited for complex computations but could also offer joy and entertainment. This breakthrough laid the groundwork for future advancements in the gaming industry, positioning video games as a staple in modern culture.

It demonstrated the entertainment potential of digital games.

Pong's success was a testament to the entertainment value inherent in digital gaming. Despite its simplicity, the game's engaging mechanics—focused on two players rallying a digital ball back and forth—captured the attention and imagination of a broad audience. Players were drawn in by the game's deceptively straightforward design, finding themselves engrossed in its competitive nature.

More importantly, Pong proved that video games could captivate diverse audiences, from children to adults, and could sustain interest beyond novelty. This realization sparked interest among tech enthusiasts and entrepreneurs, leading to significant investments in video game development. Ultimately, Pong inspired the creation of more complex and entertaining games, expanding its legacy and impact on the future of the gaming industry.

Arcades became social gathering spots largely due to Pong's appeal.

Pong transformed arcades into popular social hubs, kicking off a phenomenon that encouraged communal gaming experiences. Before Pong, arcades were frequented by a limited audience looking for pinball machines and other mechanical games. However, Pong's instant popularity attracted a diverse crowd eager to experience and engage in this new form of gaming competition.

As a result, arcades evolved into vibrant social gathering places where people could meet, compete, and socialize. The presence of Pong machines in bars, amusement parks, and restaurants further encouraged community interaction. This social aspect of gaming has endured, influencing modern multiplayer and online gaming experiences, and cementing Pong's role as a pioneer in community-based digital entertainment.

Pong inspired countless people to pursue careers in game development.

The success of Pong inspired a generation of programmers, designers, and entrepreneurs to explore careers in game development. Its widespread acclaim revealed the vast potential of the burgeoning gaming industry. Many enthusiasts saw how a simplistic design could achieve international acclaim and wanted to be part of this exciting field.

This inspiration contributed to the development of video game technology and the expansion of gaming as an artistic medium. The enthusiasm sparked by Pong led to the establishment of numerous gaming companies and institutions focused on honing game design skills. Today, the legacy of Pong is evident in the vibrant and dynamic games industry, which continues to push technological and creative boundaries.

Pong had lasting importance in pop culture, being referenced in movies and shows.

Pong's cultural impact is evident through its persistent presence in pop culture. The game has been referenced and parodied across various media, from films to television shows, indicating its iconic status. These references often highlight Pong's simplicity and nostalgia, underscoring its essential role in gaming history.

Movies about gaming or technology frequently nod to Pong as a pioneering force that shaped the digital entertainment landscape. Moreover, its representation extends to art and music, where its minimalist design and sound effects evoke a sense of nostalgia. Such cultural nods affirm Pong's enduring relevance, as it continues to be celebrated as a foundational piece of gaming history.

Technical Innovations

Underneath its simplicity, Pong showcased several notable technical innovations.

Pong used an on-screen score display, which was unique at the time.

Pong broke new ground with its on-screen scoring system, a feature that has become ubiquitous in modern gaming. Prior to Pong, most games did not have digital score displays, relying instead on physical counters or external means to track scores. **This innovation** allowed for a more immersive gaming experience, as players could focus entirely on the screen without needing to look away to check who was winning.

By integrating the score directly into the gameplay, Pong not only enhanced user engagement but also set a precedent for how games could use real-time data to enhance the gaming experience. This was a key factor in establishing the game's competitive nature and contributed significantly to its popularity.

The game relied on analog electronics, as microprocessors were not yet prevalent.

During Pong's development era, digital technology was in its infancy. Instead of relying on microprocessors, which were not yet widespread or affordable, *Pong leveraged analog electronics* to achieve its groundbreaking gameplay. The game's circuitry was elegantly simple, consisting of discrete components that facilitated the paddle movement and ball mechanics.

This analog approach not only defined Pong's distinctive play style but also presented a cost-effective solution for mass production. The game's structure was a brilliant exercise in achieving maximum entertainment with minimal technology, paving the way for future digital innovation in gaming.

Pong's use of paddle controllers set a standard for future games.

The introduction of **paddle controllers** in Pong gave players an unprecedented level of control and interaction. Unlike earlier games that relied on buttons or simple switches, paddle controllers allowed for more nuanced movement and precision, directly impacting gameplay.

This innovation set *a new standard* for player input, influencing the design of future arcade games and home consoles. The paddle controller became synonymous with precision games like Breakout and Arkanoid and highlighted the importance of intuitive and tactile game interfaces, a concept still evident in today's gaming peripherals.

The efficient design made it possible to mass-produce affordable arcade machines.

Pong's success was largely attributed to its efficient, cost-effective design, which made the mass production of arcade units feasible. Unlike complex custom-designed systems that dominated prior to its release, Pong's circuitry was simple and utilized commonly available electronic parts. **This approach** drastically reduced manufacturing costs and allowed for rapid scaling.

The affordability of these machines contributed to a wide distribution network, placing Pong units in bars and game rooms worldwide. By setting a standard for economically viable arcade machine production, Pong created a business model that countless other arcade games followed.

Its success paved the way for experiments with other input methods and game designs.

Pong's immense popularity opened doors to an era of experimentation in the gaming industry. Following its launch, developers began exploring new input methods and varying game designs, unshackled from the constraints of traditional gameplay mechanics. **Pong's success validated** the demand for interactive digital entertainment, encouraging innovation and diversity in game development.

Games began incorporating different controllers, from joysticks to trackballs, as developers sought fresh and engaging ways to interact with players. This spirit of innovation catalyzed the creation of varied gaming experiences and genres, establishing a rich, diverse gaming landscape that continues to evolve today.

Legacy of Pong

Pong's legacy lived on far beyond its initial release, influencing generations of games and developers.

Pong is often credited with launching the video game industry.

Pong, developed by Atari and released in 1972, is widely recognized as a groundbreaking title that helped establish the video game industry. Its commercial success marked a pivotal moment, transforming video games from mere novelties into a viable business.

The game's accessible design and entertaining gameplay captured the interest of a broad audience, encouraging other developers to explore this budding field. By demonstrating that video games could be both entertaining and profitable, Pong laid the foundation for the industry's explosive growth.

The game laid the groundwork for future sports and simulation games.

Pong's intuitive gameplay, simulating a simple game of table tennis, set the stage for future sports and simulation games. Its mechanics introduced players to the concept of controlling paddles and reflected the real-world dynamics of a ball bouncing between two surfaces.

As one of the first sports simulations, Pong's straightforward design inspired developers to pursue more complex and realistic simulations in various sports genres. This legacy is apparent in the diversity of sports games available today, from intricate football simulations to motor racing and even niche sports.

Its simplicity inspired the minimalist approach seen in many modern indie games.

The minimalist design of Pong, characterized by its basic graphics and core gameplay mechanics, continues to influence modern indie game developers. By emphasizing fun and accessibility over complexity, Pong showed that engaging gameplay could be achieved with minimal resources.

This philosophy of simplicity has been embraced by countless indie developers, who often focus on creative concepts and unique gameplay innovations rather than cutting-edge graphics. This legacy is evident in many successful indie titles that prioritize player experience and creativity.

Pong has been resurrected in numerous forms, from sequels to mobile apps.

Over the decades, Pong has been adapted and resurrected in numerous forms, ensuring its continued presence in the gaming landscape. From sequels and spin-offs to remakes for modern consoles and even mobile apps, Pong's enduring appeal remains evident.

Developers have experimented with various interpretations, adding new features, updated graphics, and innovative twists while maintaining the essence of the original game. These modern iterations demonstrate Pong's adaptability and its ability to captivate new generations of players.

The nostalgia for Pong remains strong, symbolizing the dawn of a new form of entertainment.

Pong evokes a powerful sense of nostalgia, symbolizing the origins of the arcade gaming era and the dawn of interactive entertainment. As one of the first video games to achieve mainstream appeal, it holds a special place in the hearts of gaming enthusiasts and collectors.

Its iconic status is celebrated through retro gaming events and collections, reminding us of the humble beginnings of the video game industry. Pong's legacy endures, not only as a symbol of early gaming history but also as an inspiration for today's innovative developments in interactive entertainment.

Chapter 10: Adventure - The First Text Adventure

Text adventures like *Adventure* (also known as Colossal Cave Adventure) brought the thrill of exploration to the screen. With nothing but text to guide players, these games captured the imagination and inspired the genre that would become known as Interactive Fiction.

The Birth of Adventure

The story of Adventure begins with its creation in the 1970s, where it laid the groundwork for the interactive fiction genre.

Developed by Will Crowther in 1976, Adventure was initially inspired by his love for caving.

Will Crowther, a programmer and avid caving enthusiast, drew from his experiences exploring real caves to create *Adventure* in 1976. His fascination with spelunking is mirrored throughout the game's setting, which invites players into a labyrinthine cave laced with hidden treasures and complex routes. Unlike the visual spectacle of modern games, *Adventure* engaged players' imaginations through vivid text descriptions, painting mental images of subterranean marvels.

At its core, *Adventure* wasn't just a game; it was an invitation to a simulated journey, an abstract space where one could visualize corridors, ancient stone chambers, and underground rivers. This connection to real-world caving fostered a sense of authenticity, differentiating the game from other nascent digital experiences. As players navigated its depths via textual commands, they encountered the mystery and excitement Crowther intended, bridging his passion for adventure with the nascent tech world of the 70s.

The game was further developed by Don Woods, adding fantasy elements like magic and mythical creatures.

In 1977, computer scientist Don Woods discovered *Adventure* and was immediately captivated by its potential. Seeking Crowther's permission, he expanded the game's world, infusing it with a rich tapestry of fantasy elements that are now iconic. Woods introduced mythical creatures, magical items, and enchanting landscapes, transforming the original realist setting into a realm of wonder.

This infusion of fantasy not only enhanced the game's allure but also broadened its appeal beyond caving enthusiasts. Woods' additions introduced players to an imaginative space filled with dragons, elves, and other folklore staples, setting a new standard for storytelling in gaming. The blend of reality and fantasy in *Adventure* proved pivotal, inspiring future developers to explore narrative depth and complex world-building in their interactive creations.

Adventure became a shared experience, distributed widely across ARPANET, one of the early networking technologies.

The impact of *Adventure* stretched far beyond its pioneering gameplay; it became a phenomenon on ARPANET, the precursor to the modern Internet. Enthusiastic players distributed the game across this nascent network, marking it as one of the earliest instances of digital content sharing. This widespread distribution turned *Adventure* into a communal experience, transcending geographic boundaries and connecting a burgeoning community of tech enthusiasts.

This ease of access contributed significantly to the game's success, allowing it to reach audiences far beyond Will Crowther's initial circle. As it spread, *Adventure* not only entertained but also educated players, introducing many to the possibilities of networked gaming. This early embrace of network technology exemplified how games could bridge cultures and communities, laying groundwork for the interconnected gaming landscape we know today.

Its creation spurred an entire genre, allowing amateur developers to create their own text adventures.

With the powerful influence of *Adventure* as a guiding precedent, the realm of interactive fiction was born. The game's success inspired developers worldwide, including hobbyists and amateurs, to explore and expand on textbased adventures. Leveraging basic programming skills, creators could construct elaborate narratives and worlds purely through text, democratizing game development in an era dominated by large companies.

The genre's accessibility led to the creation of countless "Zork-like" games throughout the late 1970s and early 1980s, wherein individuals could explore their own creativity without needing advanced graphics or hardware. This new wave of text adventures nurtured a community-driven approach to gaming, where storytelling and imagination were as valued as technical prowess. In an industry often defined by its cutting-edge visuals, *Adventure* remains a testament to the enduring power of words and narrative in digital entertainment.

The Gameplay Mechanics

Adventure's mechanics, though simple, set the template for future interactive fiction games, focusing on exploration and puzzle-solving.

Players input text commands to interact with the game world, exploring a vast cave system.

Adventure's groundbreaking gameplay used a simple yet powerful command-line interface that allowed players to engage directly with its meticulously crafted world. By inputting text commands, players would interact with their surroundings, seeking out hidden treasures within a sprawling underground cave system. This interaction system, although straightforward, was highly immersive. It offered players a sense of agency and freedom seldom seen at the time.

Navigating this intricate environment required not only curiosity but also patience, as each command fed into a larger narrative tapestry that unfolded through play. Thus, players became storytellers, shaping their journey with each typed word. This approach laid the groundwork for countless future titles in the text adventure genre.

Basic commands like 'go north' or 'take lamp' were used to progress through the adventure.

The simplicity of Adventure's command-based interface was one of its most innovative features. Basic directives such as "**go north**" or "**take lamp**" invited players to engage intuitively with the game world. This clear, straightforward interaction design allowed players to focus on exploration and discovery without the need for complex inputs.

Despite their simplicity, these commands were integral to the unfolding experience, opening doors to new locations and possibilities within the game. Players learned quickly that every action had a consequence, fostering a deeper engagement as they navigated the labyrinthine cave systems. These foundational mechanics set a standard for textbased games, emphasizing clarity and accessibility.

Players had to solve puzzles and navigate mazes, making logical deductions based on descriptions.

A hallmark of Adventure's design was its intricate puzzles and maze-like challenges that demanded keen observation and logical thinking. Players were required to interpret textual descriptions to deduce solutions to numerous obstacles and secrets hidden within the cave system. These challenges were far from superficial; they were crafted to encourage critical thinking and problem-solving.

With each success, players derived a sense of accomplishment that fueled their desire to delve deeper into the game. This strategic layer of gameplay was pivotal, offering both excitement and frustration in equal measure. It was this aspect that not only entertained but also educated, cementing Adventure's place as an intellectual and engaging title in gaming history.

The game relied heavily on player imagination, as only text descriptions painted the picture of the locations and actions.

At its core, Adventure was a masterclass in minimalism, relying solely on textual descriptions to craft its immersive world. This design choice put a powerful tool at the player's disposal: imagination. With no graphics to guide or distract, the rich narrative and evocative descriptions painted vivid mental images, making each player's experience uniquely personal.

This reliance on the player's creativity to animate the world set a precedent for interactive fiction games. It allowed for an individualized exploration where each command forged new paths in the mind's eye. This minimalistic approach showcased the power of narrative and text, offering a distinct form of escapism that has captivated players for decades.

The Cultural Impact

Adventure left a lasting impact on both the gaming industry and culture, influencing how stories could be told interactively.

It introduced a new form of storytelling that focused on player agency and creativity.

Adventure, or Colossal Cave Adventure, was groundbreaking for its time. Unlike previous games which primarily involved straightforward objectives or simulations, *Adventure* presented players with an open-ended story. This unique approach allowed players to make their own decisions, influencing the narrative's direction. The game shifted the focus from fixed paths to a more flexible experience, granting players unprecedented control over their journey.

This emphasis on agency enabled players to become co-authors of their adventures, fostering creativity and personal investment in the narrative. This novel storytelling method paved the way for future game designs where the player's choices shaped the game's world, offering endless possibilities and replayability. Thus, *Adventure* not only entertained its audiences but also encouraged them to explore the boundaries of interactive narratives.

The game inspired countless developers, leading to the rise of interactive fiction in the late 70s and 80s.

The impact of *Adventure* on the gaming industry cannot be overstated. Its success demonstrated the potential of interactive fiction, inspiring a new wave of developers eager to explore this innovative medium. The late 70s and 80s saw a surge in interactive fiction titles, with companies such as Infocom at the forefront, producing classics like *Zork* and *Enchanter*.

The creativity sparked by *Adventure* encouraged designers to experiment with storytelling methods, expanding the scope and depth of narratives within games. These pioneering works laid the foundation for the rich, story-driven games we see today, proving that games could be more than just entertainment—they could be immersive, interactive stories, resonating deeply with players.

Adventure's legacy is visible in modern games, which continue to incorporate interactive narrative elements.

Even decades after its release, the influence of *Adventure* permeates the gaming world. Modern games, from sprawling RPGs to indie titles, often incorporate elements of interactive storytelling. These games allow player choices to alter outcomes, echoing the agency-first approach pioneered by *Adventure*.

Titles such as *The Witcher* series, *Life is Strange*, and *The Stanley Parable* owe part of their narrative depth to the framework established by these early text adventures. By placing players at the heart of the story, modern games continue to build on *Adventure*'s legacy, proving how foundational this early text adventure was to evolving game design principles toward player-centered experiences.

It also brought about the use of computers as platforms for entertainment, expanding their role beyond simple computation.

Before *Adventure*, computers were largely viewed as utilitarian machines, primarily used for computation or data processing. This game shifted the perception of computers, highlighting their potential as entertainment devices. By turning the screen into a portal for adventure and exploration through text, *Adventure* demonstrated that computers could be used for storytelling and leisure.

This paradigm shift was crucial in the evolution of computer usage. As a result, more developers and companies saw the potential for computer games, leading to a burst of creativity and technological advancements in the field. The groundwork laid by *Adventure* helped transform computers into personal entertainment systems, a status they maintain to this day.

The Technology Behind Adventure

The technology of the time was quite limited, yet Adventure managed to captivate players by leveraging these constraints creatively.

Adventure was initially designed to run on a DEC PDP-10, a mainframe computer, showcasing computational resourcefulness.

The game *Adventure* was originally developed to run on the DEC PDP-10, a mainframe computer popular in the 1970s. This choice was not merely incidental; the DEC PDP-10 was a symbol of computational prowess at the time. Given the limited processing power and memory available, the creators of *Adventure* had to be exceptionally resourceful.

The PDP-10's architecture required efficient use of its capabilities, pushing the developers to design a game that was both engaging and computationally feasible. As a result, the game was predominantly text-based, which minimized the use of graphical displays and optimized memory usage.

This reliance on text created a narrative depth that became a hallmark of the genre.

The game utilized a system of text-based input and output, an efficient way to engage users given the hardware limitations.

Given the technological constraints of the era, *Adventure* employed a text-based input and output system. Players interacted with the game by typing commands, which the game interpreted and responded to in text form. This method of interaction was not only efficient but also immersive, allowing players to engage deeply with the narrative.

Through simple commands like "go north" or "take lamp," players navigated the fictional world. This system leveraged the minimal screen and processing capabilities of the PDP-10 effectively. The text interface encouraged players to use their imagination to visualize the scenes and events described, a powerful way to engage the player beyond the screen.

Despite its simplicity, Adventure offered a large virtual world, demonstrating the potential of virtual exploration.

Adventure introduced players to a vast fictional realm despite its seemingly simple framework. The game contained a series of interconnected rooms and locations, each filled with puzzles and treasures. This expansive design showcased early virtual exploration and provided players with a sense of freedom and discovery.

The complexity of the world rested not in graphics, but in the rich textual descriptions and the intricate layout of locations. This imaginative world inspired future games to explore how vast and intricate a game's universe could become, setting a precedent for open-world gameplay experiences in years to come.

Its design encouraged shared play and collaboration, as players often shared tips and strategies on how to advance.

While playing *Adventure*, many players found themselves stymied by the challenging puzzles and vast environments.

This led to an unexpected but significant social interaction—players began to share notes, tips, and strategies with each other. This communal problem-solving became an integral part of the game's experience.

Friends would gather, excitedly discussing how to solve the latest puzzle or where the elusive treasure might be hidden. This collaborative spirit not only enriched the gaming experience but also fostered a burgeoning community around the game. Sharing knowledge became just as much a part of the adventure as the game itself, highlighting how games could unite people through shared challenges and achievements.

Chapter 11: Donkey Kong - The Ladder to Greatness

Ready to climb ladders, leap over barrels, and shout at a giant ape? Travel back to the days of **Donkey Kong** and discover how this barrel-tossing simian boosted a certain plumber's career and became a stepping stone to greatness in gaming lore.

The Genesis of Donkey Kong

Unpacking the quirky origin story of Donkey Kong and how this lovable gorilla stumbled onto the arcade scene.

A humble start with Nintendo's Radar Scope flop.

Nintendo's journey into the arcade market was anything but smooth. It all began with *Radar Scope*, a game intended to rival the likes of *Space Invaders*. Unfortunately, it ended up being a dud, leaving warehouses filled with unsold units. This misstep nearly spelled doom for Nintendo's ambitions in North America. The company's bold aspiration to conquer America was suddenly in jeopardy, and they needed a hit, fast. Enter the realm of creativity.

The commercial failure of *Radar Scope* pushed Nintendo to try something different. This was a pivotal moment that sparked the creation of *Donkey Kong*. It's fascinating how a setback served as a stepping stone for innovation. The challenge was now to salvage these unused cabinets and convert them into a new, engaging experience. The mission was clear: transform failure into Fortune.

Miyamoto's challenge: Revive a failing arcade machine.

Enter Shigeru Miyamoto, a budding, imaginative game designer tasked with a monumental challenge. While many would buckle under the pressure of reviving a subpar product, Miyamoto saw it as an opportunity. Armed with boundless creativity and little prior experience, Miyamoto ventured into the unfamiliar territory of game design. His fresh perspective turned out to be a blessing in disguise.

The mission was ambitious: repurpose the lifeless *Radar Scope* cabinets into something players would love.

Miyamoto's approach was unorthodox yet brilliant. His vision was centered on telling a story through gameplay, a concept relatively unexplored in that era. This narrative-driven strategy laid the groundwork for the emergence of a new kind of arcade game, one that was engaging and fun at its core.

Birth of a gorilla: How Donkey Kong came to be.

The creation of *Donkey Kong* is as charmingly peculiar as the game itself. Miyamoto envisioned a game starring a love-struck carpenter (later evolving into the world-famous Mario) rescuing his girlfriend from a giant ape. The key to its success was simplicity blended with an engaging storyline. Instead of elaborate design, the focus was on character appeal and intuitive gameplay.

The game featured a giant gorilla atop a series of platforms, throwing barrels to stop the hero. This straightforward concept broke away from the alien invasions and spaceships prevalent at the time. Instead, it offered players something refreshingly whimsical and original. *Donkey Kong* was not just a game; it was a budding storyline complete with intrigue and adventure.

Embracing King Kong vibes with a twist.

In creating *Donkey Kong*, Miyamoto drew inspiration from pop culture, particularly the iconic film *King Kong*. However, this was not merely an imitation but a clever twist on a familiar theme. Where the enormous gorilla in *King Kong* was fearsome, Donkey Kong was almost endearing, with a playful edge that added to his charm.

The whimsical interpretation of King Kong transformed the game into a delightful parody. The hero's journey up ladders to confront the ape presented a new kind of conflict—one that was more about fun than fear. Players found themselves charmed by the humor and innovation that *Donkey Kong* delivered, which cleverly kept them coming back for more.

A make-or-break game for Nintendo in the early 80s.

The stakes for *Donkey Kong* were astronomical. Nintendo's future in the gaming world was hanging in the balance. Success would mean a foothold in the lucrative North American arcade market; failure could spell disaster. It was a classic underdog story for the company, relying on an unconventional game to achieve redemption.

When *Donkey Kong* hit the arcades, it was not just a hit—it was a phenomenon. The game's unprecedented popularity catapulted Nintendo to the forefront of the gaming industry, transforming a precarious situation into triumph. *Donkey Kong* didn't just save Nintendo; it reshaped the entire landscape of video gaming and paved the way for countless beloved franchises that followed.

Meet the Jumpman

Who is this jumpsuit-wearing hero leaping across the screen? It's a him, Jumpman!

Jumpman as the predecessor to Mario.

Before the world knew him as Mario, he was simply **Jumpman**. In 1981, when *Donkey Kong* hit the arcades, players got their first glimpse of the character who would become a global icon. Shigeru Miyamoto, the game's creator, envisioned Jumpman as a relatable, everyman hero whose only prowess was his ability to jump. This concept set the stage for players to root for this plucky protagonist, a character design that laid the groundwork for Mario's future adventures.

Jumpman's humble beginnings were essential in establishing a bond with players. Unlike other characters of the time, he wasn't a powerful warrior or a superhero. Instead, he was an everyday man thrown into extraordinary circumstances, a carpenter battling a giant ape to save his girlfriend. It was this relatability and underdog charm that captivated audiences and paved the way for Jumpman's evolution into Nintendo's beloved mascot, Mario.

The everyday hero with red overalls and a mission.

Donning red overalls and a cap, Jumpman embodied the quintessential 1980s protagonist—a simple guy in an extraordinary situation. His quest was straightforward: save his girlfriend Pauline from the clutches of the mischievous

Donkey Kong. The visual design was dictated as much by the technical limitations of the era as it was by character development.

In this pixelated world, Jumpman's red outfit contrasted sharply against the arcade cabinet's backgrounds, making it easy for players to follow him as he navigated various obstacles. His dynamic actions and determination resonated with players, making them cheer for their favorite blocky hero. This unassuming carpenter soon became the face of a new era in gaming, highlighting that heroes don't need superpowers to be memorable—they just need heart.

Saving Pauline: The damsel in distress trope.

In *Donkey Kong*, Jumpman's mission is classic yet compelling: rescue the damsel in distress, Pauline. This narrative trope was prevalent in the early 80s, and it provided a simple yet effective storyline for an arcade game. While this concept is now viewed with a critical eye, at the time, it was a key storytelling device for immersing players in Jumpman's daring rescue.

Pauline's plight establishes the stakes that push Jumpman to climb ladders and dodge barrels, delivering an adrenaline-fueled gaming experience. The simplicity of the narrative fit perfectly with the arcade format, offering quick and thrilling gameplay. This foundational storyline not only captured the hearts of the gaming public but also set the stage for more nuanced character narratives in future video games.

Why a carpenter? A look at early character design.

Jumpman's initial job as a carpenter might seem odd given his later career as a world-famous plumber, but it was a decision rooted in practicality and creativity. With limited pixels, Shigeru Miyamoto crafted a character whose role could be easily conveyed visually. The red overalls and cap were not just a stylistic choice; they helped distinguish him amid the colorful chaos of the arcade screen.

The decision to make Jumpman a carpenter was influenced by the game's construction site setting, which involved climbing and jumping over obstacles. This environment naturally led to the choice of a profession that would fit seamlessly into the game's narrative. Thus, Jumpman's carpentry background was not only a clever design element but a crucial piece of his identity in his inaugural adventure.

From Jumpman to Mario: A legend is born.

As Jumpman transitioned to Mario, a legend was indeed born. The change of name came about as Nintendo chose to honor Mario Segale, an American landlord who rented a warehouse to the company. This decision marked the beginning of Mario's ascension to gaming superstardom.

Mario's transformation from a generic, unnamed hero to a character with a memorable identity signified a new era for Nintendo. The development team expanded on Mario's story, eventually establishing him as a plumber in the bustling streets of Brooklyn. These enhancements not only paved the way for Mario's iconic status but also gave Nintendo a mascot that brought worlds of joy to gamers everywhere.

Through his evolution, Mario encapsulates the spirit of adventure that continues to enthrall audiences to this day.

Gameplay Mechanics at Their Finest

Dodge, jump, and climb your way through barrels and girders! The game that keeps players on their toes.

The linear simplicity of climbing ladders.

In the pixelated world of **Donkey Kong**, the art of climbing ladders serves as a straightforward mechanic that belies its true genius. At first glance, it might seem like basic navigation, but the ladders introduce a layer of strategy that adds depth to the gameplay. Every climber knows the anxiety of reaching the top only to have a barrel come rolling their way.

This linear simplicity is deceptive, as players must make split-second decisions—ascend with haste, or wait cautiously for a clear path? The genius lies in the blend of timing and anticipation. Ascending too early could spell doom, while waiting too long may cost valuable time. This mechanic transforms ladders from mere passageways to potential pitfalls, keeping players engaged and on edge with every step.

Barrels everywhere: A new kind of challenge.

What do barrels have in common with arch-nemeses? In **Donkey Kong**, they're one and the same! Introduced as a relentless threat, the barrels add a dynamic element of chaos to the mix. Unlike static foes, these cylindrical menaces follow gravity's whim, bouncing unpredictably and forcing players to stay alert.

The barrels ensure no two games are alike. Each playthrough presents a distinct pattern and speed, challenging even the most seasoned gamers. The unpredictability of their roll keeps players guessing, testing not just their reflexes, but also their ability to adapt on the fly. Surviving this constant barrage requires skill, timing, and a bit of luck.

How timing and reflexes defined gameplay.

In the frenetic realm of **Donkey Kong**, success hinges on two key attributes: keen timing and razor-sharp reflexes. The game's design pushes players to synchronize their movements with the on-screen action, turning each leap and dodge into a test of precision. Time it right, and you dance past obstacles with ease; falter, and your plumber ends up as a plumber's pancake.

The integration of these elements is what made **Donkey Kong** so addictive. The satisfaction of timing a flawless barrel jump or climbing a ladder to safety under the wire is unmatched. It highlights the essential skill-based nature of early arcade games, offering players the same thrill every time they play, but also inviting them to master their technique for a higher score.

The escalating difficulty across levels.

In **Donkey Kong**, as players prove their prowess, the game expertly escalates the challenge, deftly increasing the stakes with each level. Just when you think you've conquered one stage, you're thrown into a more chaotic scenario where barrels roll faster, enemies appear more frequently, and the platform layouts more confoundingly complex.

This escalating difficulty not only serves to keep players engaged but also stokes the fires of challenge and mastery. Each level feels like a personal gauntlet set by Donkey Kong himself, pushing you to adapt and improve. This crafted journey from simplicity to complexity keeps the experience fresh and invigorating, inviting players to step up and elevate their game.

A winning formula: Simplicity meets challenge.

Donkey Kong is a masterclass in game design, proving that simplicity and challenge can coexist in perfect harmony. The beauty of the game lies in its ability to be easily grasped by newcomers, while simultaneously offering layers of difficulty that challenge veterans. It's a delicate balance, but one that pays off in spades as players find themselves drawn back to the action time and again.

The straightforward mechanics—jumping and climbing—provide an accessible entry point. Yet, as players delve deeper, they encounter the game's inherent complexity, with ever-increasing obstacles to overcome. This formula has cemented Donkey Kong's place in gaming history, showcasing that even simple elements, when combined thoughtfully, can create a deeply satisfying gaming experience.

A launching pad for Nintendo's global success.

When **Donkey Kong** hit arcades in 1981, it did more than just introduce gamers to barrels and ladders. It propelled

Nintendo from a playing card company to a titan in the gaming industry. Prior to this, Nintendo had moderate successes with games like *Radar Scope*, but the explosive popularity of Donkey Kong firmly established them on the global stage.

This game was not just a hit; it was the cornerstone of Nintendo's strategy to dominate the arcade market. It also laid the groundwork for future console successes like the *NES*. The game's financial triumph enabled Nintendo to expand its reach, leading to the creation of many more beloved franchises that continue to capture imaginations worldwide.

Setting the stage for legendary characters.

Without **Donkey Kong**, there would be no Mario jumping around the Mushroom Kingdom today. The game marked the first appearance of the now-iconic plumber – originally called Jumpman. This game was Donkey Kong's stage, but it was also Mario's first leap into gaming immortality, paving the way for his starring roles in countless future titles. Moreover, the game's villain, Donkey Kong himself, would also go on to headline his own series, becoming another staple of Nintendo's character roster. The interplay between these characters created a narrative depth that was groundbreaking for its time, influencing character development in future games.

Influencing game design with its simple yet addictive mechanics.

The genius of **Donkey Kong** lies in its simplicity. The game introduced a multi-level progression system with the goal of saving the damsel in distress, which became a staple in gaming. Its straightforward yet challenging gameplay session kept players hitting the 'continue' button, a phenomenon every game designer aspired to replicate.

Donkey Kong's mechanics of using obstacles and timing challenges demonstrated how limited graphics could still result in deeply engaging gameplay. This principle has continued to inform game design, emphasizing that sophistication doesn't always rely on graphics but on engaging the player's mind.

Replicating arcade success in home consoles.

The leap from arcade to home console was a crucial step in gaming's evolution. **Donkey Kong**, adapted for systems like the Atari 2600 and ColecoVision, was instrumental in bringing that arcade magic home. Its transition was a technical marvel for its time, displaying the potential of home gaming consoles.

Though the graphical fidelity was reduced, the essence of the game was retained, proving that home systems could offer arcade-like thrills. This success helped push consoles into mainstream households, reshaping how and where people experienced video games, and setting a precedent for future arcade-to-home game adaptations.

Donkey Kong in pop culture: Cartoons and beyond.

Donkey Kong's impact wasn't confined to the realm of gaming. The enormous popularity of the game soon spilled over into pop culture, leading to animated adaptations and merchandise. The *Saturday Supercade*, a 1980s cartoon series, featured Donkey Kong prominently alongside other iconic video game characters.

These adaptations further cemented Donkey Kong's place in popular culture, exposing the character to audiences beyond gamers. Donkey Kong's pervasive influence as an early gaming icon underscores how video games were becoming contributors to the larger tapestry of entertainment media, blending the lines between mediums.

Technical Aspects That Wowed Us

From the unique hardware to brilliant software, let's peek under the hood of Donkey Kong.

Unique cabinet design for the arcade era.

In an age where arcades were the social hubs of gaming, **Donkey Kong** stood out with its bold blue and red cabinet design. This aesthetic choice was not just about visual appeal; it was a strategic marketing move. The vibrant colors ensured that the machine captured attention even amidst a crowded sea of arcade games. Gamers flocked to these machines like moths to a flame, eager to experience the latest in video game excitement.

Moreover, the cabinet wasn't just about looks. It was built to withstand the rigorous demands of enthusiastic players, providing a robust and durable housing for the electronics within. The joystick and buttons were designed for quick reflexes, allowing players to control Jumpman (later known as Mario) with precision. Each cabinet also featured a mesmerizing lit marquee that was impossible to ignore. Overall, this iconic design invited players into an engaging world where they could climb ladders and dodge barrels while vying for the high score.

Breaking boundaries with vibrant graphics.

When **Donkey Kong** entered the scene, it did so with graphics that were nothing short of revolutionary for its time. Each sprite was meticulously crafted to provide clarity and distinction. The titular ape resembled a more complex and expressive character compared to the simplistic enemies seen in other games of the era. Meanwhile, Jumpman's iconic red overalls made him instantly recognizable and easy to follow amidst the chaos of falling barrels and cunning flames.

The color palette, though limited by today's standards, utilized its constraints to dazzling effect. Warm oranges, deep blues, and lush greens were cleverly used to create a vivid, immersive world. The multi-layered backgrounds added depth to a relatively flat 2D plane, making players feel as though they were escaping through a concrete jungle. These graphics not only captivated young eyes but also hinted at the graphical evolution video games would undergo in the years to come.

Sophisticated sound effects for immersive experience.

The soundscape of **Donkey Kong** played a critical role in its immersive game play. From the catchy, upbeat tunes that greeted players on the start screen to the tense percussion of impending danger, the sound design was crafted with precision. Each jump, barrel clash, and successful rescue was punctuated with a distinctive sound effect, enhancing the player's immediate emotional response.

The auditory cues served an essential gameplay function as well; they indicated impending hazards, timing challenges, and even communicated success. The clever composition was achieved despite the limited audio channels available on the arcade hardware at the time. Collectively, these sounds created an atmosphere that players could feel deeply, turning simple actions into heart-thumping moments that kept everyone coming back for more.

Challenging programming for smooth gameplay.

Creating **Donkey Kong** was no small feat from a programming perspective. During the early 1980s, game designers had to be judicious with memory and processing power. Yet, Nintendo's team managed to deliver gameplay that was nothing short of smooth, thanks to *ingenious coding and optimization*. Jumpman's controls felt intuitive and responsive, allowing players to react in real-time to the obstacles ahead.

The game's level design, along with its environmental interactions like moving platforms and ladder mechanics, demanded meticulous programming precision. Each level was a carefully orchestrated challenge, balancing the perfect amount of difficulty with fun. Behind every fall and leap was a line of code acting as an invisible puppeteer, ensuring the game ran fluidly without hiccups, making it one of the cornerstones in the foundation of platform gaming.

Innovative use of microprocessors.

Donkey Kong was a trailblazer in using cutting-edge microprocessors to elevate arcade gaming. The game employed a Zilog Z80 microprocessor, which allowed for greater complexity in gameplay mechanics and graphics rendering. This microprocessor empowered developers to push boundaries, enabling them to include multiple characters, realistic animations, and dynamic environmental elements.

The innovation did not stop there. The microprocessor also facilitated more intricate background music and sound effects, all while ensuring the game run seamlessly without sacrificing performance. This technology was pivotal in setting the stage for subsequent advancements in gaming hardware. Overall, **Donkey Kong** not only showed what was possible at the time but also set a precedent for how microprocessors could be utilized to craft engaging and enduring interactive entertainment.

The Legacy of Donkey Kong

The game that keeps on giving, with a legacy cemented in gaming folklore.

How Donkey Kong inspired future game developers.

Donkey Kong's daring design and engaging gameplay have inspired generations of game developers. It was one of the first games to feature a coherent narrative, paving the way for storytelling in video games. The premise, involving a plucky carpenter saving a damsel in distress, set the stage for more complex plots.

Moreover, the game's innovative use of vertical movement through ladders introduced a new dimension to platform mechanics. Future developers took cues from its level design, creating intricate worlds with multi-directional movement. Donkey Kong's success showed that originality in character design and gameplay could create an enduring classic.

Spawning numerous sequels and spinoffs.

The runaway success of Donkey Kong led to a proliferation of sequels and spinoffs. Nintendo recognized the potential of their accidental hero, Mario, originally Jumpman, and built a franchise around him. Titles like Donkey Kong Jr. and Donkey Kong Country continued the legacy, introducing new characters and gameplay elements.

These sequels cemented Donkey Kong's place in gaming, each iteration borrowing from the original while adding its unique twist. The franchise's evolution reflects the industry's shift towards more narrative and character-driven experiences, with Donkey Kong being a constant inspiration.

Special place in hardcore gamers' hearts.

Donkey Kong holds a special place in the hearts of hardcore gamers, many of whom cherish it as their first taste of challenging gameplay. The game's difficulty curve, requiring precise timing and strategic thinking, resonated with players looking for a genuine test of skill. It's often cited in the context of speedrun communities, where gamers showcase their expertise and compete for the fastest completion times. Beyond its gameplay, Donkey Kong is celebrated for its historical significance. It represents a pivotal moment in gaming history, a time when innovation and creativity blossomed, leaving an indelible mark on its audience.

The ongoing appeal: Classic yet everlasting fun.

Despite the decades since its release, Donkey Kong remains a staple in arcades and retro gaming events. Its timeless appeal lies in its simplicity; the basic premise of climbing levels and dodging obstacles is as engaging now as it was then. Modern gamers appreciate the straightforward challenge amidst today's often complex gaming landscapes. This classic title is a reminder of the roots of gaming, where raw gameplay mechanics powered the experience. Donkey Kong's blend of nostalgia and fun keeps both veteran and newer audiences coming back for more barrelhopping antics.

Modern revivals and nostalgic callbacks.

Donkey Kong's legacy continues through modern revivals and nostalgic callbacks. Games like Donkey Kong Country: Tropical Freeze keep the brand alive, updating the classic feel with new graphics and mechanics. Meanwhile, Donkey Kong references regularly pop up in other media, from cameos in contemporary games to nods in popular films. These revivals highlight Donkey Kong's enduring charm, captivating new fans while delighting long-time followers. The big ape's continued presence in modern gaming is a testament to its iconic status, proving that great gaming experiences never fade away.

Chapter 12: Space Invaders - When Aliens Attacked

Before we were afraid of zombies, it was the aliens who had us wide-eyed and button-mashing. Dive into the thrilling tale of how **Space Invaders** not only brought sci-fi to our fingertips but also kickstarted a demand for video games that would shape the industry forever.

The Birth of Space Invaders

Long before high-definition graphics and complex stories, there was Space Invaders, the simplest alien invasion game that changed the gaming landscape forever.

Space Invaders debuted in 1978, created by Tomohiro Nishikado in Japan.

It was the late 1970s, a time when disco balls glittered overhead, and bell-bottoms swept the dance floors. Enter **Space Invaders**, a game that would leave a lasting impact as vibrant as the era itself. In 1978, Tomohiro Nishikado, a talented developer from Japan, introduced the world to this groundbreaking video game. Back then, games were simple affairs, but Space Invaders challenged this simplicity with a gripping twist.

Nishikado's creation marked a pivotal moment; Japan was known for its penchant for technological innovations, and now it was aiming for the amusement arcades. The debut not only expanded gaming horizons but also set a new bar for interactive experiences globally. A masterpiece of the time, Space Invaders attracted not just gamers, but anyone with a penchant for the mysterious and the fun of defending humankind from digital alien threats.

Inspired by movies like Star Wars and the invasion genre, the game had players defending Earth from descending aliens.

In the shadow of movie classics like *Star Wars* and other alien invasion flicks, Space Invaders emerged as a digital reflection of our fascination with the cosmos. Players found themselves at the helm of Earth's defense, tasked with thwarting a relentless wave of descending extraterrestrial foes. As pixels danced across the screen, so did players' imaginations, fueled by the allure of sci-fi cinema.

This game expertly tapped into our fears and fantasies about the unknown. The idea of battling otherworldly invaders resonated deeply with players, providing an adrenaline rush as they shot at waves of blocky alien ships. With each level, the game intensified its grip on its audience, turning casual players into dedicated defenders of digital Earth.

Nishikado faced challenges with technology, hand-crafting his own tools to develop the game.

Developing Space Invaders was no simple feat in an era when computer technology was still unfolding its mysterious petals. Tomohiro Nishikado encountered numerous technical hurdles, given the limited capabilities of contemporary technology. Like a digital-age Da Vinci, he hand-crafted his own development tools, piecing together the hardware with the finesse of a watchmaker.

Undeterred by limitations, Nishikado modified circuits and created bespoke hardware to render his vision into reality. His ingenuity laid the foundation for future video game developments, showcasing the necessity of innovation in overcoming technological constraints. Through this process, he not only crafted a historical game but also carved his name into the hall of fame of video game design pioneers.

The game's technical limitations turned into iconic features, like the incremental speed-up of alien movement.

What a delightful quirk that a technical limitation became a game-changer. Space Invaders' signature feature, the incremental speed-up of descending alien invaders, was a serendipitous result of hardware constraints. As players destroyed aliens, the game had fewer objects to render, allowing the processor to handle information more swiftly. This unintended acceleration heightened tension, turning a quirk into a landmark gameplay feature that kept players on their toes. The characteristic frenetic pace at later stages of the game became a hallmark, celebrated as much for its ingenuity as for its entertainment value. Masterfully, the limitation was embraced, proving that sometimes restrictions can birth creativity.

Space Invaders was initially supposed to have tanks, but shifted focus to aliens after the impact Star Wars had on science fiction.

In its conceptual stages, Space Invaders was to feature tanks as protagonists in the battle scenario, but inspiration struck like a bolt of lightning. As *Star Wars* soared across cinema screens, altering the landscape of science fiction, Nishikado saw the potential of incorporating alien invaders instead. This shift from earthly tanks to cosmic threats transformed the game's dynamic completely.

The decision was timely; it aligned perfectly with public intrigue surrounding aliens, fueled by cinematic exploits. The evocative imagery of defending the planet from space invaders was far more compelling and capitalized on the growing cultural fascination with extraterrestrial life. This change made Space Invaders not just a game, but an exploration into our collective dreams of battling across the stars.

Beep, Boop, Blast: Game Mechanics

Forget complicated rules and tutorials. Space Invaders thrived on simplicity, as gamers engaged in escalating alien battles with every quarter.

Players controlled a laser cannon, moving horizontally while shooting vertical barrages at aliens.

In *Space Invaders*, players took command of a laser cannon, gliding effortlessly from left to right at the screen's bottom. This straightforward control scheme made the game accessible to newcomers while providing a skillful challenge to veterans. The laser cannon's main role was to send waves of vertical shots skyward, aimed at a relentless procession of descending aliens.

The beauty of this mechanic lay in its simplicity. The laser cannon was limited by its single-shot capacity, requiring players to carefully time their attacks. Mastering the art of repositioning across the screen to dodge alien fire added an exhilarating layer to the gaming experience. It ensured that every shot counted, and players had to keep an eye on the entire screen, ensuring no alien crept too close.

The gameplay loop was addictively simple: shoot the aliens before they landed on Earth.

The core gameplay loop in *Space Invaders* was both ingenious and beguilingly simple. Your mission: obliterate the wave of menacing aliens before they reached the planet's surface. This premise provided an intuitive goal that was clear from the get-go, needing no backstory or tutorial. What kept players glued to the screen was the innate drive to protect Earth, as alien formations methodically descended, their tempo increasing with fewer invaders on the screen. This provided a perfect blend of both immediate and emergent challenge, as every play session demanded quick reflexes and strategic positioning. The adrenaline rush of a very narrowly averted alien touchdown contributed to its 'just one more game' appeal.

The alien 'swoosh' became memorable, increasing tension as the pace quickened with each kill.

The eerie "swoosh" of the alien fleet in motion became one of the most iconic soundscapes in gaming history. As invaders methodically inched closer to the bottom, this hypnotic sound increased in pace, creating an escalating sense of urgency. Each successful hit transformed the rhythmic pulse into a rapid-fire conundrum.

This audio feedback not only tilled the soil for increasing tension but also synced seamlessly with the gameplay's visual cadence. In essence, each "swoosh" provided a heartbeat rhythm, intertwining player actions with a tangible auditory tension that kept players on the edge of their seat. The game's auditory experience was fundamental to its suspense, reminding players that the battle was far from over.

Space Invaders' escalating difficulty was revolutionary, increasing player engagement.

One of the game's groundbreaking features was its dynamic difficulty adjustment, paving the way for future games.

As players dispatched more aliens, the pace of the remaining swarm quickened, increasing pressure and difficulty.

This mechanic required heightened precision and quicker reflexes from players.

This shifting tempo was a clever way to prolong player engagement, invoking a continuous push towards mastery. Each new wave of aliens not only reset the challenge but also introduced a subtly different speed and pattern, requiring players to adapt constantly. This ensured that no two playthroughs felt exactly the same, laying the groundwork for contemporary game design strategies.

Sound effects: The ever-accelerating beats of the soundtrack were compared to a heartbeat, ramping up the tension.

As you played *Space Invaders*, the relentless drumming of the soundtrack mimicked the acceleration of a heartbeat.

This escalating audio tempo was no accident; it mirrored the increasing tension as swarms of aliens closed in. With each alien you downed, the rhythm subtly quickened, until it reached a fever pitch.

Experts often liken this auditory device to the more subconscious effects in thriller movies, where the swell of music heightens tension. The game's soundtrack synced perfectly with the gameplay, always reminding players of the impending doom. The composition effectively heightened the experience, making each session a nerve-wracking battle that players craved to conquer.

Impact on Pop Culture and Economics

Who knew a silent arcade machine could shout so loud? Space Invaders was more than a game; it was a pop culture phenomenon and a pivotal economic force.

Space Invaders was one of the first games to stir national demand, even causing a coin shortage in Japan!

In 1978, when **Space Invaders** hit the arcade scene in Japan, it was more than just a hit; it was a sensation. The game's popularity soared so high that it triggered a shortage of the ¥100 coin, which was needed to play the game. It's not every day a video game can claim to have disrupted a country's monetary circulation! Players found themselves hunting down these precious coins as if they were hidden Easter eggs.

This phenomenon highlighted the burgeoning enthusiasm for interactive entertainment and demonstrated how a single game could drive an entire nation into a fervor. The coin shortage incident became a quirky historical footnote, showcasing Space Invaders' early influence on economic systems.

The game's success contributed to a boom in arcade culture globally, peaking in the 1980s.

Space Invaders wasn't just a game; it was the cornerstone of a cultural movement. Its success heralded the golden age of arcade games, leading to their peak in the early 1980s. Arcades became bustling social hubs where gamers gathered to compete, collaborate, and conquer new challenges. The sight and sounds of arcade machines lined up in rows became emblematic of the era's entertainment landscape. The game triggered a surge in arcade openings worldwide, fostering a community of avid gamers eager to top high scores and master new releases. Space Invaders paved the way for classics like *Pac-Man* and *Donkey Kong*, forever altering the world's gaming and cultural landscape.

Merchandise flooded the market: from toys and T-shirts to home furnishings and even foods.

As Space Invaders took the world by storm, it seeped into all aspects of popular culture, including merchandise. Fans of the game could express their devotion through an array of themed products. From alien-adorned T-shirts to Space Invaders bedspreads, the game became a lifestyle. The pixelated invaders were printed on notebooks, trading cards, and lunchboxes, turning everyday items into nerdy treasures. The market even saw edible Space Invaders in the form of snacks and candies, allowing players to munch on their way to high scores. This wave of merchandising helped blur the lines between gaming and everyday life, solidifying Space Invaders' place not just in arcades, but in homes and daily routines worldwide.

Spawned the first strategy guide, changing how games were played and solo missions were conquered.

Before *cheat codes* and online walkthroughs, **Space Invaders** spawned a new era in gaming strategy. The game inspired the first-ever video game strategy guide, a revolutionary tool for avid players. This guide provided invaluable tips and tricks for mastering the game, giving strategists an edge in their battle against pixelated extraterrestrials.

This innovation heralded a new approach to gaming, allowing players to refine techniques and achieve new highscores. It marked a shift from solitary gameplay to a more communal knowledge-sharing culture, ultimately transforming how players approached and enjoyed video games.

Influence extended to music and television, with its pixelated aliens appearing almost everywhere.

Space Invaders' impact was not confined to arcades and merchandise; it infiltrated the entertainment industry, appearing in television shows and music videos. Its iconic pixelated aliens became symbols of an era, capturing the imagination of artists and creators across mediums.

The game's distinctive sound effects and visual style influenced musicians, who incorporated them into tracks, further embedding the game in pop culture. Television shows featured references and parodies, showcasing the aliens as a cultural touchstone. Even decades later, Space Invaders' legacy continues to inspire creative works, testament to its enduring influence and nostalgic charm.

Space Invaders: The Tech Revolution

While players were battling extraterrestrials, Space Invaders was quietly sparking a revolution in tech and hardware development.

The game was one of the first to overlay characters on top of a background, an advance for graphics.

In the world of vintage video games, **Space Invaders** stood out as a pioneer by being one of the first to introduce the concept of overlaying characters on top of a static background. This was groundbreaking for its time, offering a richer visual experience compared to the flat, static screens of earlier games. Until then, games were mostly limited to basic shapes on a stark, empty canvas.

By making use of a layered presentation, *Space Invaders* brought its alien foes and player's cannon to life, igniting player's imaginations. This graphical advancement set a precedent, heavily influencing the design of future games. Suddenly, it was not just about the gameplay but also about creating an immersive environment that could draw players in. Players felt like heroes defending Earth—not just angry rectangles firing dots.

Developed using a microprocessor, it increased the game’s complexity and playability.

The use of a microprocessor in **Space Invaders** was a forward-thinking move that revolutionized gaming at the time.

Microprocessors enabled greater complexity in gameplay and more intricate game mechanics, distinguishing Space Invaders from its predecessors like Pong. This leap provided developers with more room to innovate, by allowing richer animations and new dynamics in enemy behavior.

Players were captivated by the strategic depth the game offered, where enemy waves increased in speed as players successfully eliminated them. This created an escalating challenge that kept players engaged longer. The microprocessor was like the magical wand that, when waved, transformed a simple video game concept into a thrilling battle that kept gamers returning to the arcade for just one more round.

Space Invaders' success prompted rapid growth in video game hardware demands and innovations.

The unprecedented success of **Space Invaders** sent shockwaves through the industry, creating a burgeoning demand that drove hardware innovations. Arcades filled with towering machines, and many tech companies rushed to develop both diverse and powerful gaming platforms.

This demand fueled the creation of specialized chips and circuits that just a few years prior would have seemed futuristic. Today's gamers can thank innovations prompted by Space Invaders for the rapid evolution of graphics processing speed, memory capacity, and user interface complexity, forging a technological path that modern video games would navigate toward their massive potential.

The limitation of monochrome graphics led to creative game design and gameplay focus.

Despite its monochrome graphics, **Space Invaders** showcased an incredible ability to captivate players through its ingenious game design. The absence of flashy colors meant greater emphasis on gameplay, sound effects, and player engagement. Designers had to think outside the box, and this limitation became a powerful catalyst for creativity. The resulting game was a perfect harmony of simplicity and challenge, where every pixel was a tool, and every sound was deliberate. The monochrome screen forced players and developers to focus intensely on the game's mechanics, fostering a level of immersion and excitement that became *the heartbeat* of the gaming experience. It proved that innovation isn't hampered by constraints; rather, sometimes, constraints can be the spark that ignites innovation. **The success of arcade machines pushed future development in home consoles like the Atari 2600.**

The popularity and profitability of **Space Invaders** arcade machines had a domino effect on the gaming industry, directly influencing the development and success of early home consoles like the Atari 2600. As players fell in love with video games in arcades, there was a growing desire to bring that excitement into homes, packaging it in a more intimate, accessible way through consoles.

This shift marked a significant turning point, as console manufacturers recognized the potential for home gaming. *Space Invaders* set the gold standard for what a successful game could achieve, leading to the porting of games onto consoles which expanded the audience. This move not only preserved classic experiences but also helped proliferate the home gaming market, forever altering how the world engaged with video games.

Space Invaders' Legacy Today

The aliens might have retreated, but Space Invaders' influence on video games remains indelible in our digital DNA.

Modern games still draw inspiration from Space Invaders' simplistic yet challenging mechanics.

Many modern games, believe it or not, often nod back to the straightforward yet exhilarating dynamics of **Space Invaders**. It pioneered the "easy to play, hard to master" model, a backbone of contemporary game design philosophy. The game's core mechanics—simple controls paired with an escalating challenge—remain a benchmark in game development.

Today's indie developers, in particular, have adopted these principles, as seen in many successful titles that prioritize accessible gameplay yet manage to demand finesse and strategy. Titles like *Geometry Wars* and *Super Stardust* owe their existence to the foundational simplicity yet addictive progression that *Space Invaders* popularized. It seems clear that while aliens have taken a backseat, their legacy continues to drive the pulse-pounding intensity of today's digital challenges.

It's often cited in discussions about game design for its pacing and difficulty level.

Space Invaders is a prime example in any discourse about game design due to its impeccable timing and balance. Its gradual increase in difficulty keeps players engaged—a well-tuned art that persists in modern gaming. The notion of pacing, where the earliest waves lull players in, and then it ramps up the suspense and action, set a standard.

Game designers frequently study **Space Invaders** to understand how a few simple elements can combine to create a captivating experience. It's like a lesson in suspense, akin to a Hitchcock film but without the tuxedo-clad villains.

Even with today's advanced graphics and deep narratives, the flow and rhythm originally set by *Space Invaders* remain influential and ever-relevant in game design classrooms around the world.

Space Invaders saw continuous re-releases, keeping its classic charm alive for new generations.

Like a classic rock band on a never-ending tour, **Space Invaders** continues to strum its iconic tune across gaming platforms of all kinds. Through every leap in video game technology—from arcade machines to home consoles and now smartphones—this retro masterpiece has experienced numerous reincarnations.

Each re-release is like a time capsule opened anew, allowing both nostalgic players and curious newcomers to experience the original thrill. Whether in color, with upgraded graphics, or in its pure, unaltered form, *Space Invaders* connects gaming generations, keeping the fervor of alien attacks ever-relevant. This ongoing adventure solidifies its status as not just a game, but a timeless experience.

The game is part of gaming museums and halls of fame, celebrated for its lasting impact.

Step inside any gaming museum or peruse the annals of gaming hall of fames, and you're sure to find **Space Invaders** showcased with pride. Its cultural and technical significance has earned it a pedestal among the premier relics of gaming history.

As visitors immerse themselves in gaming nostalgia, *Space Invaders* stands as a testament to how a simple concept can revolutionize an entire industry. Its presence in these revered spaces not only celebrates its past glory but also educates the public on the formative stages of gaming history, reinforcing its impact on the gaming giants we admire today.

Its alien sprite and game format have become symbolic in gaming iconography.

The iconic alien sprite from **Space Invaders** has morphed from a mere pixelated enemy into a universal symbol of the gaming culture. Its distinct design is instantly recognizable to both gamers and non-gamers alike, epitomizing the retro gaming era and spurring a sense of nostalgia.

Beyond just the sprite, the game's format itself—a cascading wave of challenges—has been mimicked and referenced in countless forms of media. The symbols of *Space Invaders* have transcended the screen to appear on everything from T-shirts to tattoos, branded as emblems of the digital age's golden beginnings.

Chapter 13: Pac-Man - An Icon is Born

Few games are as universally recognized as **Pac-Man**. Released in 1980, this game's bright colors, simple but challenging gameplay, and lovable character design made it a standout hit worldwide. Pac-Manmania swept through arcades and cemented the game's place in cultural history.

The Birth of Pac-Man

Pac-Man was originally developed by Namco and designed by Toru Iwatani. The game's creation marked a significant shift in the gaming industry.

Conceived as 'Pakkuman,' a character inspired by the Japanese onomatopoeia 'paku-paku,' which means to gobble up.

Pac-Man's development began with a simple yet inventive idea: a character whose purpose was to "gobble" everything in its path. This concept was derived from the Japanese onomatopoeia 'paku-paku,' which imitates the sound of a mouth opening and closing in quick succession. The game was conceived by Namco designer Toru Iwatani, who wanted to create a non-violent game with a universal appeal.

The character's round, puck-like shape was inspired by a pizza missing a slice, representing Pac-Man's voracious appetite. This innovative character design not only defined the game but also differentiated it from the era's dominant themes of space battles and blocky pixels. Pac-Man's simplicity captured players' imaginations, making it an instant classic in gaming history.

The game was intended to appeal to both genders, breaking away from the war and sports themes of the time.

At a time when most video games were themed around war and sports, Pac-Man marked a departure from the norm. Toru Iwatani's vision was to create a game that could draw in a more diverse audience, including women. He saw an opportunity to design a game that diverged from typical violent themes, thus widening its appeal.

This strategic move broadened the scope of the gaming audience, making arcades places of social gathering for both genders. The simple yet challenging maze layout, engaging gameplay mechanics, and charming character design helped Pac-Man transcend the typical demographic barriers of its time, making it a global sensation and a staple in popular culture.

Released in Japan as 'Puck Man,' it was renamed 'Pac-Man' for its international release to prevent vandalism of the arcade cabinets.

Originally released in Japan as 'Puck Man,' the game underwent a name change when Namco prepared it for the international market. The decision to rename it 'Pac-Man' was largely a preventive measure against potential vandalism. English-speaking audiences could easily alter

'Puck' to something vulgar by modifying arcade cabinet graphics.

This change proved fortuitous, as 'Pac-Man' became a name synonymous with arcade gaming. The catchy and concise name contributed to its iconic status. It doesn't just represent a linguistic tweak for marketing; it symbolizes the strategic thinking that contributed to the game's global success and enduring popularity.

Pac-Man was a technological marvel with advanced maze algorithms and innovative character AI.

Pac-Man's success wasn't just about concept; it also highlighted significant technological advancements. The game's maze algorithms offered players an array of challenging yet rewarding paths that kept them coming back for more.
This was paired with the artificial intelligence of the ghosts, which was highly advanced for its time.

Each ghost in the game had its own personality and behavior pattern, contributing to its unpredictability and excitement. The strategic element of understanding and predicting ghost movements gave players a reason to hone their skills, promoting replayability and setting benchmarks in AI design for future video games.

Its simplistic controls—just imitating eating—made it accessible to a wide audience.

One of the key reasons behind Pac-Man’s widespread popularity was its accessibility. The game utilized a joystick control system that was intuitive and simple, mimicking an action as common as eating. This allowed players of all ages and backgrounds to pick up the game with ease.

The game's simple control mechanics—navigate Pac-Man through the maze to eat dots and avoid ghosts—eliminated steep learning curves. This ease of access encouraged extended play and appealed to casual and hardcore gamers alike, further embedding Pac-Man into the fabric of gaming culture.

Gameplay and Mechanics

Pac-Man's gameplay involved guiding Pac-Man through a maze to eat all the dots and avoid ghosts. Simple yet engaging, the mechanics set Pac-Man apart.

The maze contains 240 dots and 4 larger 'power pellets' that enable Pac-Man to eat the ghosts temporarily.

Pac-Man's maze is ingeniously designed with 240 small dots laid out in a pattern that continuously challenges players to navigate efficiently. The objective is deceptively simple: eat all the dots to progress to the next level. The inclusion of four strategically placed **power pellets** elevates the gameplay. Once consumed, these power pellets temporarily empower Pac-Man with the ability to turn the tables on his pursuers, making the ghosts vulnerable for a brief period.

This dynamic adds a layer of strategy, allowing players to choose whether to chase down the now defenseless ghosts for additional points or to clear another section of the maze. The placement and timing of these power pellets introduce an exciting risk-reward scenario that keeps the game engaging and strategic, despite its initially simple appearance.

Four ghosts—Blinky, Pinky, Inky, and Clyde—with different personalities create strategic challenges for the player.

The ghosts in Pac-Man are more than mere obstacles; they are key to the game's enduring challenge and charm. Each ghost—**Blinky, Pinky, Inky, and Clyde**—has its own distinct personality and behavior pattern, compelling players to adapt their strategies. Blinky is known for his aggressive chasing of Pac-Man, while Pinky tries to position herself ahead to trap the player.

Inky's movements are more unpredictable, often causing players to second-guess their strategies. Clyde, on the other hand, occasionally veers away from the chase, adding another layer of unpredictability. This diverse array of ghost behaviors ensures that no two gameplay experiences are exactly alike, encouraging players to tirelessly hone their skills and strategies to outmaneuver their relentless adversaries.

The game increases in difficulty as levels progress, providing a continuous challenge.

As players advance through Pac-Man, they encounter progressively challenging levels that demand quicker reflexes and sharper strategic thinking. Each new level ramps up the speed of the ghosts, reducing the reaction time available to the player. This escalation keeps the game engaging and tests even the most seasoned of players.

Moreover, the ghosts' behavior becomes more synchronized and aggressive as the game progresses, compelling players to continuously adapt and refine their strategies to survive. This progressive difficulty curve is expertly balanced to maintain the game's addictive nature, ensuring players remain invested in mastering the increasingly complex mazes and ghost patterns.

The cyclical nature of the game and the absence of an 'end' drove players to achieve high scores.

Pac-Man’s cyclical nature, characterized by its continual loop without a definitive 'end,' encouraged a culture of high score competition. The lack of a final level meant players could theoretically play indefinitely, provided they had the skill to survive the increasing challenges. This "endless" gameplay was revolutionary for its time and spawned countless leaderboard contests among arcade goers.

The drive to achieve a higher score than before, or to outscore competitors in the arcade, became a significant part of Pac-Man's appeal. Leaderboards became a social hub, where players’ names and scores were immortalized. The pursuit of high scores pushed players to explore and exploit every nuance of the game's mechanics, ensuring each playthrough contributed to a deeper understanding of the game itself.

Cultural Impact

Pac-Man didn't just influence the gaming industry; it became a cultural icon, leading to widespread merchandise and even an animated TV series.

Pac-Man inspired music, with the hit song 'Pac-Man Fever' reaching the top 10 on the Billboard charts in 1982.

In the early 1980s, **'Pac-Man Fever'** became a testament to the game's cultural phenomenon. Created by Buckner & Garcia, this catchy song captured the 1980s arcade frenzy and managed to climb into the top 10 of the Billboard charts in March 1982. The track serves not just as an anthem for gaming enthusiasts but also highlights how deeply Pac-Man had penetrated mainstream culture. Through witty lyrics and upbeat melodies, the song celebrated the thrill of arcade gaming while solidifying Pac-Man's status as an icon.

'Pac-Man Fever' was more than just a novelty; it reflected the changing cultural landscape, where digital entertainment began influencing other entertainment forms. This cross-pollination between gaming and music was unprecedented at the time, showcasing Pac-Man's extraordinary reach beyond the confines of arcade walls.

Merchandise ranged from toys and clothing to board games.

The success of Pac-Man translated into a surge of merchandise, reflecting the game's immense popularity. In the early 1980s, Pac-Man-themed products became a craze, with everything from plush toys to clothing and accessories suddenly synonymous with cool. The familiar yellow character was emblazoned on t-shirts, hats, and even shoes, becoming a mainstay in youth fashion.

Board games and puzzles brought the Pac-Man experience into homes, allowing fans to engage with their favorite character beyond arcade walls. This merchandising success not only generated significant revenue but also helped establish a new marketing paradigm for future games. By monetizing character appeal, Pac-Man paved the way for future franchises to expand their brand presence through diverse merchandise offerings.

The character's design became a staple in pop culture, recognizable by people worldwide.

Pac-Man became an icon largely due to its simple yet striking character design. With a bright yellow circle, a large open mouth, and a playful personality, Pac-Man's visual simplicity ensured widespread recognition. This unique design was inspired by a simple concept: a pizza with one slice removed. Over time, it transcended gaming, appearing in numerous forms of media and advertising across the globe.

The character's simplicity allowed it to be adaptable and relatable, making it accessible to people of all ages and backgrounds. This design efficiency has cemented Pac-Man's image in pop culture as not just a game character but also as a symbol of the early gaming revolution. Such widespread recognition continues to be a testament to the timeless appeal of this iconic character.

Pac-Man influenced future games by demonstrating the appeal of a lovable mascot.

With Pac-Man's unprecedented popularity, the gaming industry recognized the power of creating memorable and lovable mascots. The character set a precedent for game developers who began focusing on developing engaging protagonists that could captivate audiences and drive merchandise sales. This shift in strategy was instrumental in the evolution of character design in video games.

The appeal of a lovable mascot was clear - they could create brand loyalty and enduring fanbases, as seen later with characters like Mario, Sonic the Hedgehog, and Pikachu. Pac-Man's success showed that compelling characters could transcend gaming, influencing other media and becoming icons themselves. This concept continues to be integral to developing successful and lasting game franchises today.

Legacy and Evolution

Pac-Man's legendary status has led to numerous sequels, spin-offs, and adaptations in various media over the years.

Games like 'Ms. Pac-Man' introduced new challenges and are considered classics in their own right.

Ms. Pac-Man, released in 1981, took the foundation laid by the original Pac-Man and built upon it with added complexity and charm. The introduction of new maze designs, multiple warp tunnels, and unpredictable ghost movements provided players with refreshing challenges. Each level presented a unique pattern, requiring new strategies to navigate successfully.

Additionally, Ms. Pac-Man featured an expanded narrative with the iconic intermission animations, depicting the evolving relationship between Pac-Man and Ms. Pac-Man. This subtle storytelling introduced a layer of personality to the characters, enhancing the game's appeal. The game's vibrant colors and improved graphics further captivated audiences, making Ms. Pac-Man a beloved title in its own right and a staple of arcade gaming history.

Pac-Man Championship Edition revived the arcade classic with modern twists, updating graphics and gameplay styles.

Released in 2007, the **Pac-Man Championship Edition** breathed new life into the arcade legend by implementing innovative gameplay mechanics while preserving the essence of the original. This updated version boasted highdefinition graphics and new neon visual effects, which provided a contemporary glow-up to the classic mazes.

The introduction of time-limited sessions and dynamic mazes added layers of strategy, rewarding players for their speed and adaptability. The game also featured evolving mazes that changed as players advanced, increasing the excitement and replay value. This modernization allowed both veteran fans and new players to engage with the nostalgia and thrill of Pac-Man in an entirely fresh way.

The game is featured in modern gaming consoles, ensuring that new generations experience the classic maze chase.

Throughout the decades, **Pac-Man** has endured through numerous different gaming platforms, evolving alongside console technology. Available on major modern gaming consoles such as PlayStation, Xbox, and Nintendo, Pac-Man has reached audiences far beyond its arcade origins.

Various adaptations of the game introduce younger players to the timeless joy of navigating mazes and chasing scores. The charm of Pac-Man's simplistic yet challenging gameplay continues to capture imaginations, making it a perfect introduction to the world of gaming for younger generations. The accessibility across diverse platforms ensures the legacy of Pac-Man remains strong in today's digital era.

Pac-Man's influence is evident in countless games that followed, cementing its role as a pioneering game in the industry.

The impact of **Pac-Man** extends far beyond its immediate commercial success, having paved the way for numerous games that followed. It was among the first titles to introduce the concept of character-based gameplay, inspiring countless developers to create engaging characters and narratives within their games.

Pac-Man's iconic gameplay mechanics, such as the power-up system and non-violent conflict resolution, have been emulated and expanded upon in various genres over the years. From stealth action games to puzzle-based adventures, elements of Pac-Man's design have become a foundation for innovative game development. Its pioneering role has left an indelible mark on the industry's evolution, demonstrating the power of simple yet compelling game design.

Critical Reception

Upon its release, Pac-Man was met with critical acclaim, praised for its innovative design and unrivaled entertainment value.

Reviewers highlighted its approachable yet challenging gameplay mechanics, appealing to a broad audience.

When **Pac-Man** first hit arcades, its gameplay mechanics were celebrated for being both accessible and intriguing.

The simple objective of navigating a maze while avoiding ghosts made it easy for anyone to pick up and play. However, the strategic element of collecting power pellets to turn the tables on those ghosts added a layer of complexity that kept gamers coming back.

This balance of simplicity and depth was something that resonated with a broad spectrum of players, from casual gamers to those seeking a more demanding challenge. The intuitive controls and increasing difficulty levels provided a perfect blend that engaged players across different skill levels. Reviewers of the time noted this unique balance, leading to high praise and contributing significantly to the game's enduring popularity.

The game's audio, particularly the cheerful tunes and sound effects, was noted as memorable and engaging.

One of **Pac-Man**'s standout features upon its release was its distinctive audio experience. The cheerful music and iconic sound effects, including the "wakka wakka" sound as Pac-Man eats dots, became defining auditory symbols for the game. These sounds were not just delightful but served an integral role in enhancing the gameplay experience.

The audio design was crafted to heighten the tension and excitement of the game, with faster-paced music tracks signaling critical moments as players neared completing a maze. This thoughtful integration of audio not only immersed players more deeply but also left a lasting impression, making the soundtrack as enduring as the game itself. Critics consistently pointed to the ingenuity of Pac-Man's sound design as a hallmark of its innovation.

Its non-violent nature was a refreshing change, drawing in diverse players and families.

At a time when many arcade games focused on shooting or combat, **Pac-Man** offered a refreshing, non-violent alternative. This distinct departure from violence allowed the game to appeal to a wider and more diverse audience, including young children and families. The non-threatening nature of Pac-Man's world, characterized by colorful ghosts and harmless dot-munching, was inviting and inclusive.

This aspect of Pac-Man was particularly noted by critics, who praised it for opening up the gaming world to more people and demonstrating that games could be both challenging and engaging without relying on violent themes. The game's universal appeal was a major factor in its success and helped establish it as a family-friendly option in arcades worldwide, contributing to its legendary status.

Critics continue to hold Pac-Man in high regard, often citing it in discussions of the best video games of all time.

More than four decades since its release, **Pac-Man** remains a highly revered title among both critics and gamers. The game's influence on popular culture and its pioneering contributions to gaming are often brought up in discussions of the greatest video games ever made. Its simplicity, strategic depth, and iconic status make it a frequent point of reference for game developers and historians alike.

Critics continue to acknowledge Pac-Man's role in shaping the gaming industry, highlighting its impact in terms of game design and cultural importance. As a testament to its endurance, Pac-Man consistently ranks on "greatest of all time" lists, showcasing its timeless appeal and the high regard in which it is still held. The game's ability to remain relevant in ever-changing times underscores its status as an icon of gaming history.

The Birth of Pac-Man

Pac-Man was born out of a desire to create a game that would appeal to a broader audience, beyond the typical shooting games popular at the time. Designed by Toru Iwatani, Pac-Man's development reflected a shift in gaming culture.

Pac-Man was developed by Namco and released in Japan in 1980.

The groundbreaking arcade game **Pac-Man** was developed by the Japanese company *Namco* and made its debut in May 1980. As the gaming industry was dominated by space shooters like Space Invaders, Namco's release represented a significant shift. Its innovative concept brought about a new era of arcade gaming. Pac-Man's introduction was a calculated risk by Namco, which paid off dramatically as the game quickly captured the public's attention in Japan.

The game's subsequent North American release in October 1980 through a collaboration with Bally Midway led to an unprecedented boom in popularity. Players were drawn to its simple yet engaging gameplay, marking a pivotal moment in the global arcade scene. Pac-Man became a staple in arcades everywhere, ushering in what is known today as the "Golden Age of Video Games."

Designer Toru Iwatani aimed to create a non-violent game that could be enjoyed by both genders.

The mastermind behind Pac-Man, **Toru Iwatani**, set out with a clear vision: to create a game that differed from the violent themes present in most games of the era. His goal was to design an experience that could entertain and attract a broader audience, including women, who were often overlooked in the gaming community. This inclusive approach broke away from conventional gaming design and introduced an appeal that extended beyond the male demographic.

This innovation is credited with creating a welcoming gaming environment. By focusing on non-violent, strategic, and entertaining gameplay, Iwatani laid the groundwork for a universal appeal that pacified traditional gender roles in gaming. As a result, Pac-Man not only entertained but also brought a diverse group of players into arcades worldwide.

The game's design was inspired by the shape of a pizza with a missing slice.

One of the most whimsical aspects of Pac-Man is its design origin story. The iconic shape of **Pac-Man** was inspired when Toru Iwatani saw a pizza with a single slice removed. This simple yet effective design choice became a hallmark of video game iconography. Iwatani wanted a character that was both recognizable and endearing, aided by the approachable design of a circular, smiling figure.

The character’s simplicity resonated with players and made the game instantly recognizable. Pac-Man's design perfectly complemented the bright arcade aesthetics of the time and aligned with Namco's vision of creating something entirely different in terms of arcade games. This departure from typical gaming icons helped cement PacMan as a beloved fixture in arcade history.

Pac-Man introduced a unique maze-chase genre that captivated players worldwide.

Pac-Man stands out not only for its iconic character but also for pioneering a new genre of gaming: the maze chase. This gameplay style involves navigating intricate mazes while avoiding enemy characters. Unlike many games of the era, which relied heavily on action and shooting, Pac-Man emphasized strategy and planning. Players had to carefully navigate the maze to eat all the dots, escape ghosts, and capture power pellets to change the tables on their pursuers.

This new genre offered a fresh and engaging experience that was easy to grasp but challenging to master. The worldwide reception was extraordinary as players delighted in this new type of arcade fun that required both skill and strategy. Pac-Man's success ensured that the maze-chase concept would influence countless other games in the years to come.

The game was originally titled 'Puck-Man' in Japan.

Before becoming the legendary Pac-Man we know today, the game was first released under the name **'Puck-Man'** in Japan. The name stemmed from the Japanese onomatopoeia "paku-paku," which evokes the sound of a mouth opening and closing. This original title aptly described Pac-Man's characteristic chomping action.

However, in preparation for the game's international release, concerns arose that the name 'Puck-Man' could be easily altered to an inappropriate word in English-speaking regions. Consequently, the decision was made to rename the game 'Pac-Man,' ensuring it maintained its original playful spirit while avoiding potential mischief. This careful consideration of cultural nuances contributed to the game's universal appeal and enduring success.

Gameplay Mechanics

Pac-Man's gameplay was both simple and innovative, centered around navigating mazes, collecting dots, and avoiding ghosts. Its mechanics were straightforward yet challenging, contributing to its mass appeal.

Players navigate Pac-Man through a maze while eating dots.

In the iconic **Pac-Man** game, players take control of the titular character to guide him through intricate mazes. The goal is straightforward yet engaging: consume all the dots within the maze. Players use directional controls to navigate Pac-Man, who moves continuously until redirected. The simplicity of such a mechanic took the gaming world by storm, offering a pick-up-and-play experience.

The fundamental challenge lies in the maze's twists and turns, which require players to plan routes strategically, anticipating both dead ends and ghost movements. The more dots Pac-Man eats, the closer players get to progressing to the next level. This basic yet compelling loop has charmed generations, laying the foundation for its timeless appeal.

The maze contains four power pellets that allow Pac-Man to eat ghosts.

Scattered throughout each maze are four larger pellets known as *power pellets*. When consumed, a power pellet gives Pac-Man the temporary ability to turn the tables on his ghostly pursuers, allowing him to eat them for bonus points. The ghosts, normally dangerous, turn blue and flee, marking a rare opportunity for Pac-Man to eliminate them from the game temporarily.

This mechanic introduces a strategic element, as players must decide when to use these limited resources. Timing is crucial, as the invincibility effect is brief, lasting only moments. Successfully consuming ghosts during this window not only scores extra points but also provides a brief respite from pursuit, enhancing the player's sense of empowerment.

Each ghost in the game has its own behavior pattern, adding complexity to the game.

Adding depth to the maze-chase dynamics, each of Pac-Man's ghostly adversaries follows its unique behavior pattern. Blinky, the red ghost, aggressively chases Pac-Man, while Pinky attempts to ambush him by moving ahead of his path. Inky, the blue ghost, exhibits erratic behavior based on a mix of factors including Pac-Man's position and Blinky's movement.

Clyde, the orange ghost, seems to oscillate between chasing and avoiding Pac-Man. This diversity in ghost behavior not only challenges players to adapt their strategies but also ensures that no two plays feel exactly alike. Mastering these patterns is key to maintaining an advantage, as understanding the ghosts' movements enables more effective navigation through each maze.

The game progressively becomes more challenging as the player advances.

As players advance through the levels in **Pac-Man**, the difficulty gradually intensifies. The pace of both Pac-Man and the ghosts increases, demanding quicker reflexes and more decisive movements. Additionally, the game's Artificial Intelligence adjusts, making the ghosts' movements less predictable and more aggressive.

While the mazes maintain their layout, the incremental difficulty shifts encourage players to refine their strategies continuously. Timing, precision, and an understanding of ghost patterns become increasingly crucial to surviving deeper into the game. This progressive escalation sustains engagement, as players are constantly challenged to improve their skill level in pursuit of higher scores.

A session typically ends when all lives are lost.

In *Pac-Man*, players start with a set number of lives, usually three, though additional lives can be earned by reaching specific score thresholds. The game session proceeds until all lives are depleted, with each lost life bringing the player one step closer to a game over.

Survival hinges on avoiding ghost encounters, which result in a life loss each time Pac-Man is caught. This looming threat requires constant vigilance and adept use of power pellets and strategic maneuvers. Emphasizing skill and persistence, the finite nature of lives in Pac-Man adds a layer of tension, driving players to refine their approach and aim for higher achievements.

Cultural Impact

Pac-Man was more than just a game; it was a cultural phenomenon that had a profound impact on gaming and popular culture. Its legacy is still felt today in various forms.

Pac-Man became a household name and a cultural icon of the 1980s.

Pac-Man's rise to fame in the 1980s is a testament to its universal appeal and trendsetting nature. Its simplistic yet captivating gameplay quickly caught the attention of players worldwide. As arcades became social hubs, Pac-Man emerged as the flagship game, drawing players of all ages and backgrounds.

Its character design, a yellow, dot-munching protagonist, became instantly recognizable. Within a short period, PacMan transcended gaming, making appearances in TV shows, films, and even on advertisements. The game's influence extended beyond entertainment, embodying the spirit of the era and becoming a symbol of the burgeoning digital age. It's challenging to think of the 1980s pop culture without visualizing the familiar face of Pac-Man.

The game's success spurred a range of merchandise, including a chart-topping song and an animated TV series.

At its peak, Pac-Man was not only a game but a multimedia powerhouse. The demand for anything Pac-Man-related resulted in a vast array of merchandise. From lunchboxes and t-shirts to board games, Pac-Man was omnipresent. The commercial success of this merchandise underscored the game's impact on consumer culture.

Adding to its media penetration, "Pac-Man Fever" by Buckner & Garcia topped music charts, a rarity for a song inspired by a video game. The animated TV series further solidified Pac-Man's status, bringing the character to life on television screens and expanding its story universe. Such ventures diversified Pac-Man's audience, embedding it further into cultural consciousness.

Pac-Man's popularity contributed to the growth of the arcade industry.

Pac-Man's release was a pivotal moment for the arcade industry, which was gaining momentum at the time. Arcades, once niche establishments, blossomed into bustling centers of entertainment, largely due to Pac-Man's draw. The game attracted a broader audience compared to other arcade games, including diverse age groups and genders, thereby expanding the player base.

This broadened demographic appeal translated into heightened foot traffic and sales for arcades, prompting them to install multiple Pac-Man units to meet demand. This frenzy spawned numerous arcade imitators and competitors, seeking to capitalize on Pac-Man's success. Ultimately, the game played a significant role in positioning arcades as mainstream entertainment venues of the era.

The game's simple yet addictive design influenced numerous subsequent video games.

Pac-Man introduced a level of simplicity that belied its deep and addictive gameplay mechanics. Its intuitive design allowed anyone to play, but its increasing difficulty challenged even the most experienced gamers. This balance of simplicity and depth became a guiding principle for future game designers.

Many video game developers drew inspiration from Pac-Man's design, innovating with their versions of maze chases, collectible items, and escalating challenges. Its timeless formula has been revisited time and again, proving that elegant design is often the keystone to engaging gameplay. Through its influence, Pac-Man set a foundational example for game mechanics in the video game industry.

It was one of the first games to feature a character with a personality and story.

Before Pac-Man, many games relied solely on abstract mechanics rather than character-driven experiences. Pac-Man broke this mold by introducing a character with a distinct personality and a simple narrative. Players weren't just controlling pixels; they were guiding a character with a purpose, eating dots and evading ghosts.

The emergence of Pac-Man as a character invited players to emotionally connect, weaving a basic story with a clear protagonist and antagonists—the iconic ghosts. This was groundbreaking, opening new avenues for storytelling in games. It paved the way for future games to develop more elaborate narratives and character-driven stories, influencing how games would be crafted for decades to come.

Technological Innovations

Pac-Man introduced several technological advancements that were revolutionary for its time. These innovations were key in shaping the development of future video games.

Pac-Man featured one of the first video game characters with an identity and personality.

One of Pac-Man's groundbreaking aspects was its introduction of a character with a distinct identity. Unlike previous games, which often featured abstract shapes or simple avatars, Pac-Man brought to life a character that resonated with players through its simplistic yet charming design. The circular, yellow figure with a wide mouth not only served as the protagonist but also became a cultural icon.

Pac-Man's character wasn't just a visual gimmick; it played a central role in the game's appeal. It acted as a relatable entity that players could root for, marking a significant departure from the faceless characters of early video games. This move towards character-driven games paved the way for countless iconic video game characters in the years that followed.

Its AI system included varying ghost behaviors, creating different challenges for players.

Pac-Man was also notable for its use of AI to distinguish the behavior of its antagonists, the ghosts. Unlike typical enemy patterns that were predictable and repetitive, the ghosts in Pac-Man each had unique movement strategies. For example, Blinky, the red ghost, was programmed to chase Pac-Man aggressively, while Pinky and Inky had more strategic approaches to corner the player.

This variety in AI behavior meant that players needed to develop diverse strategies to succeed, adding layers of complexity to the game. Such innovation in enemy AI provided a template for future games, demonstrating the potential for AI to greatly enhance gameplay dynamics.

The colorful graphics and sound effects set a new standard for visual and audio elements in games.

Pac-Man's visual appeal was unrivaled at the time of its release, featuring vibrant, colorful mazes and distinct character designs. The bright hues not only attracted players but also made the game recognizable, even from a distance in bustling arcades. This shift towards enticing graphics was a significant leap from the monochrome displays of earlier games.

Equally important were Pac-Man's sound effects, which included catchy jingles and distinctive 'waka-waka' eating sounds. These audio elements became iconic, elevating the gaming experience beyond visuals. The combination of engaging graphics and sound showcased the potential for games to be sensory-rich experiences.

The intermissions between levels were among the first examples of cutscenes in games.

Pac-Man introduced players to one of the earliest forms of cutscenes through its intermission animations between levels. These short, entertaining clips provided a break from the gameplay and added a narrative element to the experience.

In these intermissions, humorous interactions between Pac-Man and the ghosts were displayed, fostering a storytelling aspect that engaged players beyond the immediate level challenges. This innovation not only enhanced the game's charm but also set a precedent for narrative elements in games, influencing many future titles to incorporate story-driven cutscenes.

Pac-Man's design utilized a looping feature where characters exited one side of the screen and reappeared on the opposite side.

The loop feature of Pac-Man's design was a revolutionary concept that added a strategic dimension to gameplay. As Pac-Man or the ghosts exited one side of the screen, they would reappear from the opposite side, allowing for endless, seamless exploration without encountering borders or barriers.

This mechanic added a spatial puzzle aspect to the game, as players could use it to evade ghosts or optimize their path through the maze. The looping design was a creative solution to the limitation of screen real estate in arcades, demonstrating innovative thinking that inspired similar mechanics in future game designs.

Chapter 14: The Legend of Zelda - Adventure Reimagined

1986 saw the release of *The Legend of Zelda*, a game that redefined what adventure games could be. Combining exploration, puzzle-solving, and combat, this game provided an immersive experience that set the benchmark for future titles.

The Birth of a Legend

The Legend of Zelda emerged in a time when video games were just starting to explore deeper narratives and complex gameplay. This section discusses how the game came into existence and its early reception.

Shigeru Miyamoto's Vision: The creator, Shigeru Miyamoto, was inspired by his childhood explorations of caves and forests, leading to the game's focus on exploration.

Shigeru Miyamoto, often hailed as one of the most brilliant minds in gaming, drew on his own childhood adventures when creating *The Legend of Zelda.* As a child, Miyamoto spent countless hours traversing the countryside near his home in Kyoto, stumbling upon hidden caves and dense forests. These explorations sparked his imagination and curiosity, forming the backbone of the game's design.

Miyamoto's vision was to create a game that captured the thrill and wonder of discovery. He wanted players to experience the excitement he felt as a child, never knowing what lay around the next corner. This aspiration was realized through an expansive world filled with secrets and challenges, encouraging a sense of awe and adventure that deeply resonated with gamers worldwide.

Combining Genres: The game combined elements of action, adventure, and puzzle-solving, offering a new kind of interactive experience.

The Legend of Zelda was groundbreaking for its time, seamlessly merging multiple gaming genres into a cohesive experience. It blended action, where players engaged in combat with various enemies, with deep adventure elements that encouraged exploration and interaction with the world.

Furthermore, the game incorporated intricate puzzle-solving components, requiring players to think strategically and use items creatively to progress through dungeons and obstacles. This fusion of genres created a multifaceted gameplay experience that was both engaging and unprecedented, setting a new standard for immersive storytelling in video games.

Innovative Gameplay: Players were given an open-world experience which was rare at the time, allowing choices on how to explore Hyrule.

In an era where linear progression was the norm, *The Legend of Zelda* offered players a remarkable degree of freedom through its open-world design. The land of Hyrule was vast and filled with possibilities, allowing players to chart their own course through the game.

This non-linear approach was a novel concept, empowering players to tackle challenges in the order they chose, and to explore every nook and cranny at their own pace. The sense of agency and autonomy invigorated players, inviting them to immerse themselves fully in the game's world and lore, making each adventure unique and personal.

Initial Reception: At launch, the game was praised for its innovation, quickly becoming a bestseller and setting a high bar for future games.

Upon its release in 1986, *The Legend of Zelda* was met with widespread acclaim for its innovative gameplay mechanics and engaging narrative. Critics and players alike praised the game for pushing boundaries and exploring new frontiers in gaming.

The game swiftly rose to commercial success, becoming a bestseller and captivating audiences with its rich world and challenging gameplay. Its impact was profound, setting a high bar for future adventure games and establishing a legacy that would influence game design for decades to come.

Core Gameplay Mechanics

The Legend of Zelda introduced several gameplay mechanics that were pioneering at the time, transforming how players interacted with video games.

Inventory System: Players could collect items and manage an inventory, a feature that added depth to the gaming experience.

One of the most influential aspects of *The Legend of Zelda* was its innovative inventory system. This feature allowed players to collect, manage, and strategically use various items found throughout the game. Each item, from swords to bombs, played a crucial role in puzzle-solving and combat, adding a layer of complexity and engagement.

The ability to manage an inventory was groundbreaking at the time, as it required players to make strategic decisions about which items to use in different scenarios. This system not only enhanced the gameplay by offering more interactive and personalized experiences but also set a precedent for future adventure games. By empowering players with choices, the inventory mechanic significantly contributed to the game's depth and replayability.

Save Progress: The ability to save progress using a battery-backed save option was groundbreaking and allowed for longer gameplay sessions.

The introduction of a battery-backed save feature in *The Legend of Zelda* was nothing short of revolutionary. Before this, most games required players to complete them in one sitting, an often daunting task given the challenging nature of early video games. With this new save system, players could preserve their progress, encouraging longer and more intricate gaming sessions.

This feature was particularly appreciated as it alleviated the frustration of losing progress after turning off the console. It allowed players to explore the expansive world of Hyrule at their own pace, deepening their connection with the game's narrative and characters. Ultimately, the saving system set a new standard for future games, emphasizing convenience and player-centric design.

Puzzle Elements: Integrating puzzles into the game design challenged players to think strategically, beyond mere combat.

Puzzle elements were intricately woven into the fabric of *The Legend of Zelda*, elevating it beyond a simple actionadventure game. Players encountered complex puzzles that required critical thinking and strategic planning to solve. These challenges were seamlessly integrated into the environment, making them feel like an organic part of the world.

The puzzles added a layer of intellectual engagement, pushing players to look beyond swords and shields to solve problems. This blend of mental and physical challenges helped to diversify the gameplay and maintained player interest over extended periods. The successful use of puzzles helped establish *The Legend of Zelda* as a blueprint for future games that seek to balance combat with cerebral challenges.

Non-linear Exploration: The openness of Hyrule encouraged discovery and exploration, offering freedom rare in games of that era.

The Legend of Zelda's non-linear exploration was a refreshing innovation that set it apart from its contemporaries. Unlike many games of the time, which were largely linear, Zelda offered an expansive, open world that encouraged players to roam freely and discover secrets at their own pace.

The vastness of Hyrule invited players to explore uncharted territories, fostering a sense of adventure and curiosity. This open-ended design allowed for personal storytelling, as each player could encounter different paths and objects in a unique order. By prioritizing exploration and player agency, the game broke new ground in how virtual worlds were constructed, influencing countless titles that followed.

Story and Lore

The game featured a rich story that drew players into the mystical world of Hyrule, establishing a deep lore that continues to captivate.

The Quest: Players took on the role of Link, tasked with rescuing Princess Zelda and defeating the evil Ganon.

In *The Legend of Zelda*, players assume the role of Link, a courageous young hero whose mission is nothing short of epic. The primary objective is to rescue Princess Zelda, whom the malevolent Ganon has captured. Ganon, a formidable antagonist, seeks to use his powers to conquer the realm of Hyrule. As Link, players embark on an adventurous quest filled with perilous challenges and dangerous enemies.

The journey involves navigating through intricate dungeons, solving complex puzzles, and engaging in combat with a variety of foes. By overcoming these obstacles, players gain the tools and skills necessary to face Ganon's sinister forces. The narrative unfolds through exploration and discovery, with each conquered dungeon bringing Link a step closer to his ultimate goal. This quest not only defined the player's journey but also created an enduring blueprint for future adventure games.

Triforce Mythology: Central to the game's plot was the Triforce, an important element of Zelda lore, representing power, wisdom, and courage.

The Triforce is a central mythological element within *The Legend of Zelda*, embodying the virtues of power, wisdom, and courage. This sacred relic, divided into three golden triangles, plays a pivotal role in the game's lore. Each piece is connected to the series' main characters: Zelda embodies wisdom, Link represents courage, and Ganon seeks power.

The quest for the Triforce is integral to the conflict between Link and Ganon. Throughout the game, players are driven by the need to reconstruct the Triforce to restore balance to Hyrule. Its influence resonates throughout the series, symbolizing the eternal struggle between good and evil. This mythology enriches the game's narrative complexity and leaves a lasting impact on both the plotline and the player's engagement with the story.

A Living World: The game world featured a variety of NPCs, each contributing to the immersive storytelling and world-building.

A hallmark of *The Legend of Zelda* is its immersive and interactive world, where non-playable characters (NPCs) add depth to the player's experience. The vibrant land of Hyrule is inhabited by a diverse cast of characters, each with unique stories and personalities. These NPCs offer crucial information, lore, and side quests that enrich the game's narrative.

From the wise old man offering hints to the merchant with vital items, each interaction contributes to building a believable and captivating world. The game encouraged players to engage with these characters, fostering a sense of community within the game. This living world concept was revolutionary, providing players with a sense of agency and connection seldom seen before in video games, setting a standard for future titles.

Timeless Themes: Themes of good versus evil, courage, and destiny resonated deeply, setting a narrative foundation for future games in the series.

The Legend of Zelda weaves timeless themes into its narrative, grounding the story in universal concepts that resonate with players. The battle between good and evil is at the heart of the game, with Link standing as a symbol of courage against Ganon's malevolent forces. The theme of destiny is also prominent, as Link is often portrayed as the chosen hero fated to save Hyrule.

The interplay of these themes creates an enduring narrative that is both compelling and relatable. Players find inspiration in Link's journey, where courage triumphs over overwhelming odds. These foundational themes have not only established the game's iconic status but have also laid the groundwork for subsequent titles in the series, each expanding on this rich tapestry of narrative depth.

Impact on the Gaming Industry

The Legend of Zelda's influence on the gaming industry is undeniable, setting new standards and inspiring countless other titles.

Standard Setting: The game's design elements became benchmarks for quality in adventure games.

The Legend of Zelda introduced core design elements that set a new standard in adventure gaming. One of the game's major contributions was its innovative approach to non-linear gameplay. Players were given the freedom to explore the game world at their own pace, creating a sense of autonomy that was rare at the time.

The open-ended design, combined with the integration of exploration, puzzle-solving, and combat, established a comprehensive adventure framework that many games still emulate today. The seamless blend of these elements became a benchmark, with subsequent titles seeking to replicate its immersive experience. Additionally, the game's emphasis on detail and quality in graphic design and soundscape set a high bar for production values in the gaming industry.

Innovation: It inspired the introduction of open-world environments and complex narratives in future games.

The innovation showcased by *The Legend of Zelda* was groundbreaking, particularly in its introduction of open-world environments. This concept allowed players to wander freely, creating a sandbox-style experience that many future games would draw inspiration from.

Furthermore, the game laid the groundwork for embedding more complex narratives within the gaming experience. The storyline, though simplistic by today's standards, was intricate for its time. It interwove elements of fantasy with strategic gameplay, influencing countless future titles to incorporate deep, engaging plots. Nintendo's approach demonstrated that games could offer more than just action—they could tell stories and captivate gamers on multiple levels.

Cult Following: The game's success led to a series that remains influential, with a dedicated fanbase and numerous sequels.

The Legend of Zelda quickly gained a cult following, thanks to its captivating gameplay and unique style. The game's profound success paved the way for an enduring franchise that continues to thrive decades after its inception. With each new installment, the series consistently delivers fresh innovations while preserving the beloved mechanics that fans adore.

This dedicated fanbase has grown with each sequel, fueling a cultural phenomenon within the gaming community. The game's characters, world, and lore have become iconic symbols, influencing not only players but developers, who strive to capture the magic of Zelda in their creations. This longstanding influence highlights its pivotal role in shaping the future of adventure gaming.

Industry Influence: It showed that video games could offer rich storytelling and cinematic experiences, moving the industry towards more mature content.

The impact of *The Legend of Zelda* on the gaming industry extends beyond gameplay innovations. It was pivotal in demonstrating that video games could extend beyond simple entertainment to deliver rich storytelling and cinematic experiences.

This shift towards narrative depth and engaging content helped transform public perception of video games, paving the way for more mature and diverse content. Titles that followed began incorporating sophisticated plots and character development, elevating games to an art form capable of conveying emotion and complex themes. This evolution has had lasting effects, encouraging the development of games that are both entertaining and thoughtprovoking, contributing significantly to the industry's growth and maturity.

Genesis of a Legend

Learn how *The Legend of Zelda* was conceptualized and developed by Nintendo, leading to the creation of one of the most beloved franchises in gaming history.

The creative forces of Shigeru Miyamoto and Takashi Tezuka

Shigeru Miyamoto and Takashi Tezuka, two visionary game designers at *Nintendo*, were instrumental in the creation of *The Legend of Zelda*. Drawing from their complementary skill sets, they orchestrated a game that defied conventional norms of the time. Miyamoto, already renowned for his work on *Super Mario Bros.*, brought a unique storytelling ability and a penchant for creating captivating worlds. Tezuka, on the other hand, contributed his expertise in level design and narrative structure.

The collaboration between Miyamoto and Tezuka set a new standard for adventure games. Their shared vision to create an interactive, nonlinear experience laid the groundwork for what would become a defining title in gaming history. Together, they crafted a world that invited players to explore, experiment, and engage with the story at their own pace, which at the time was a groundbreaking approach to game design.

Inspired by childhood adventures in Kyoto

The inspiration for *The Legend of Zelda* can be traced back to Miyamoto’s childhood experiences in the countryside around Kyoto, Japan. As a child, Miyamoto often explored forests and caves, which later served as the creative basis for the game’s expansive, interconnected world. This sense of wonder and discovery is central to the game’s design, encouraging players to uncover hidden secrets and solve puzzles.

Miyamoto's childhood adventures translated into the game's core philosophy—**freedom of exploration** without a fixed path. This open-ended gameplay allowed for a personal connection between the player and the virtual world, akin to the memorable adventures of Miyamoto’s youth. Emphasizing curiosity and exploration, the game invites players to recreate the magic of discovering new places in a digital format.

A new approach to open-world gameplay

The Legend of Zelda broke new ground by introducing players to a non-linear, open-world gameplay experience. Unlike other games of its time, which typically followed linear paths with predefined checkpoints, Zelda offered an open terrain where players could explore at their own pace. This open-world design was both innovative and risky, as players were given little direction, encouraging them to chart their own course through Hyrule.

This groundbreaking approach fostered a sense of liberation that resonated deeply with players, establishing an immersive and interactive experience. The open-world concept challenged gamers to think strategically and adaptively, rewarding exploration and problem-solving. This laid the foundation for future open-world games, making *The Legend of Zelda* a pioneer in game design.

Nintendo's ambitious vision for the Famicom Disk System

When *The Legend of Zelda* was initially released in Japan, it was launched as a flagship title for the Famicom Disk System, an add-on to Nintendo's popular console. Nintendo aimed to showcase the capabilities of this new hardware, which promised enhanced features like expanded storage and the ability to save game progress—unheard of in home console games at that time.

This ambitious vision allowed developers to experiment with more complex game designs, including the save feature, which let players return to their adventure without starting over. This innovation was a fundamental shift in gaming, transforming how narratives could be woven throughout extended gameplay sessions. The success of *The Legend of Zelda* on the Famicom Disk System not only demonstrated Nintendo's innovative drive but also marked a pivotal moment in gaming history.

Gameplay Mechanics and Design

Explore the innovative mechanics and design elements introduced by *The Legend of Zelda*, which laid the groundwork for adventure games to follow.

The introduction of non-linear exploration

The Legend of Zelda broke new ground by introducing non-linear exploration, allowing players to venture into the game's world in a flexible manner. Unlike many games of its era, which guided players along a predetermined path, Zelda encouraged a sense of discovery and freedom. Players could choose their own routes, explore different areas without being forced to follow a linear storyline, and uncover secrets organically.

This design choice was revolutionary, as it empowered players to engage with the game world on their own terms. It provided a sense of control and agency that was relatively unheard of at the time. By allowing the game to unfold in a non-sequential manner, Nintendo paved the way for future open-world games, fundamentally changing player expectations about what a video game's world could offer.

Puzzle-solving elements that challenged players

The hallmark of The Legend of Zelda is its intricate puzzle-solving mechanics, which challenged players to think critically and creatively. Each dungeon presented a unique series of puzzles that required observation, deduction, and experimentation to solve. Players had to manipulate objects, discover hidden switches, and use items cleverly to progress.

These puzzles added depth and complexity to the game, rewarding players for their problem-solving skills and persistence. The sense of achievement upon solving a difficult puzzle became a key part of the gaming experience, transforming how players interacted with adventure games. It set a new standard for the intellectual engagement expected from players, encouraging developers to incorporate more sophisticated challenges in their titles.

Inventive use of items and inventory management

The Legend of Zelda introduced a groundbreaking inventory system that allowed players to collect, manage, and use various items strategically throughout their journey. Each item offered unique abilities, and mastering their use was crucial to overcoming enemies and solving puzzles. This mechanic encouraged experimentation, as players had to figure out which items were best suited for specific challenges and scenarios.

This approach significantly enhanced gameplay depth by ensuring that items were not mere collectibles, but essential tools for progress. The seamless integration of this system fostered an engaging layer of strategy, influencing future adventure games to adopt similar item mechanics. As a result, Zelda set the standard for how inventory systems could enrich storytelling and gameplay interactivity.

Seamless integration of combat and exploration

The seamless blend of combat and exploration in The Legend of Zelda created a cohesive and dynamic gameplay experience. Players could transition smoothly between exploring environments and engaging in battles, with neither aspect feeling secondary or out of place. This integration was achieved through intuitive controls and a world design that naturally accommodated both elements.

The game's combat was straightforward yet required quick reflexes and tactical thinking, complementing the exploration components. This balanced approach ensured that players remained engaged and invested in both combat scenarios and the game's vast, open world. It set a precedent for future titles, proving that adventure games could successfully harmonize action with exploratory components to deliver an immersive and unified experience.

Narrative and World-Building

Understand how *The Legend of Zelda* crafted a compelling narrative and immersive world that captured the imaginations of players worldwide.

The creation of the magical land of Hyrule

The magical land of Hyrule serves as the iconic backdrop to *The Legend of Zelda*, a world filled with adventure and mystery. Created by Shigeru Miyamoto and Takashi Tezuka, Hyrule is a vibrant, open landscape that invites exploration. This meticulously crafted environment is populated with diverse terrains, including lush forests, daunting mountains, and vast lakes, each providing unique challenges and secrets.

Hyrule's structure was groundbreaking for its time, offering players a non-linear experience that allowed them to choose their path through the game's various dungeons and quests. Players are encouraged to explore every corner, unveiling hidden treasures and powerful items critical for advancing in their heroic journey. The inclusion of recurring symbols and motifs throughout the land, like the sacred Triforce, entrenched the game's mythos and added depth to the storyline.

A story of courage and the quest to defeat Ganon

At the heart of *The Legend of Zelda* lies a classic tale of courage versus evil. Players step into the shoes of Link, a young hero tasked with rescuing Princess Zelda from the clutches of the dark sorcerer Ganon. This narrative unfolds through a series of challenges that test the player's wit and bravery.

The game eschews detailed dialogues, instead relying on gameplay mechanics and sparse textual cues to convey its plot. The quest to assemble the shattered pieces of the Triforce of Wisdom is central to the story, symbolizing the struggle between light and darkness. Each successfully completed quest unveils more of the plot, ensuring players remain engaged and invested in the narrative's outcome.

Link: The silent protagonist with a heroic journey

Link, the silent protagonist of *The Legend of Zelda*, personifies the archetypal hero's journey. His character, though devoid of spoken words, resonates deeply with players through his actions and the journey he undertakes. This silence allows players to project themselves onto Link, fostering a personal connection with the game's challenges and triumphs.

Link's journey is one of growth and discovery, enhanced by the acquisition of powerful items and skills that aid him in his quest. As players guide Link through Hyrule, battling enemies and overcoming obstacles, they witness a transformation from a humble adventurer to a legendary hero. This narrative technique not only enriches the gameplay experience but also solidifies Link's status as an iconic figure in gaming history.

Layered storytelling through environmental details

The Legend of Zelda employs a unique form of storytelling that relies heavily on environmental details rather than direct exposition. Players find clues about the historical and cultural backdrop of Hyrule through objects, landscapes, and architecture. Each dungeon and location tells a part of Hyrule's rich lore, from ancient ruins whispering stories of past civilizations to enchanted forests teeming with mythical creatures.

This layered storytelling approach rewards keen-eyed players, encouraging them to piece together the larger narrative puzzle from scattered fragments in the game world. The interplay between gameplay and narrative through environmental storytelling not only immerses players deeply into Hyrule’s lore but also invites them to reflect on the broader themes of adventure and bravery that the game embodies.

Critical Acclaim and Legacy

Examine the critical reception of *The Legend of Zelda* upon its release and the lasting impact it has had on the gaming industry.

Widespread acclaim from critics and players alike

The release of *The Legend of Zelda* in 1986 sparked widespread acclaim from both critics and players. Its innovative blend of action, adventure, and puzzle-solving set a new standard in gaming. Critics praised the game’s open-world design, which encouraged exploration and offered a sense of freedom that was rare at the time. Alongside its engaging gameplay, the vibrant pixel art and memorable soundtrack contributed to a highly immersive experience.

Players were particularly impressed by the game's intricate world, filled with secrets and challenges that rewarded curiosity and skill. This level of interactivity was unprecedented, drawing both casual and dedicated gamers. *The Legend of Zelda* not only garnered high scores from gaming publications but also built a dedicated fan base that would grow with each subsequent release. Its critical success underscored the potential of video games as a means of storytelling and artistic expression.

Influence on subsequent adventure and RPG titles

The Legend of Zelda profoundly influenced future adventure and RPG games, setting a template for the genres. Its open-world exploration and non-linear gameplay have become staples in gaming design. Titles like *Final Fantasy* and the *Secret of Mana* series drew inspiration from Zelda's blend of action, exploration, and puzzle-solving.

The concept of acquiring items to unlock new areas became a ubiquitous element in future games, fostering a feeling of continuous progression and discovery. Moreover, Zelda's balance of combat, exploration, and puzzle-solving triggered developers to innovate in ways that would challenge players' strategy and planning skills. The game's pioneering spirit continues to influence game designers, helping adventure and RPG genres evolve into richer cxperiences.

Legacy as a foundational game in Nintendo's lineup

The Legend of Zelda is not just a game; it's a cornerstone of Nintendo's history and identity. As one of the company's flagship titles, it established Nintendo as an innovator and leader in the gaming industry. The game's success laid the foundation for a franchise that would become one of Nintendo's most cherished and profitable series.

Beyond commercial success, Zelda has become synonymous with Nintendo's brand, showcasing their ability to deliver engaging and groundbreaking gaming experiences. Over the years, the series has adapted to new technologies and gaming platforms, maintaining its relevancy and allure. Its status as a foundational game is evident in how each new installment is met with anticipation by fans and critics alike, continuously shaping Nintendo's legacy in the gaming world.

Ongoing impact on game design and storytelling

The influence of *The Legend of Zelda* on game design and storytelling endures to this day. Its narrative design introduced players to a rich, immersive world where story and gameplay are seamlessly integrated. The multi-layered storytelling, combined with the freedom of exploration, has paved the way for more complex and interactive narratives in gaming.

Designers have looked to Zelda's innovative approach to crafting engaging and meaningful stories that react to player choices. Moreover, its emphasis on environmental storytelling, where the world's history is told through exploration and discovery, continues to inspire developers. The game's approach to nonlinear gameplay and exploration remains a benchmark in the industry, guiding the creation of expansive, engaging worlds that captivate players' imaginations worldwide.

Enduring Popularity and Cultural Impact

Discover how *The Legend of Zelda* has remained a beloved title and how it has permeated popular culture throughout the years.

A franchise evolved and expanded over decades

The *Legend of Zelda* franchise has undergone significant evolution since its debut in 1986. Originally released on the Nintendo Entertainment System (NES), it introduced players to the vast kingdom of Hyrule and the timeless battle between good and evil. Over the decades, this series has expanded across various platforms, including handheld devices, modern consoles, and even mobile services, each iteration bringing new gameplay mechanics and stories.

Every main installment has pushed the boundaries of gaming, from the transition to 3D environments in *Ocarina of Time* to the open-world exploration seen in *Breath of the Wild*. The series' ability to innovate while preserving its core essence of exploration and adventure has kept it at the forefront of the gaming industry. This successful marriage of tradition and innovation has ensured its enduring presence and continued evolution.

Memorable music and symbols recognizable worldwide

The impact of *The Legend of Zelda* extends beyond gameplay, with its music and symbols becoming iconic elements of gaming culture. The game's main theme, composed by Koji Kondo, is recognized worldwide and has been performed by orchestras globally, testament to its enduring appeal. Similarly, recognizable symbols like the Triforce have transcended the game, representing wisdom, courage, and power, themes central to the series.

From the simple yet enchanting melody that plays as Link opens a treasure chest to the ominous Ganon theme, the music of Zelda is as crucial to its identity as its gameplay. This musical legacy enhances the epic feel of the series, making each adventure an unforgettable auditory experience. Such elements ensure that Zelda remains etched in the minds of enthusiasts and resonates with audiences across diverse cultures.

Influence in media beyond games, including TV and comics

The Legend of Zelda has left its mark not just in the gaming world but across various media, including television, comics, and manga. The animated series in the late 1980s introduced the world of Hyrule and its characters to a broader audience, while various comic adaptations have further explored and expanded the Zelda narrative.

These portrayals helped cement Link, Zelda, and other characters as cultural icons. Additionally, manga adaptations have delved into intricate plot lines, offering fans deeper insights into the mythology and lore of the series. By establishing a presence beyond video games, Zelda continues to captivate audiences and maintain its relevance as a multifaceted piece of pop culture.

Ongoing fan community and annual Zelda-themed events

The *Legend of Zelda* boasts a passionate and dedicated fan community that spans generations. This vibrant fanbase is kept alive through forums, fan fiction, and art, ensuring an ever-renewing interest in the franchise. Annually, Zeldathemed events such as 'Zelda Symphony of the Goddess' concerts celebrate the rich musical history of the series, drawing crowds from around the world.

Beyond music, events like 'Zelda-thon' and fan conventions highlight creativity and dedication, fostering a community that actively keeps the spirit of Zelda alive. These gatherings serve not just as tributes but as platforms for fans to share experiences and discover new facets of the beloved series. Such initiatives underline the game's profound impact on its audience, ensuring its stories and adventures continue to inspire future generations.

Innovations that Changed Gaming

Identify the groundbreaking features of *The Legend of Zelda* that have had a lasting influence on game development and design.

Saving progress: Introducing battery-backed saves

The Legend of Zelda was a pioneer in game design with its introduction of battery-backed save functionality, an innovation that fundamentally changed how games could be played. Before this innovation, players typically relied on passwords or had to restart from the beginning each time they played, which could be frustrating and timeconsuming.

With battery-backed saves, players could save their progress directly onto the game cartridge, allowing them to pick up exactly where they left off. This feature was a game-changer for The Legend of Zelda and laid the groundwork for save systems in games for years to come. It paved the way for more complex and prolonged gaming experiences without the fear of losing all progress, thus increasing the game's appeal and longevity.

Revolutionary open-world design concepts

The Legend of Zelda introduced an unprecedented sense of freedom with its revolutionary open-world design. Contrary to the linear progression seen in many games before it, this title offered players a vast, interconnected world to explore at their own pace.

This freedom was a significant innovation, as players could choose to venture in any direction and tackle challenges in a non-linear order. This approach fostered a sense of discovery and adventure, encouraging players to explore, experiment, and engage with the game world in new ways. The success of this design has influenced countless other titles, solidifying open-world concepts as a staple in game design.

The blend of action, exploration, and role-playing elements

The Legend of Zelda expertly combined elements of action, exploration, and role-playing, creating a game experience that was both diverse and engaging. This blend allowed players to engage in dynamic combat, solve intricate puzzles, and follow a narrative-driven adventure.

The integration of these elements created a rich gameplay experience that went beyond the straightforward mechanics of earlier games. By offering a mix of challenges and a compelling storyline, The Legend of Zelda set a new standard for interactivity and depth in video games, influencing subsequent game design across multiple genres.

Benchmark for adventure games that followed

The Legend of Zelda established itself as a benchmark for adventure games by setting a high standard in storytelling, gameplay mechanics, and immersive world-building. It brought together groundbreaking innovations that others aspired to emulate and build upon.

Its compelling narrative, combined with an expansive world and innovative gameplay features, has inspired generations of developers and remains a touchstone in game development. As a result, The Legend of Zelda has had a lasting impact on the adventure genre, influencing numerous titles and solidifying its place in gaming history as a monumental achievement.

Chapter 15: Tetris - The Puzzle Phenomenon

Designed by Alexey Pajitnov in the Soviet Union, **Tetris** is one of the most addictive puzzle games ever created. Its simple yet deep mechanics have kept players captivated for decades, making it a timeless classic.

Genesis and Design

The story of Tetris begins in the mid-1980s, conceived by a Soviet software engineer with a passion for puzzles.

Alexey Pajitnov, a Soviet computer scientist, developed Tetris while working at the Dorodnitsyn Computing Centre in Moscow.

Alexey Pajitnov, a skilled software engineer with an affinity for puzzles, embarked on a journey to create Tetris in June 1984. At the time, he was employed at the Dorodnitsyn Computing Centre of the Soviet Academy of Sciences in Moscow. His primary objective was to produce a game that captured the simplicity and engagement of traditional puzzles through the digital medium.

Pajitnov's innovative use of basic geometric shapes redefined how interactive entertainment was perceived in an era largely dominated by arcade-style video games. Despite the technological constraints, his deep understanding of algorithmic design and player motivation allowed him to craft a game that was as mentally stimulating as it was enjoyable. Tetris emerged as a true testament to his ingenuity amidst the creatively restrictive environment of 1980s Soviet Union.

Tetris was inspired by a traditional puzzle game called 'Pentominoes,' which involves arranging geometric pieces to fit in a specific area.

The inspiration for Tetris can be traced back to the ancient game of Pentominoes. Pentominoes is a mathematical puzzle that requires players to arrange twelve unique shapes made from five squares into a designated area without gaps or overlaps. This spatial challenge intrigued Pajitnov, sparking the idea of translating it into a video game format.

Pajitnov's adaptation involved the simplification of Pentomino shapes into tetrominoes, geometric figures composed of four squares each. This adjustment made the game more accessible while still retaining its puzzle-based challenge. By incorporating the mechanics of falling pieces, a novel concept at the time, Pajitnov transformed a traditional pastime into an addictive and universally appealing digital experience.

The name 'Tetris' comes from the combination of 'tetra,' meaning four (since all of the game's pieces, known as 'tetrominoes,' are made of four blocks), and 'tennis,' Pajitnov's favorite sport.

The etymology of 'Tetris' reflects Pajitnov's personal interests and the game's foundational mechanics. The term 'tetra' is derived from the Greek word for 'four,' signifying the four-block structure of the tetrominoes that are the game's building blocks. Each piece in Tetris consists of four squares arranged in differing patterns, providing just the right balance of complexity and simplicity.

The addition of 'tennis' to the name adds a personal touch, highlighting Pajitnov's love for the sport and drawing a parallel to the game's fast-paced, strategic play style. By intertwining these two elements, Pajitnov not only coined a catchy and memorable title but also encapsulated the game's essence: simple yet profound, with an appeal that transcends cultural and geographical boundaries.

Initially coded on an Elektronika 60, Tetris quickly spread across Moscow, capturing the fascination of local programmers and students.

Tetris began its life as a text-based game on the Elektronika 60, a computer with limited graphical capabilities. Despite its rudimentary appearance, the addictive gameplay quickly captivated those who encountered it. The minimalist design did not detract from its appeal; instead, it enhanced the focus on strategic thinking and pattern recognition.

The game rapidly gained popularity among local programmers and computer science students, spreading across Moscow like wildfire. This was facilitated by the distribution of copies on floppy disks, passed from one enthusiast to another. The grassroots success in Moscow set the stage for Tetris to transcend borders, eventually reaching the Western world where it became a global phenomenon, beloved by generations of gamers.

Global Spread and Impact

Tetris moved beyond Moscow, becoming a global sensation and one of the most recognized games in the world.

Its simplistic design allowed it to be easily ported to various platforms, starting with the IBM PC.

Tetris's minimalist design was a key factor in its broad adaptability and success. Initially developed for the Electronika 60, its simple graphics and straightforward mechanics made it easy to port to various systems. One of the earliest and most significant ports was to the IBM PC, opening the game to a broader audience and showcasing its potential beyond the Soviet Union.

This portability was crucial during an era when personal computers varied widely in hardware capabilities. Tetris's basic requirements meant it could run on almost any machine, from high-end systems to more modest setups. The game's accessibility on diverse platforms helped cement its status as a global gaming phenomenon.

In 1989, Nintendo bundled Tetris with its Game Boy, skyrocketing both the game and the handheld device to enormous success.

Bundling Tetris with the Game Boy was a landmark decision that would impact the trajectory of both the game and the handheld market. With the Game Boy, Nintendo made a strategic move by choosing a puzzle game that appealed to a wide demographic, transcending age and gender barriers. This accessibility contributed to the Game Boy's rapid sales.

By including Tetris, Nintendo ensured that new Game Boy owners had an addictively engaging title from the start. The synergy between the game and the device led to millions of units sold, establishing Tetris as a household name and confirming the Game Boy as a dominant force in gaming.

Tetris set the standard for future puzzle games, demonstrating that ingenious mechanics can drive immense popularity and longevity.

Tetris's success laid the groundwork for future puzzle games, influencing design philosophies across the genre. Its elegant mechanics—simple to understand but challenging to master—highlighted the importance of gameplay over flashy graphics or complex narratives. This focus on core gameplay became a template for numerous subsequent puzzle games.

The game's enduring popularity proved that innovative design could result in both commercial success and cultural impact. Tetris showed that a game didn't need elaborate storytelling to captivate audiences; instead, compelling mechanics could sustain a game's relevance for decades.

The game's addictive nature coined the term 'Tetris Effect,' referring to how players visualize Tetris patterns even when not playing.

The term 'Tetris Effect' emerged from the game's ability to permeate players' thoughts, even when they weren't actively engaged in gameplay. Many players reported seeing Tetris shapes in their minds or dreaming about fitting blocks together, a testament to the game's hypnotic pull. This phenomenon highlights the psychological impact games can have on individuals.

The 'Tetris Effect' is not just folklore; it has been studied by psychologists as an example of how immersive experiences can alter cognitive processes. This enduring effect has not only entered popular culture but has also influenced how developers think about player interaction and immersion.

Mechanics and Gameplay

Tetris' core mechanics are intuitively simple yet provide deep strategic challenges.

The player's objective is to manipulate falling tetrominoes to create complete lines across the playing field.

In Tetris, players are tasked with maneuvering tetrominoes—geometric shapes composed of four square blocks—so they fit together perfectly as they descend the playing field. The ultimate goal is to form uninterrupted horizontal lines.

When a line is complete, it disappears, earning the player points and freeing up space for new tetrominoes. Players can rotate each tetromino and guide its descent to ensure the best fit, requiring quick reflexes and careful planning. This simple yet captivating objective is a core reason behind Tetris's enduring appeal, as it challenges players to strategize on the fly and make split-second decisions.

Completed lines disappear, allowing for more pieces to be stacked, and the game speeds up as the player clears more lines.

The disappearing line mechanic in Tetris not only keeps the playfield clear but also introduces increasing levels of challenge. As players successfully clear lines, the game steadily increases in speed, requiring quicker responses and more strategic thinking.

This progressive difficulty curve is what keeps players engaged and constantly tests their abilities. The speed increase urges players to not only continue eliminating lines but also to carefully consider each move, lest the tetrominoes stack to the top. The balance between clearing lines and preparing for increasingly challenging levels is a hallmark of Tetris's thrilling and rewarding gameplay loop.

Tetris challenges players to think quickly and adaptively, promoting skills in spatial reasoning and forward planning.

Tetris is more than just a game; it's a mental exercise that hones crucial cognitive skills. By forcing players to adapt to the random sequence of tetrominoes and strategize accordingly, it fosters excellent spatial reasoning abilities.

Players must plan several moves ahead, visualizing how different shapes will stack together. This forward-thinking approach improves problem-solving abilities and mental agility. Tetris's demand for quick thinking under pressure is beneficial beyond the game, as it trains the brain to process information rapidly and efficiently, skills valuable in many areas of life and work.

The game's music, particularly the Russian folk tune 'Korobeiniki,' has become iconic and synonymous with the Tetris experience.

One cannot discuss Tetris without mentioning its memorable music, especially the theme based on the Russian folk song 'Korobeiniki.' This tune, with its upbeat tempo and catchy melody, has become inseparable from the Tetris gameplay experience.

Its consistent, driving beat mirrors the escalating pace of the game, enhancing both urgency and player focus. The synergy between the evolving gameplay challenge and the dynamic soundtrack contributes significantly to the sense of immersion and excitement. The music has not only become a hallmark of Tetris but also a cultural icon in the gaming world, remembered fondly by generations of players.

Cultural Significance

Tetris has left an indelible mark on popular culture, becoming a symbol of gaming's early impact.

The distinct look of Tetris blocks has been utilized in fashion, art, and architecture, reinforcing its status as a cultural icon.

The instantly recognizable Tetriminos of Tetris have transcended the digital screen to become a staple in various artistic expressions. Fashion designers have drawn inspiration from the vibrant colors and geometric precision of these blocks to craft unique clothing lines that reflect the game's playful essence.

In the art world, Tetris has been celebrated through installations and exhibits that reinterpret the game's visual motifs, highlighting its influence on modern aesthetics.

Architects, too, have dabbled in Tetris-inspired designs, using the clean lines and interlocking shapes of the Tetriminos to create structures that are both innovative and nostalgic.
This widespread adoption in creative fields underscores Tetris's lasting impact as a cultural icon.

Merchandise such as Tetris-themed plushies, lamps, and even home décor items help keep the game in the public consciousness.

Tetris-themed merchandise bridges generations, bringing the game's charm into everyday life. From plushies mimicking the familiar block shapes to quirky lamps casting colorful shadows evocative of falling Tetriminos, these products captivate fans both old and new.

Beyond toys and gadgets, Tetris has found a place in home décor, with designs that incorporate the game's aesthetic into functional items like shelving units and wall art. This range of merchandise not only fosters nostalgia among longtime players but also introduces the iconic puzzler to new audiences. The commercial success of these items continues to reinforce Tetris's presence in global pop culture.

Tetris has inspired academic research into game design, psychology, and the cognitive benefits of gameplay.

Academia has long recognized Tetris as a subject ripe for exploration, owing to its deceptively simple yet complex mechanics. Researchers in game design study Tetris to understand how minimal elements can lead to deeply engaging experiences, shaping the development of future games.

Psychologists have delved into the Tetris Effect, where prolonged play results in players visualizing falling Tetriminos in real life. This phenomenon has been linked to spatial awareness and cognitive flexibility, making Tetris a valuable tool in studying brain functions. Research continues to reveal how its unique gameplay fosters problem-solving skills and mental dexterity, adding to its legacy beyond entertainment.

Events like the Classic Tetris World Championship showcase the game's enduring appeal and competitive nature.

Since its inception in 2010, the Classic Tetris World Championship (CTWC) has brought together players from across the globe to compete in this timeless puzzle game. The event highlights the competitive spirit Tetris evokes, turning a solitary pastime into a shared spectacle.

The annual tournament not only preserves the legacy of the NES version but also emphasizes the strategic depth and split-second decision-making that Tetris demands. With live streams and growing viewership, the CTWC has become a celebrated part of gaming culture, solidifying Tetris's role as a game that transcends its era to continually captivate enthusiasts worldwide.

Reviews and Legacy

Tetris is consistently touted as one of the greatest games of all time, maintaining influence across generations of gamers.

Critics praise the game's elegant simplicity and challenging gameplay, highlighting its accessibility and universal appeal.

Tetris is often celebrated for its straightforward yet inviting gameplay, which strikes a perfect balance between ease of understanding and depth of challenge. Critics have marveled at its elegant simplicity, where players only need to rotate and position falling tetrominoes to clear lines. This intuitive mechanic makes Tetris remarkably accessible to players of all ages and skill levels.

The universal appeal of Tetris is largely due to its minimalistic design and the satisfaction derived from its increasingly challenging gameplay. Players are continually motivated to improve their skills, as the game encourages both strategic planning and quick reflexes. These elements have made Tetris a staple in video game history, earning accolades from reviewers and gamers alike.

Tetris has received numerous awards, including entry into the World Video Game Hall of Fame and a BAFTA Special Award for a lifetime of achievement.

Throughout its illustrious history, Tetris has been showered with accolades, a testament to its profound impact on the gaming industry. Inducted into the World Video Game Hall of Fame in 2015, Tetris stands as a pioneering force in gaming culture, honored for its enduring popularity and influence.

In addition to this prestigious honor, Tetris was also the recipient of the BAFTA Special Award, recognizing its lifetime of achievement and the significant role it has played in shaping modern gaming. These awards reflect the game's excellence and far-reaching impact, contributing to its status as an iconic masterpiece in video game history.

It has inspired numerous sequels and spin-offs, each offering a new twist while maintaining the essence that made the original so beloved.

Over the years, Tetris has inspired a plethora of sequels and spin-offs, each offering fresh takes on the classic formula while preserving the core mechanics that made the original game so beloved. From the multiplayer antics of Tetris 99 to the aesthetically pleasing Tetris Effect, the game has constantly evolved.

These iterations introduce novel modes, graphics, and audio experiences, yet all retain the fundamental blockdropping gameplay that characterizes Tetris. Developers have creatively expanded the Tetris universe, ensuring that each new release not only pays homage to its origins but also pushes the boundaries of innovation and engagement.

Despite changes in technology and gaming trends, Tetris remains relevant and is available on virtually every gaming platform imaginable.

As technology continues to advance and gaming trends evolve, Tetris has seamlessly adapted, maintaining its relevance across the ever-changing landscape of the gaming industry. Its timeless design ensures that it remains a beloved fixture, appealing to both nostalgic players and new generations.

Tetris's ubiquity is evidenced by its presence on nearly every gaming platform available, from classic consoles to modern smartphones. Whether on handheld devices or the latest gaming systems, its widespread availability underscores its universal appeal. This enduring presence reaffirms Tetris's role as a cornerstone of gaming history.

Chapter 16: Mario Bros. - Platforming Perfection

The world was introduced to Mario, *Nintendo's* legendary plumber, in **Super Mario Bros.** This game helped save the North American video game industry in the 1980s and established the platforming genre.

Mario's Origins and Impact

Super Mario Bros. was a groundbreaking title that set the stage for modern gaming. Let's explore how Mario transformed the gaming landscape.

Super Mario Bros. debuted in 1985, reviving a struggling video game market.

The release of *Super Mario Bros.* in 1985 came at a crucial time when the video game market was in turmoil. The early 1980s had witnessed a collapse due to oversaturation and poor-quality games, leading many to believe the industry was a passing fad. However, *Super Mario Bros.*, with its innovative gameplay and engaging design, breathed new life into the gaming world. It showcased what a well-crafted video game could achieve, both commercially and culturally. This pivotal moment not only rejuvenated the market but also proved that video games could be a sustainable and creative form of entertainment.

The game was pivotal for Nintendo's success, showcasing the potential of home consoles.

Super Mario Bros. was instrumental in securing Nintendo's dominance in the burgeoning home console market. The game capitalized on the hardware of the Nintendo Entertainment System (NES), which offered superior graphics and sound compared to previous consoles. By demonstrating the NES's capabilities, *Super Mario Bros.* helped solidify Nintendo's brand as synonymous with quality gaming experiences. This success paved the way for Nintendo's future as a leading force in the industry, with a legacy that continues to influence console designs today.

Mario quickly became an iconic symbol for video games worldwide.

Mario, with his distinctive red hat and blue overalls, rapidly ascended to become one of the most recognizable characters in video game history. His enduring appeal transcended cultural and language barriers, resonating with players around the globe. Mario's image became emblematic of video gaming itself, often used to represent the medium in broader cultural contexts. This universal recognition not only drove the popularity of the *Super Mario* franchise but also helped solidify video games as a major entertainment sector.

The simplicity and charm of Mario's character appealed to a wide audience.

One of the key reasons for Mario's widespread appeal lies in the simplicity and charm of his character. Designed to be approachable and non-threatening, Mario's persona resonated with a broad demographic, including both children and adults. His adventures were imbued with a sense of fun and wonder, encouraging players of all ages to participate in his quests. This universal allure helped establish video games as a family-friendly form of entertainment, expanding the potential audience for future gaming titles.

Super Mario Bros. demonstrated the importance of engaging gameplay mechanics.

At the heart of *Super Mario Bros.*'s success are its engaging gameplay mechanics. The game introduced players to precise platforming that required both skill and timing, offering a perfect balance between challenge and accessibility. The level design ensured progressive difficulty, keeping players engaged and motivated. These mechanics set a new standard for gameplay, showing developers the importance of playability and satisfaction, effectively setting the bar for what players would expect in a video game experience.

The game laid the foundation for future platformers with its design and control.

Super Mario Bros. established a blueprint for future platformers through its innovative level design and intuitive controls. Each level was crafted to introduce new obstacles and strategies, encouraging exploration and mastery. The responsive controls made Mario's movements feel fluid and natural, a hallmark that later platformers would strive to emulate. By setting these foundational principles, *Super Mario Bros.* ensured its legacy, influencing countless games that would follow in its footsteps, each building on its pioneering design.

Gameplay Mechanics and Innovation

Super Mario Bros. introduced innovative gameplay mechanics that were ahead of its time. Here's a look at what made the gameplay so compelling.

Players experienced seamless horizontal scrolling for the first time.

One of the groundbreaking innovations in *Super Mario Bros.* was its introduction of seamless horizontal scrolling, a feature that set it apart from earlier games. Prior to this, most video games used single-screen gameplay or jumpy transitions between screens, which could disrupt the immersive experience. With horizontal scrolling, players could explore vast and expansive levels that felt like real worlds. This created a fluid sense of movement, contributing significantly to the game's dynamic and engaging nature.

By eradicating the limitations of single screens, the game provided an unparalleled sense of progression and adventure. Players could move smoothly from one side of the level to the other, uncovering hidden secrets as they progressed. This innovation not only enhanced the visual appeal but also pioneered a new era of platform gaming that many subsequent titles would adopt. The fluid scrolling became a benchmark for the genre, elevating *Super Mario Bros.* into a league of its own.

The game introduced the concept of power-ups, like the Super Mushroom and Fire Flower.

Super Mario Bros. revolutionized gameplay with the introduction of power-ups, a concept that became integral to the platforming genre. The Super Mushroom, a now-iconic feature, allowed Mario to grow larger, symbolizing strength and empowering players by giving them an extra hit point. This simple yet effective mechanic provided a tangible sense of growth and progression in the game.

Moreover, the Fire Flower became a game-changer by granting Mario the ability to shoot fireballs, thus adding a layer of strategy and combat to the gameplay. Players had to master using these power-ups strategically to overcome various obstacles and enemies. This innovation not only influenced Mario's gameplay but also set a precedent across the genre, making power-ups a standard feature in platformers, enhancing both challenge and engagement for players.

Each level offered unique challenges, keeping the gameplay fresh and engaging.

Every level in *Super Mario Bros.* was meticulously crafted to offer unique challenges and environmental puzzles, ensuring that players constantly faced new obstacles. From navigating treacherous underground passages to timing precise jumps over pitfalls, the game presented a diverse range of challenges that kept gameplay fresh and interesting.

The progression through levels was carefully designed to introduce new elements gradually. As players progressed, they encountered different types of enemies and platform types, requiring players to adapt their strategies. This ongoing variation maintained player interest and set a standard for level design in video games. By constantly introducing innovative obstacles and scenarios, *Super Mario Bros.* kept players engaged and eager to discover what lay beyond the next screen.

Players could break bricks and collect coins, adding layers of interaction.

The interactive environment of *Super Mario Bros.* marked a significant leap forward for platformers. Players were encouraged to break bricks, often revealing hidden power-ups or secret areas, creating a rewarding exploration experience. This mechanic fostered curiosity and exploration, encouraging players to interact with the game world actively.

Moreover, collecting coins provided an additional layer of engagement. Every 100 coins earned players an extra life, offering a tangible reward for their exploration efforts. This feature introduced a level of strategy, as players decided between focusing on survival or exploration. These interactive elements became staples in gaming, setting the foundation for future titles and encouraging games that rewarded exploration and curiosity.

Super Mario Bros. featured a symphony of sound effects that enhanced the experience.

The soundscape of *Super Mario Bros.* played a pivotal role in creating an immersive gaming experience. Koji Kondo's iconic compositions, combined with innovative sound effects, brought the game to life. Each action, from collecting a coin to stomping on a Goomba, was accompanied by a unique and responsive sound effect that provided immediate audio feedback to players.

This attention to audio detail enhanced the gameplay, making each action feel satisfying. The music also changed according to the level's theme, with upbeat tunes in overworld stages and more suspenseful music in underground sections, creating a rich and varied audio experience. These elements came together to enhance the emotional response, making sound integral to the immersive experience of *Super Mario Bros.*

The controls were tight and responsive, which was crucial for player satisfaction.

The precise and responsive controls of *Super Mario Bros.* were crucial in delivering its celebrated gameplay experience. The intuitive control scheme allowed players to make accurate movements, jumps, and maneuvers, which was essential for navigating its challenging levels. Mario's running and jumping mechanics were finely tuned, enabling players to react quickly to obstacles and enemies.

Such tight controls ensured that any mistakes felt fair, attributed to player error rather than game design flaws. This precision in gameplay was a hallmark of the game's design philosophy, setting a standard for future platformers. Ensuring that players had complete control over their character was vital in maintaining a rewarding experience, making the game both accessible to newcomers and challenging for veterans.

Design and Artistic Influence

The design of Super Mario Bros. was not just functional but also artistically influential. Here's how its art and design made a mark.

The colorful pixel art style was both charming and technically impressive.

The visual appeal of *Super Mario Bros.* lies in its vibrant pixel art, which was both eye-catching and a technical marvel for its time. The use of a limited color palette forced the developers to be creative, resulting in an iconic and colorful world. This design choice was not only vital for defining the game's aesthetic but also for maximizing the capabilities of the Nintendo Entertainment System (NES) hardware.

The charm of these visuals played a crucial role in making the world of Mario both accessible and memorable. Players were immediately drawn into the Mushroom Kingdom with its bright greens and blues, enhanced by the cleverly designed tilesets. Despite the graphical limitations of the era, the game's pixel art stood out and set a standard for future side-scrolling platformers.

Miyamoto, the game's designer, prioritized simplicity and clarity in design.

Shigeru Miyamoto, the visionary behind *Super Mario Bros.*, focused on creating a game that emphasized simplicity and clarity. This design philosophy ensured that players of all ages could easily understand and navigate the game world. By prioritizing intuitive controls and clear objectives, Miyamoto made the game approachable and enjoyable without sacrificing depth.

Each level was crafted to gradually introduce players to new mechanics and challenges, creating a seamless learning curve. This approach allowed players to explore and experiment within the game's mechanics without feeling overwhelmed. Miyamoto's emphasis on usability and simplicity was a significant factor in the game's widespread appeal and lasting impact.

Distinctive enemy designs, like Goombas and Koopa Troopas, were memorable.

One of the key aspects of *Super Mario Bros.* is its memorable enemy designs, which play a crucial role in the game's distinctive charm. Characters like Goombas and Koopa Troopas are instantly recognizable and add personality to the experience. These enemies were designed with unique silhouettes and behaviors, making them easy to differentiate and anticipate during gameplay.

The imaginative designs not only provided variety but also contributed to the game's challenge. Each enemy demanded a specific strategy, helping to keep the gameplay fresh and engaging. These iconic foes have become staples of the *Mario* franchise, highlighting the game's lasting artistic influence.

The world and level design balanced difficulty with accessibility.

The level design in *Super Mario Bros.* expertly balanced difficulty with accessibility, making it both challenging and enjoyable. The game gradually increases in complexity, providing a satisfying progression that caters to both newcomers and seasoned players. Early levels serve as training grounds, introducing players to basic mechanics through trial and error.

As the game progresses, levels become more intricate, requiring more precision and timing. Despite the growing challenge, the design remains fair, offering checkpoints and power-ups to aid in progression. This thoughtful balance was critical in ensuring that players remained engaged and motivated to continue their journey through the Mushroom Kingdom.

Environments like the Mushroom Kingdom became iconic elements of the franchise.

The environments of *Super Mario Bros.*, especially the Mushroom Kingdom, have become iconic symbols of the franchise. These environments were meticulously crafted to immerse players in a whimsical, yet perilous world. The familiar green hills, brick-lined skies, and underwater caverns are not only visually appealing but also play a significant role in gameplay.

These settings provided diverse challenges and surprises, encouraging players to explore and interact with the environment. The Mushroom Kingdom's playful and imaginative design has left a lasting impression, establishing a visual identity that continues to influence the *Mario* series and gaming culture at large.

The use of animated sprites added life to the digital world.

Animated sprites in *Super Mario Bros.* brought the game's digital world to life, creating a dynamic and engaging experience. These animations, though simple by today's standards, were groundbreaking at the time. They allowed characters like Mario and Luigi to move fluidly, jump, and interact with their environment in a lively manner.

The animation added a layer of realism and playfulness, making the characters more relatable and the world more immersive. Enemies and environmental elements also benefitted from this, moving and reacting in ways that added depth and excitement. This attention to animated detail set the stage for future developments in video game graphics.

Legacy and Ongoing Influence

Super Mario Bros. has left an indelible mark on the gaming industry. Let's discuss its lasting legacy and influence on future titles.

The game established Nintendo as a leader in the video game industry.

The release of **Super Mario Bros.** in 1985 marked a pivotal moment for *Nintendo* and the entire gaming industry. It was a product of inventive design and polished execution that captivated an audience worldwide. This single title transformed the perception of Nintendo from an emerging company into a dominant force in the realm of video games. By showcasing creative gameplay and masterfully crafted level design, Nintendo not only captivated existing gamers but also attracted new audiences, effectively establishing its foothold in North America.

The success of **Super Mario Bros.** set a high standard for future releases. It laid the groundwork for Nintendo's continued success with franchise expansions and innovations. The strategic brilliance of Nintendo's game designers established a legacy of excellence, influencing game development strategies across the industry. As a result, *Nintendo* emerged as a visionary leader, continually pushing the boundaries of what video games could achieve.

Super Mario Bros. inspired countless sequels and spin-offs over the decades.

In the wake of its success, **Super Mario Bros.** spawned numerous sequels and spin-offs, establishing one of gaming's most beloved franchises. Each iteration introduced new elements and gradually expanded what seemed possible in gaming. Titles like *Super Mario World*, *Super Mario 64*, and *Super Mario Odyssey* have each added their own unique twists while maintaining the core appeal that Mario is known for.

The franchise's success also paved the way for spin-offs that explored new genres, such as *Mario Kart* and *Luigi's Mansion*. These games retained the charm and innovation that made **Super Mario Bros.** a landmark title, ensuring Mario remained a central figure in gaming culture. The continuous evolution of the series demonstrates its creators' ability to balance nostalgia and innovation, keeping the experience fresh for every new generation of gamers.

The concept of level design in games owes much to its pioneering structure.

The revolutionary level design of **Super Mario Bros.** has become a blueprint for countless games that followed. Its impeccable balance of challenge and reward captivated players and kept them engaged. Each level was crafted to gradually introduce new challenges and mechanics, a design philosophy that is still emulated by game designers today. This careful structuring allowed players to learn and master the game's mechanics naturally.

The game's level design introduced the concept of a 'learning curve,' where players are subtly guided to increase their skills while exploring more complex stages. This approach encouraged exploration and experimentation, a hallmark of enjoyable gaming experiences. **Super Mario Bros.** has thus influenced not only platformers but also games of various genres, making it a cornerstone of effective game design.

It has influenced various genres beyond platformers, including puzzle games and RPGs.

While **Super Mario Bros.** is primarily celebrated as a pioneer in platforming, its influence extends across multiple genres. The game's emphasis on exploration, immersive environments, and character development has inspired design elements in puzzle games and RPGs. Titles like *The Legend of Zelda* and *Final Fantasy* have benefited from the level of finesse in world-building and character dynamics seen in Mario's escapades.

Additionally, its level-based gameplay and embedded puzzles have underpinned development approaches in puzzle games, where logical progression and player engagement are paramount. The design strategies that evolved from **Super Mario Bros.** inform the core mechanics of many successful games, reflecting its broad and lasting impact across the gaming landscape.

Mario's character has become synonymous with gaming and pop culture.

Since his debut, Mario has become a cultural icon akin to Mickey Mouse or Superman. The enduring popularity of this cheerful plumber extends beyond the gaming community, etching Mario into the broader realm of pop culture. His image has adorned everything from cereal boxes to major animated films, demonstrating his universal appeal and recognition.

Mario's persona encapsulates the spirit of adventure and perseverance, qualities that resonate with audiences worldwide. As a mascot, Mario symbolizes the fun and creativity of Nintendo, and by extension, gaming itself. His influence is evident in countless memes, merchandise, and cross-media adaptations, securing Mario's place as an integral figure in entertainment history.

Super Mario Bros. is studied in game design courses for its groundbreaking mechanics and design.

Super Mario Bros. is frequently referenced in game design curricula for its innovative mechanics and exemplary design. Educational courses analyze its seamless integration of gameplay elements, storytelling, and intuitive control systems to teach aspiring developers about the fundamentals of game creation.

The game's design is noted for its player-centric approach, where every aspect of the game is constructed to enhance the player's experience. Learning from **Super Mario Bros.**, students explore how its meticulous design can lead to heightened engagement and satisfaction. As a standard-bearer in the industry, the game continues to educate and inspire the next generation of game developers, underscoring its lasting educational influence.

Chapter 17: Sonic the Hedgehog - Need for Speed

Speeding past with a spin-attack and a snazzy pair of sneakers, **Sonic** showed us how fast-paced platforming and blue spikes could redefine gaming. Zip through this chapter to see how Sega's iconic hedgehog raced into our hearts and gave Mario a run for his mushrooms.

Sonic's Speedy Origins

Get ready to dash into Sonic's backstory and find out how this speedy hedgehog first hit the scene. It all started when Sega needed someone to take on Mario.

In the early 90s, Sega was on the hunt for a mascot to rival Nintendo's Mario.

The video game industry of the early 1990s was akin to a heated race, with Nintendo's Mario taking a clear lead. Sega, eager to become a formidable contender, needed a mascot who could challenge Mario's dominance in the gaming world. This called for a character with a unique appeal, capable of captivating audiences and giving Sega that much-needed breakthrough.

Sega's brainstorming sessions were a creative goldmine as teams worked tirelessly to conceptualize a character that was both memorable and marketable. They sought something new and dynamic, a mascot that would not only represent the brand but also break the mold. The result was the inception of a character who wasn't just another mascot but a game-changer.

Sonic was born from the creative mind of Yuji Naka and the artistic hand of Naoto Ohshima.

The creation of Sonic the Hedgehog was a collaborative stroke of genius from two pivotal figures. Yuji Naka, a gifted programmer, envisioned a game driven by speed—a feature that contradicted the slow-paced platformers of the era.

Complementing Naka's vision was Naoto Ohshima, whose artistry gave Sonic his iconic blue look and sleek spikes.

Ohshima's art style was crucial in making Sonic visually stand out, while Naka's programming skills ensured the game was a technical marvel. Together, they crafted a character who was not only defined by his agility but also his cool, defining aesthetic. Their collective creativity and innovative approach breathed life into what would become one of the most beloved video game characters of all time.

With his cool attitude and blazing speed, Sonic was designed to appeal to a wider, edgier audience.

Sonic didn't just run fast; he sped into the hearts of gamers looking for something more exhilarating and fresh. Sega's strategy was to design a character that embodied a more rebellious and confident spirit compared to Nintendo's jovial and friendly Mario. This was evident in Sonic's edgy personality and iconic smirk.

By focusing on Sonic's attitude and speed, Sega aimed to capture an audience that craved thrill and excitement. This persona played well with the burgeoning youth culture of the 90s, making Sonic not just a character in a game, but a cultural icon. His appeal extended beyond traditional gamers, pulling in audiences who appreciated his unique flavor and charisma.

Sonic made his debut in 1991, instantly becoming a hit with fans and critics alike.

When Sonic the Hedgehog first hit Sega Genesis consoles in 1991, it was an immediate sensation. From the moment players picked up the controller, they were hooked. Sonic's debut was not just a game release; it was an event that reshaped the gaming landscape.

Critics praised the game for its exhilarating speed and engaging level design. Fans were equally enthusiastic, flocking to grab their copy of this groundbreaking title. Sonic quickly became the face of Sega, symbolizing an exciting new era where speed, style, and skill were at the forefront of gaming innovation.

The game's cutting-edge graphics and super-fast gameplay were revolutionary for the time.

The original Sonic the Hedgehog game was a technical masterpiece that set new standards for platformers. The use of bright, colorful graphics brought the game's world to life, creating an immersive experience that was unmatched at the time. It was this visual flair that helped Sonic stand out on store shelves and in living rooms alike.

Yet, it wasn't just about appearances. The gameplay was a revolutionary experience in itself, pushing the boundaries of how fast a platformer could be. Players were thrilled by the sensation of sonic speed, as Sonic zipped through loops and dashed over obstacles with incredible fluidity. This cutting-edge combination of rapid gameplay and visual charm stamped Sega's mark on the industry and ensured Sonic's place in gaming history.

Gameplay and Mechanics

Let's dive into the gameplay that had players zipping through loops and collecting rings like never before.

Sonic the Hedgehog introduced the concept of speed as a key gameplay element.

Sonic the Hedgehog brought an exhilarating sense of speed to the gaming scene, setting it apart from the other platformers of its time. Unlike earlier games where characters plodded along at a moderate pace, Sonic blazed through levels with a velocity rarely experienced before. This was a groundbreaking shift that changed how players interacted with games. Instead of cautiously jumping from platform to platform, Sonic invited players to embrace the thrill of the rush.

This unique focus on speed was not just a gimmick; it was a core part of the identity and gameplay mechanics. Players were encouraged to maintain momentum, creating a dynamic and engaging experience that felt fresh and exciting. The result was a frenetic pace that required quick reflexes and keen decision-making, ensuring that every session with Sonic was as thrilling as the last.

Players zoomed through inventive levels, each filled with hidden paths and secrets.

The level design in Sonic was nothing short of revolutionary. Each stage was a colorful playground filled with twists, turns, and surprises that kept players coming back for more. Instead of linear stages, Sonic's worlds featured multiple routes and secrets, rewarding exploration and replayability. Players could choose to speed straight for the finish or take time to uncover hidden areas and bonuses.

This approach to level design not only complemented the game's high-speed platforming but also enhanced its strategic depth. Experienced players could experiment with different paths, discovering shortcuts and secret locations that could lead to higher scores or elusive extra lives. This innovative design kept the gameplay feeling fresh, making every playthrough a unique adventure.

The spin dash allowed Sonic to build up momentum and smash through enemies and barriers.

One of the defining mechanics of Sonic the Hedgehog was the introduction of the spin dash. With just a simple motion, players could charge up Sonic's speed, allowing him to burst forward with momentum capable of bowling over enemies and breaking through barriers. This mechanic not only emphasized Sonic's agility and power but added a new layer to the gameplay strategy.

The spin dash wasn't just about speed; it was about timing and precision. Players needed to decide the right moment to unleash this power, whether to clear a difficult section or decimate a line of enemies. The spin dash empowered players to blaze through levels with confidence, making Sonic feel like an unstoppable force in the world of 2D platformers.

Collecting rings not only kept Sonic alive but added an addictive layer of strategy to the game.

Sonic's iconic golden rings became more than just a flashy collectible; they were a lifeline. Gathered throughout the levels, these rings served a crucial purpose: they ensured Sonic's survival. Instead of a traditional health bar, holding onto just one ring meant Sonic could endure a hit without losing a life. This mechanic introduced a fun and addictive element to the gameplay.

The constant challenge was to accumulate as many rings as possible while navigating treacherous terrain and tricky foes. Losing all rings upon being hit created moments of tension, as players scrambled to collect them before they disappeared. This added a strategic dimension, pushing players to master levels to both maximize ring collection and minimize the risk of losing them.

The innovative physics engine made Sonic feel smooth and responsive, a technical marvel at the time.

The smooth and fluid motion of Sonic was made possible by its groundbreaking physics engine, which was a marvel for its era. The game delivered a seamless experience where acceleration, inertia, and momentum played crucial roles. This level of detail in character movement and interaction was unprecedented, contributing to the game's 'feel' which players adored.

It was this attention to detail in physics that allowed players to seamlessly transition from blistering speeds to precise platforming. Sonic's responsiveness to player input was remarkable, making the game not just about speed but about skillful control. This intuitive control laid the foundation for many platformers to come and set a new standard in game design.

Iconic Levels and Enemies

Remember those twisted paths and quirky foes? Let's revisit the exciting worlds that kept us hooked.

From Green Hill Zone to Labyrinth Zone, each level presented its own unique challenges and atmosphere.

The journey through Sonic's world starts with the lush landscapes of **Green Hill Zone**, a place etched in the memory of gamers with its iconic checkerboard loops and blue skies. This level offered a perfect mix of speed and exploration, providing a warm introduction to Sonic's high-speed antics.

Contrast this with the damp and treacherous **Labyrinth Zone**, where waterlogged paths tested a player's patience and precision. With slower-paced gameplay and the ever-present threat of drowning, it presented an entirely different type of challenge. These diverse environments not only showcased the variety in level design but also tested a player's adaptability to different gameplay mechanics, making each level a unique adventure.

The vibrant and colorful art style made each setting come to life.

Sonic the Hedgehog dazzled with its **vivid color palette**, contrasting sharply against its contemporaries. Each pixel was deliberately placed to craft an immersive and exciting world. The bright greens of Green Hill Zone encouraged speed, while the cooler tones in the mysterious Scrap Brain Zone hinted at danger lurking around every corner.

This dynamic and alluring art style was not just aesthetic; it actively guided players through levels, making use of color contrasts to signal paths or hidden areas. This visual richness remains a hallmark of Sonic games, inviting players to not only play but to *experience* the game's universe in its full technicolor glory.

Dr. Robotnik, Sonic's ever-menacing nemesis, challenged players with a variety of clever boss battles.

No Sonic adventure would be complete without Dr. Robotnik's diabolical machines. Each encounter with him was part puzzle, part adrenaline rush. Every level ended with the thrill of taking on one of Robotnik's inventive creations, whether dodging a fire-breathing ball and chain or evading giant wrecking balls.

These boss battles required timing, precision, and a keen observation of **patterns**. They kept players on their toes, instilling a satisfying sense of accomplishment upon victory. Robotnik's character added an extra layer of continuity and purpose to each level, establishing him as a villain as much defined by his inventive schemes as by his persistent pursuit of Sonic.

Enemies like the Buzz Bomber and Crabmeat became memorable foes with distinct attack patterns.

Sonic's world was populated with quirky adversaries, each with their own attack rhythms and defensive quirks. The *Buzz Bomber*, for example, hovered menacingly before shooting a targeted energy bolt, keeping players alert and cautious in open spaces.

In contrast, the *Crabmeat*, with its slow movement and side-shooting claws, challenged players in more enclosed or strategic encounters. These enemies were crafted with care, each uniquely complementing the level's environment they inhabited. Their memorable designs and attack patterns made each battle a small puzzle to solve, enriching the gameplay experience.

Levels were designed to encourage multiple playthroughs, rewarding exploration and mastery of mechanics.

From hidden pathways to secret rooms, Sonic's levels were a playground for players who liked to explore. Each zone had branching routes and secret passages, begging to be discovered by those curious enough to look for them.

This thoughtful design encouraged players to return time and again, mastering the mechanics to shave precious seconds off their completion times or simply to relish the joy of discovering every nook and cranny. Sonic's world was packed with intricacies that offered small but rewarding discoveries, proving that speed was not just about being fast, but about uncovering the richness of exploration.

Cultural Impact and Legacy

Sonic didn't just spin his way into our game consoles; he left a legacy that impacted pop culture forever.

Sonic became an immediate pop culture icon, appearing in movies, TV shows, and comics.

From the moment Sonic the Hedgehog zipped onto the scene in 1991, he became more than just a video game character. Sonic embodied a cool, rebellious spirit that quickly captured the imagination of audiences worldwide. His blue spikes and red sneakers went beyond the console, appearing in a vast array of multimedia.

Sonic became a household name, featuring prominently in his own TV series like "Adventures of Sonic the Hedgehog" and "Sonic the Hedgehog: The Animated Series." Comic book adaptations further expanded his universe, providing fans with more of the stories they loved. More recently, Sonic made his big-screen debut in Hollywood films, proving that his appeal transcends generations.

The rivalry between Sonic and Mario became legendary, sparking debates and friendly competition among fans.

The gaming world witnessed one of its most iconic rivalries with Sonic and Mario. This clash wasn't just about speed versus stamina or blue versus red—it was a battle of consoles, Sega against Nintendo. Sonic aimed to dethrone Mario as the king of platformers, leading to endless debates about which mascot truly reigned supreme.

Schoolyards turned into battlegrounds as kids passionately defended their hedgehog hero or stout plumber. This rivalry even spilled into friendly gaming competitions, as players tried to best each other's high scores. While the debates have mellowed with time, they left a lasting imprint on gaming culture, fueling competitive spirits and fan loyalties.

Sega's success with Sonic solidified their place in the console wars of the 90s.

Before Sonic, Sega was struggling to find footing in the intense console wars. Enter the blue hedgehog, who zoomed them into public consciousness and established Sega as a formidable player in the gaming industry of the 90s. Sonic, with his speed and attitude, provided Sega with a mascot capable of competing directly against Nintendo's Mario.

This success translated into skyrocketing sales of Sega's Genesis console, with Sonic the Hedgehog frequently bundled as the go-to game. Sega managed to grab a significant share of the market, thanks largely to Sonic's popularity, redefining the console landscape. The Sonic-sealed deal was a pivotal moment, fortifying Sega's place in the annals of gaming history.

Sonic's influence can be seen in countless platformers and games that followed.

Sonic's success set a new benchmark for the platformer genre. His emphasis on speed and unique level designs inspired countless developers to rethink how platform games could be built. The innovative gameplay mechanics—such as loop-de-loops and intricate map layouts—encouraged designers to explore bolder, cleaner graphics and faster-paced gameplay.

Many platformers that followed in Sonic's wake adopted similar elements, integrating brisk pacing and dynamic environments. Games like Crash Bandicoot and Ratchet & Clank carried forward his legacy, proving that Sonic was not just another character; he was a force pushing the genre into new directions.

To this day, Sonic is celebrated in new games, re-releases, and anniversaries, solidifying his place in the gaming hall of fame.

Even decades after his first speedy adventure, Sonic remains a vibrant part of the gaming world. Sega continuously rolls out new titles featuring the beloved hedgehog, ensuring he stays relevant in the ever-changing gaming landscape. With remasters and special anniversary releases, fans old and new can enjoy Sonic's classic escapades afresh.

Speciality releases and nostalgic events celebrate Sonic's enduring appeal. Fans globally participate in conventions and exhibitions that pay tribute to this iconic character. Sonic’s legacy isn’t just in his games; it’s in his ability to evolve and charm each successive generation, ensuring his place in the gaming hall of fame for years to come.

Chapter 18: Street Fighter II - The Fight Begins

Released in 1991, **Street Fighter II** reinvented the fighting game genre. Its competitive gameplay, diverse characters, and special moves created a blueprint that many follow even today.

The Birth of a Legend

Street Fighter II emerged during a time when arcades were cultural hubs. Its impact was immediate and transformative.

The game was released by Capcom in 1991 and became an arcade sensation around the world.

When **Street Fighter II** hit the arcades in March 1991, it quickly became a global phenomenon. Developed and published by Capcom, its release marked a turning point in the fighting game genre. Unlike its predecessor, *Street Fighter*, which struggled to leave a significant impact, **Street Fighter II** captivated players with its accessible yet deep gameplay mechanics.

The game's immediate success can be attributed to its fresh approach to competitive gaming. Players were drawn to its innovative six-button control scheme, which allowed for diverse fighting styles. The game's balanced mechanics and fluid animations set a new standard in arcade gaming. The excitement surrounding **Street Fighter II** turned local arcades into bustling hubs of activity, bringing together players eager to master its intricacies.

Heavily based on its predecessor, it improved upon the original Street Fighter with better graphics and sound.

Street Fighter II built upon the foundation laid by the original *Street Fighter* while introducing significant advancements in both graphics and sound. The improved visuals featured detailed character sprites and vibrant backgrounds, setting a new benchmark in arcade presentation. Each fighter's unique stage was a testament to the artistic prowess of Capcom's development team, providing players with a visually engaging experience.

Sound design was another area of substantial enhancement. The game offered catchy background music and distinct voiceovers for each character, contributing to its memorable gameplay experience. Sound effects became integral to the feedback loop, providing players with cues for successful hits and special moves. These improvements were not merely aesthetic; they helped create a more immersive gaming experience, drawing new fans to the burgeoning fighting game community.

Street Fighter II's success sparked countless competitions and tournaments, adding to its legendary status.

The success of **Street Fighter II** transcended the arcade floors as it sparked the formation of a thriving competitive scene. The game's balanced design made it a natural fit for tournaments, and soon local competitions began cropping up worldwide. Players dedicated countless hours to mastering combos, special attacks, and counter-strategies, elevating gameplay to an art form.

This burgeoning esports culture became a defining characteristic of the game's appeal. High-profile tournaments attracted both seasoned veterans and aspiring newcomers, fostering a sense of community and belonging among fans. **Street Fighter II** thus played a pivotal role in establishing an organized competitive gaming landscape that continues to thrive in today's gaming world.

The game's popularity contributed to a resurgence of arcade culture in the early '90s.

At the dawn of the 1990s, arcades were dwindling in popularity as home consoles became more prevalent. Yet, **Street Fighter II** breathed new life into these social gaming spaces, reversing the decline. The game's engaging mechanics and competitive allure reinvigorated interest in arcades, making them bustling centers of activity once again.

Players would flock to arcades not only for the challenge but for the camaraderie and thrill of real-time competition. The game became a social phenomenon, encouraging interactions and rivalries that transcended the screen. This revitalization of arcade culture was pivotal, extending the lifespan of arcades and ensuring their relevance well into the late '90s.

Characters with Personality

The diverse cast of characters was one of the standout features that set Street Fighter II apart.

Each character came from different parts of the world, showcasing a variety of fighting styles.

Street Fighter II introduced a truly global cast of characters, each originating from various corners of the world and representing unique fighting styles. This diversity was not just for show; it played a crucial role in the game's mechanics and strategy. Ryu and Ken brought Japanese martial arts to the forefront, showcasing Shotokan karate with powerful moves like the Hadouken. Chun-Li's lightning-fast kicks highlighted her Chinese martial arts skills, while Guile's military background was reflected in his disciplined combat style.

This international assembly allowed players to connect with characters on a cultural level, as well as enjoy a variety of gameplay experiences. The distinct fighting styles introduced layers of strategy, encouraging players to experiment and find characters that suited their personal play styles. By drawing on different cultural backgrounds, *Street Fighter II* catered to a global audience, making it appealing and relatable across different demographics. This approach was later emulated by many other games, making diversity a staple in the genre.

Iconic characters like Ryu, Ken, Chun-Li, and Guile quickly became household names among gamers.

The characters of *Street Fighter II* did more than just fight—they became cultural icons. Ryu and Ken, with their iconic headbands and martial arts gi, symbolized dedication and strength. Chun-Li was praised for breaking stereotypes as one of the first strong, female protagonists, becoming a role model for many. Guile’s stoic demeanor and recognizable theme music made him a memorable character.

These characters were more than just fighters; they represented ideals and engaged players emotionally. Their signature moves and distinctive appearances were easy to recognize, making them popular even beyond the game. Merchandise, animated series, and even live-action films expanded their reach, embedding these characters in the fabric of gaming culture. This level of character branding was unprecedented at the time and set a new standard for character design in video games.

The unique backstory of each character added depth and engaged players on a narrative level.

Unlike many of its predecessors, *Street Fighter II* offered players more than just a chance to fight; it gave them stories to dive into. Each character was equipped with a backstory that explained their motivation for entering the tournament. Ryu sought personal improvement, emphasizing a never-ending journey to become a better fighter.

Chun-Li battled to avenge her father's death, adding a narrative layer of revenge and justice.

These narratives allowed players to form a connection with the fighters, turning them from mere avatars into beloved personas with whom players could empathize. It wasn't just about mastering moves but understanding and relating to why these characters fought. This depth was pioneering, paving the way for future games in the genre to incorporate rich storytelling as an integral element of gameplay.

This variety became the blueprint for many fighting games that followed.

The innovative approach of *Street Fighter II* in character diversity and their defining traits set a standard for subsequent fighting games. By demonstrating the importance of varied character rosters, Capcom created a template that many developers would strive to emulate. Games like *Mortal Kombat* and *Tekken* followed suit, adopting the idea of unique fighters from different parts of the world.

This template wasn't limited to character diversity; it extended to the intricate balance of fighting styles and narrative depth, which heightened the competitive edge while providing richer player engagement. The concept of distinctive special moves and backgrounds not only enhanced replayability but also encouraged player loyalty to favored characters. The success of *Street Fighter II* ensured its legacy as the blueprint for character-driven fighting games, influencing countless titles in the decades following its release.

The Innovation of Combos

Street Fighter II was notably revolutionary for introducing combo moves, which became a staple in later games.

Combos are sequences of moves that could be linked together to deliver more damage.

In **Street Fighter II**, combos represent an innovative leap forward in fighting game mechanics. This concept allows players to chain several attacks into a seamless sequence, significantly amplifying the damage dealt to opponents. The power of combos lies in their ability to turn the tide of a match within seconds, creating high-stakes moments that can captivate both players and spectators alike.

Each character in the game boasts unique combo moves, enriching the strategic depth and tactics players can employ. Mastering these combinations involves not only understanding the character's moveset but also perfecting the timing to execute them flawlessly. As a result, combos add layers of complexity and excitement to the game's competitive landscape.

This mechanic began as a programming glitch, later it became an intentional feature.

Interestingly, the combo system in *Street Fighter II* emerged quite by accident. Initially conceived as a programming glitch, developers noticed certain moves could be linked to create a rapid-fire assault on unsuspecting opponents.

Realizing its transformative potential, the development team decided to embrace and refine this mechanic, embedding it as a core feature of the game.

Capcom's decision to structure the gameplay around this newfound element underscored their forward-thinking creativity. This embrace of what was initially a bug led to the creation of an entirely new gameplay dimension. In doing so, they not only enriched the game but also set a new standard for future titles within the genre.

Players quickly mastered these moves to gain a competitive edge over opponents.

As the gaming community became aware of combos in **Street Fighter II**, players realized their potential to drastically impact competitive play. The learning curve was steep; however, determined gamers invested countless hours in honing their skills. Mastering combos became a matter of pride and skill, distinguishing novice players from seasoned veterans.

Gamers began to share tips and strategies in arcades and through early online forums, facilitating a grassroots movement of knowledge exchange. This social aspect contributed to the game's enduring popularity and fostered a community of hardcore fans dedicated to perfecting their craft.

The introduction of combos significantly increased the game's skill ceiling, attracting serious players.

By incorporating combos, *Street Fighter II* raised the bar for what constituted mastery. The elevated skill ceiling ensured that the game appealed not only to casual players but also to those seeking a deeper and more challenging experience. The demand for precision, timing, and strategic foresight transformed the game into a proving ground for serious competitors.

This complexity helped fuel an emergent competitive scene, laying the groundwork for modern-day esports. Tournaments began to spring up worldwide, drawing in audiences eager to witness the best players showcase their skills. Consequently, *Street Fighter II* not only revolutionized gameplay but also catalyzed the growth of competitive gaming culture.

The Cultural Phenomenon

The influence of Street Fighter II went beyond video games, impacting pop culture significantly.

The game inspired merchandise, comics, and animated series, expanding its influence beyond gaming.

Street Fighter II quickly evolved into a multimedia sensation, extending far beyond the confines of the arcade and gaming consoles. The game's distinctive characters and dynamic style inspired a wide range of merchandise, from action figures and clothing to home décor. These products allowed fans to bring a piece of the game world into their everyday lives.

In addition to merchandise, *Street Fighter II* found new life in print and animation. The game inspired numerous comic book adaptations and animated series that explored the rich backstories of its iconic fighters. Such expansions contributed significantly to the game's lore, connecting with a broader audience and cementing its place in popular culture.

Street Fighter II had a major role in establishing competitive gaming as we know it today.

Before the esports phenomenon, **Street Fighter II** laid the groundwork for competitive gaming. With its engaging one-on-one arcade matches, it attracted players eager to demonstrate their skills. The game encouraged friendly rivalry and community bonding, fueling the growth of local tournaments across the globe.

These tournaments tapped into the burgeoning culture of competitive gaming, eventually leading to a structured framework for what is known today as esports. The competitive spirit ignited by *Street Fighter II* has influenced countless games, fostering a legacy of skill-based competition within the gaming community.

It also contributed to the fighting game community (FGC), fostering a vibrant, long-lasting culture.

The emergence of **Street Fighter II** marked the inception of the modern fighting game community (FGC). The game's intricate mechanics and vibrant roster prompted players to gather, discuss strategies, and share techniques.

Thus, *Street Fighter II* served as the catalyst for a thriving social scene dedicated to the fighting game genre.

This vibrant culture encouraged inclusivity and diversity among players. Over time, the FGC has grown to include international tournaments and forums where players from diverse backgrounds come together, united by their passion for fighting games. The enduring community spirit initially sparked by *Street Fighter II* continues to inspire future generations of gamers.

The game's catchphrases and character moves became part of gaming vernacular.

Street Fighter II introduced not only a deep and rewarding gameplay experience, but also a bevy of memorable catchphrases and character moves. Phrases like "Hadouken!" and "Shoryuken!" became synonymous with the game itself, echoing in arcades and later transitioning into mainstream lexicon.

These expressions contribute to a shared understanding among gamers, representing pivotal moments in matches and forming an integral part of gaming vernacular. The iconic moves and lines from *Street Fighter II* continue to be referenced in other media, showcasing the game's enduring cultural impact across various entertainment fields.

Legacy and Influence

Even today, Street Fighter II's impact on gaming is undeniable, with its legacy enduring over decades.

It paved the way for future fighting game franchises like Tekken, Mortal Kombat, and more.

Street Fighter II set the standard for what a fighting game could be, strongly influencing the development of future franchises such as *Tekken* and *Mortal Kombat*. It introduced mechanics like special moves and combos that became a staple in the genre. By crafting a formula that emphasized both balance and strategy, the game laid the foundation upon which other developers could build.

The success of **Street Fighter II** also created a market for more complex and innovative fighting games. As companies sought to capitalize on its success, they experimented with 3D graphics, story-driven narratives, and diverse character rosters, as seen in titles like *Tekken*. This competitive spirit pushed the envelope further, refining controls and deepening gameplay mechanics across the board.

Modern iterations of the game continue to be released, attracting both new and veteran players.

Over three decades since its initial release, **Street Fighter II** still captivates audiences. Modern versions, like *Street Fighter II: Ultra* and various anniversary editions, introduce enhancements while preserving the original's essence.

These releases attract not just nostalgic veterans but also new players curious about the roots of fighting games.

This enduring allure speaks volumes about the game's robust design and its status as a cultural icon. The iterative releases keep the community vibrant, continually introducing improvements and ensuring the legacy of **Street Fighter II** remains relevant. This has helped maintain a diverse player base, ensuring the game's elements can be appreciated by gamers across generations.

The game's design principles are studied in game development courses worldwide.

The innovative design of **Street Fighter II** has made it a subject of academic study in game development programs worldwide. The game exemplifies how to create a nuanced balance between accessibility and depth, ensuring players of varying skill levels find engagement. Its character design, each with unique strengths and weaknesses, is a masterclass in creating diversity within constraints.

By studying **Street Fighter II**, students can grasp principles of game balance, character archetypes, and playercentric design. These insights are crucial for those looking to create engaging and replayable content. As a case study, the game provides invaluable lessons on adhering to player feedback and iterating for improvement—skills vital for any aspiring game designer.

Its influence is evident in the evolution of competitive gaming, bridging the gap between casual and professional play.

Street Fighter II was pivotal in fostering the early days of competitive gaming, laying the groundwork for the esports phenomenon we see today. The introduction of versus mode directly engaged players in competitive play, encouraging them to hone their skills not just against the computer, but against each other, sparking local and international tournaments.

This evolution of competitive gaming paved the way for today's tournaments and professional gaming circuits. By bridging the gap between casual play and professional competition, **Street Fighter II** created a community where players could transition from hobbyists to professionals, contributing to the game's enduring legacy in the esports realm.

Chapter 19: Doom - The FPS Revolution

Doom changed the landscape of gaming by popularizing the first-person shooter genre. Released in 1993, its fastpaced action, networked multiplayer, and modding community influenced countless developers and games.

The Birth of a Genre

Doom was integral in giving rise to the first-person shooter genre, a form of game that allows players to experience action from a first-person perspective.

Doom was developed by id Software and first released in 1993.

Doom was crafted by the innovative team at id Software, led by industry legends John Carmack and John Romero. This development marked a significant point in gaming history when it launched in 1993. id Software had already gained prominence with *Wolfenstein 3D*, but *Doom* took things to a new level. It wasn't just a game; it was a technological marvel that challenged the capabilities of hardware at the time. Released as shareware, it provided a revolutionary business model that allowed players to explore part of the game for free before purchasing the full version. This strategy contributed to its widespread reach and appeal.

The game used a revolutionary 3D graphics engine for its time, allowing immersive gameplay.

The core of **Doom's** allure was its cutting-edge 3D graphics engine, designed by John Carmack. Unlike a traditional 2D engine, it used ray-casting techniques to simulate 3D environments, creating more realistic and engaging visuals. Although technically not "true" 3D, it was groundbreaking at the time, offering players a sense of depth and immersion previously unseen. The engine rendered the game world with an unprecedented level of detail, featuring texture mapping and variable lighting. This, combined with the speed and fluidity of movement in the game, created a fast-paced and exhilarating experience that captivated players around the globe.

Its success paved the way for future FPS games, setting a new standard for the genre.

Doom's immense success redefined expectations for what a first-person shooter could achieve. It set a high standard in terms of graphics, gameplay, and design. Competitors and successors in the genre had to innovate and evolve to match or exceed the benchmarks set by *Doom*. The game's groundbreaking mechanics, especially its seamless integration of action and exploration, became a touchstone for developers. Aspects like its non-linear level design and secret areas encouraged exploration, adding depth to gameplay. This influence ensured that *Doom* would not merely be a passing phenomenon but a foundational pillar for future FPS developments.

Doom's influence is seen in many subsequent titles like Quake and Halo, which built upon its formula.

The ripple effects of **Doom's** innovations are clearly visible in iconic titles such as *Quake* and *Halo*. *Quake* built upon *Doom's* pioneering work, introducing fully 3D graphics and further advancing multiplayer capabilities. It pushed the boundaries of what FPS games could offer. Years later, *Halo* inherited and evolved *Doom's* formula, revolutionizing console FPS gameplay with its refined mechanics and storytelling approach. Both these games owe a significant part of their heritage to *Doom*, demonstrating its lasting impact in the gaming industry and how it served as a blueprint for success.

It introduced many players to the FPS style, broadening the gaming audience.

Doom was a seminal experience for many gamers, introducing them to the first-person shooter genre. Its availability as shareware meant it reached a wider audience than most games of its time, piquing the curiosity of new players. The game's addictive mechanics and engaging design appealed to both seasoned gamers and newcomers. Its network multiplayer capabilities allowed it to tap into the nascent online gaming scene, further extending its reach. By lowering the entry barrier for players and creating a dynamic gaming community, *Doom* significantly expanded the FPS player base, setting the stage for the genre's explosive growth in subsequent years.

Innovative Multiplayer Experience

Doom was one of the first games to support multiplayer gameplay over networks, a feature that greatly increased its appeal and longevity.

The game offered a mode called 'Deathmatch' where players could compete against each other.

Deathmatch, a term that has become synonymous with multiplayer gaming, was pioneered by *Doom*. This mode allowed players to engage in competitive battles, with the objective of eliminating each other in richly designed 3D levels. It introduced gamers to an era of adrenaline-pumping action, as they faced off against human opponents rather than AI-controlled enemies.

Players explored labyrinthine maps, collecting powerful weapons and items, while constantly being aware of threats from other players. This competitive play fostered a new kind of intensity and required quick reflexes and strategic planning, factors that became essential staples in later FPS games. *Doom's* Deathmatch mode laid the foundations for the competitive eSports scene we see today.

Multiplayer options included cooperative play, enhancing player interaction and cooperation.

In addition to the competitive Deathmatch, *Doom* offered a **cooperative mode** that emphasized teamwork and collective problem-solving. This option allowed players to work together, sharing resources and strategizing to overcome challenging levels filled with demons and obstacles.

The cooperative play mode fostered camaraderie and communication among friends, as players united to achieve a common goal. This aspect of teamwork helped diversify the multiplayer experience, providing an alternative to solitary gaming and competitive play. It also laid the groundwork for countless other games that would incorporate cooperative multiplayer dynamics, highlighting the value of shared gaming experiences.

Doom popularized the LAN party concept, where players would connect computers via local networks to play together.

Doom was instrumental in popularizing the **LAN party**, a social event where players connected their computers on a local network to enjoy multiplayer gaming. This setup allowed for fast, lag-free interactions and brought players together physically, creating a social experience around gaming.

These gatherings became a cultural phenomenon, turning basements and living rooms into temporary arenas of competition and collaboration. The local aspect of LAN parties reinforced gaming as a shared hobby, fostering communities and friendships. Moreover, the success of these events showcased the potential of local network gaming, influencing the future design of multiplayer games.

The success of Doom's multiplayer mode demonstrated the potential of online and LAN gaming.

The thriving multiplayer component of *Doom* highlighted the immense potential of **online and LAN gaming**. By enabling players to connect, compete, and collaborate through networks, *Doom* expanded the possibilities of interactive entertainment beyond the boundaries of single-player gaming.

This foresight and implementation spurred innovation, leading to the development of more sophisticated networking technologies and infrastructure in gaming. As a result, *Doom* played a critical role in shaping the future of multiplayer gaming, paving the way for the online ecosystems we are familiar with today, including the widespread use of internet-based gaming platforms.

It laid the groundwork for modern online multiplayer ecosystems, influencing games like Counter-Strike and Call of Duty.

Doom's pioneering efforts in multiplayer gaming didn't just achieve success in its own right but **set the stage** for future giants like *Counter-Strike* and *Call of Duty*. These franchises have built vast online communities, drawing from the foundations established by *Doom*, such as competitive play, strategic team dynamics, and expansive multiplayer options.

The principles and innovations introduced by *Doom* have been echoed and expanded upon by modern multiplayer games, demonstrating its lasting influence. By laying the groundwork for what evolved into massive online multiplayer ecosystems, *Doom* showed the gaming industry the value and potential reach of interconnected play, forever changing the landscape of interactive digital entertainment.

Community and Modding Impact

In a groundbreaking move for its time, id Software provided players with the tools to create their own content for **Doom**. This initiative included level editors and other development resources that allowed enthusiasts to craft custom levels and share them with others. By openly distributing these tools, id empowered players to experiment creatively, adding significant replay value to the game.

This practice of allowing end-users to modify a game was relatively novel in the early '90s. It played a considerable role in Doom's lasting popularity, setting a foundation for the idea that games could be endlessly reshaped by their communities, thus pioneering a user-driven content culture.

This openness led to the emergence of a passionate modding community that extended the game's lifetime.

The open modding framework introduced by Doom was instrumental in creating a thriving community that has been active for decades. Enthusiastic players quickly organized into collaborative groups, sharing knowledge and resources. These communities grew into forums and websites dedicated to Doom mods, fostering a constant exchange of ideas and support.

This vibrant community didn't just help in developing mods; it also helped maintain the game's relevance long past its initial release. The communal effort made Doom more than just a game; it became a platform, enabling continuous innovation and engagement.

Mods varied from simple level packs to total conversions, showcasing creativity and innovation.

One of the most fascinating aspects of Doom's modding scene was the diversity of content produced. Mods ranged from simple map packs that introduced new challenges to complex total conversions that radically changed the game's setting and mechanics. Mods like these demonstrated the significant creative potential the game toolkit unlocked.

Some conversions were so extensive that they seemed like entirely new games sharing only Doom's underlying engine. This not only showcased the adaptability of the game but also highlighted the artistry and ingenuity of its community. Such creativity set a precedent in game design that is still evident today.

The modding culture that Doom inspired can be seen in modern gaming through platforms like Steam Workshop.

The legacy of Doom's modding culture continues to influence modern gaming. Today, platforms like the Steam Workshop owe much of their success to the pioneering steps taken by id Software. By making modding tools accessible, Doom demonstrated the potential for community-driven content creation.

Steam Workshop now hosts thousands of mods for contemporary games, providing players with an extensive range of content that adds depth and variety to gaming experiences. These platforms reflect Doom's legacy, where the lines between developers and players blur, encouraging collaborative world-building and story-telling.

Many aspiring game developers got their start by creating mods for Doom, leading to careers in the industry.

Doom's modding community not only created content but also nurtured talent. Many well-known game developers found their initial footing by experimenting with Doom mods, gaining practical experience in level design, coding, and storytelling. This early exposure to game development skills was instrumental in shaping their careers.

These individuals often cite Doom as their inspiration and stepping stone into the professional gaming industry. By lowering the entry barrier to game design, Doom's modding tools democratized game development, fostering a generation of developers who contribute significantly to today's gaming landscape.

Cultural and Industry Influence

Doom's influence extended beyond gaming, entering popular culture and setting trends across the entertainment industry.

The game's simple but engaging narrative inspired many media adaptations, including books and movies.

The release of **Doom** brought about a narrative that was as straightforward as it was captivating. Set on a space marine battling demons unleashed in a UAC facility, the minimalistic but engaging story has prompted the development of several media adaptations. The lore expanded beyond the screen into novels such as the *Doom Series* authored by Dafydd ab Hugh and Brad Linaweaver.

Furthermore, Doom's influence reached Hollywood, leading to the 2005 release of a movie adaptation that attempted to encapsulate the game's essence. Although not critically acclaimed, it demonstrated the game's reach and impact on popular culture. These adaptations, by retaining the core excitement of the original game, highlight Doom's narrative as a significant source of inspiration for diverse storytelling in different media formats.

Doom set a precedent for game soundtracks, with its heavy metal-inspired music becoming iconic.

One of the standout features of **Doom** was its rousing soundtrack, which drew significant inspiration from heavy metal music. Composed by Bobby Prince, the soundtrack featured tracks that echoed the aggressive energy of bands like Metallica and Slayer. This approach to music in video games broke new ground and set the standard for future game soundtracks.

The metal-inspired music became synonymous with the intense gameplay, further immersing players in its frenetic pace. This heavy emphasis on soundtrack would go on to influence other genres, making music a critical factor in game design and player engagement. The integration of these rhythms contributed to shaping how soundtracks are perceived and appreciated in modern gaming.

The controversy surrounding its violent content sparked discussions about video game violence and regulation.

Doom did not shy away from showcasing explicit violence, which quickly made it a focal point in the debate over violence in video games. The graphic imagery and intense combat scenarios stirred significant controversy upon its release, prompting discussions among politicians, researchers, and media outlets.

This dialogue often revolved around the potential effects of gaming on young audiences and pushed for stricter regulations on video game content. While Doom was not the first to encounter such criticism, its immense popularity put it under the spotlight, making it a cornerstone reference in the ongoing discussion about the impact of interactive media on society. The controversy underscored the need for a nuanced examination of video game content and its potential influence.

Its impact is evident in the shooter mechanics and design choices of many later titles.

The influence of **Doom** on subsequent first-person shooters is unmistakable. Its pioneering use of 3D graphics and fast-paced shooter mechanics laid the groundwork for the intrinsic design of the FPS genre. Features like weapon variety, enemy AI, and multiplayer capabilities became standard expectations due to Doom's innovative approach.

Games such as *Quake*, *Counter-Strike*, and even modern titles like *Call of Duty* and *Battlefield* inherit many of Doom's groundbreaking elements. This legacy is rooted in its gameplay design, which emphasized speed, precision, and strategy, inspiring developers to continue evolving the FPS landscape by building on its unmistakable formula.

Doom continues to be referenced in various forms of media, cementing its legacy in entertainment history.

Even decades after its release, **Doom**'s presence in media is pervasive. The game's iconic elements—such as its enemies, sound effects, and gameplay innovations—are regularly referenced in films, TV shows, and other video games, illustrating its deep-rooted cultural significance.

From humorous nods in animated series to thematic inspiration in other gaming titles, Doom's footprint can be seen across a broad array of content. This persistent referencing underscores not just its past influence but its ongoing role as a cultural touchstone, cementing Doom's place as a legendary entity in the tapestry of entertainment history.

Chapter 20: Final Fantasy VII - A Story Transcending Pixels

Final Fantasy VII, released in 1997, showed the world that video games could deliver deep and emotional narratives. It's a masterpiece that brought RPGs to the forefront of gaming.

Origins of Final Fantasy VII

Final Fantasy VII was born out of Square's desire to evolve the RPG genre. Let's explore how this landmark game came to be.

Development started in 1994 as Square aimed to revolutionize RPGs.

In 1994, Square began the ambitious journey of creating Final Fantasy VII, aiming to push boundaries and redefine the role-playing game (RPG) genre. The developers wanted to create an experience that not only entertained but also resonated emotionally with players. They envisioned a game that would combine compelling storytelling with engaging gameplay.

As Square embarked on this project, they recognized the potential for technological advancements to enhance narrative depth and player immersion. The idea was to craft a world where players could lose themselves, feeling connected to the characters and story. This vision laid the groundwork for what would become a landmark in gaming history, drastically changing the expectations for RPGs moving forward.

The decision to move from Nintendo to Sony's PlayStation platform was pivotal.

Switching from Nintendo to Sony's PlayStation was a critical decision that shaped the future of Final Fantasy VII. Initially, Square considered developing the game for the Nintendo 64, but the limitations of cartridge storage became a concern. The PlayStation, on the other hand, could utilize CD-ROMs, offering significantly greater storage capacity.

This platform change allowed Square to incorporate extensive video sequences, higher-quality audio, and expansive worlds, elements that were vital for the ambitious scope envisioned for Final Fantasy VII. This decision not only facilitated the realization of a more immersive game but also cemented Sony's position as a key player in the gaming industry.

Utilizing 3D graphics and pre-rendered backgrounds was a bold innovation.

Final Fantasy VII's use of 3D graphics and pre-rendered backgrounds represented a bold leap in game design during its time. This blend of technology allowed for more detailed and visually appealing environments, enhancing the game's storytelling capabilities. The characters, rendered in 3D, moved through intricate and beautifully crafted backgrounds that captivated players' imaginations.

The visual aesthetics provided a richness that contributed to the emotional impact and immersion of the game. It was an innovative approach that not only captured the essence of the world but also set new standards for visual storytelling in video games, influencing future RPGs and other genres.

Final Fantasy VII was the first in the series to use CD-ROMs, offering expansive content.

By utilizing CD-ROMs, Final Fantasy VII was able to expand its content exponentially compared to its predecessors. This shift enabled the inclusion of expansive environments, full-motion video sequences, and a richly orchestrated musical score. The storage capacity of CDs offered the creative freedom necessary to deliver a complex and captivating narrative.

The transition to CD-ROMs marked a turning point in the gaming industry, allowing developers to think bigger and more creatively. It facilitated a comprehensive gaming experience that intertwined intricate storytelling with gameplay, ultimately solidifying Final Fantasy VII's legacy as a groundbreaking RPG.

Story and Characters

The engaging story and memorable characters of Final Fantasy VII drew players into its epic narrative.

The protagonist, Cloud Strife, is a complex character with a mysterious past.

Cloud Strife stands as one of the most intriguing protagonists in gaming history. At first glance, his stoic demeanor and formidable sword suggest a traditional hero archetype. However, as players delve deeper into the game, they uncover layers of complexity woven into his character.

The narrative reveals Cloud's troubled past, marred by identity crises and memory manipulation. These elements create a sense of suspense and curiosity, driving the story forward. Unraveling Cloud's true identity becomes a central theme, with players embarking on a journey of self-discovery alongside him. This exploration of Cloud's psyche not only enhances the storytelling experience but also invites players to reflect on their own perceptions of identity.

The game's profound narrative touches on themes of identity and environmentalism.

Final Fantasy VII is renowned for its profound thematic exploration, particularly its focus on identity and environmentalism. Identity is a recurring motif, manifested through various characters' struggles with self-image and truth. Cloud's personal journey serves as a powerful commentary on the search for self, prompting players to question the nature of existence and memory.

Simultaneously, the game's narrative tackles environmentalism with a bold critique of corporate greed and its impact on the planet. The fictional corporation Shinra epitomizes destructive capitalism, harvesting the planet's life force for profit. This motif resonates with real-world environmental concerns, making the game's message both timeless and timely.

Sephiroth, the game's antagonist, is one of gaming's most iconic villains.

Sephiroth, the primary antagonist in Final Fantasy VII, is etched into the pantheon of gaming's greatest villains. His journey from revered hero to embittered antagonist adds depth to an already intricate plot. Sephiroth's transformation is rooted in a profound betrayal, fueled by revelations about his origins and the experiments that created him.

His chilling presence and formidable power elevate the game's stakes, underscoring a complex narrative of revenge and ambition. Sephiroth's theme, a haunting symphony that accompanies his appearances, becomes synonymous with impending doom. Ultimately, his character embodies the struggle between destiny and free will, challenging players philosophically while maintaining narrative tension.

Supporting characters like Tifa, Aerith, and Barret enrich the storyline.

The supporting cast of Final Fantasy VII, including Tifa, Aerith, and Barret, brings richness and diversity to the game's narrative tapestry. Tifa, with her steadfast loyalty and personal ties to Cloud, provides an emotional grounding that counterbalances the game's darker themes. Her complexity challenges traditional female roles in gaming, offering strength, vulnerability, and depth.

Aerith, with her mysterious past and connection to the planet, introduces spirituality and mysticism to the storyline.

Her character arc, marked by tragedy, resonates deeply with players, reinforcing the themes of sacrifice and destiny.

Barret, meanwhile, adds layers of social commentary, confronting issues of loss and resistance against oppression. Together, these characters create a dynamic narrative, each contributing uniquely to the epic story of Final Fantasy VII.

Gameplay Mechanics

Final Fantasy VII introduced innovative gameplay mechanics that reshaped the RPG landscape.

The Materia system allowed for deep customization of character abilities.

The Materia system in **Final Fantasy VII** represented a breakthrough in character development and customization within the RPG genre. Players could equip characters with 'Materia,' magical orbs unlocking various abilities and spells. This system enabled an unprecedented level of strategy, allowing for unique character builds based on the chosen Materia combinations.

What made the Materia system innovative was its impact on both abilities and character stats. For example, some Materia increased magic power but decreased physical prowess, compelling players to think carefully about who received which Materia. This balancing act added layers of complexity, requiring players to constantly assess their strategies and adapt to different combat situations. The system was praised for its depth and the freedom it provided to experiment, a feature that enhanced replayability and engaged players in endless tactical evaluations.

Turn-based combat, combined with Active Time Battle, keeps players engaged.

The combat system in **Final Fantasy VII** was a key component of its success, integrating the classic turn-based style with the innovative Active Time Battle (ATB) system. Unlike traditional turn-based setups where actions proceeded strictly in turns, the ATB system created a dynamic and engaging experience. Each character had a time gauge that filled in real-time, regardless of whether the player was actively taking action.

As a result, players had to make tactical decisions rapidly, balancing risk with reward. This system introduced tension and urgency to battles, keeping players engaged and on their toes. Additionally, the variety of enemy types and abilities required players to adapt their approach constantly, further enhancing the game's strategic depth. The marriage of turn-based methodology with real-time decision-making in the ATB system was a hallmark of *Final Fantasy VII*'s gameplay that captivated players worldwide.

Exploration across various landscapes adds depth and variety to gameplay.

Final Fantasy VII excels in providing a rich tapestry of environments for players to explore, each with distinct visual styles and atmospheres. From the bustling, industrial cityscape of Midgar to the serene and mystical landscapes of the Forgotten Capital, the game offers a diverse range of settings that captivate the imagination.

This varied world design not only contributes to the visual allure of the game but also affects gameplay. Each location presents unique challenges and opportunities, whether it's navigating the winding paths of a mountainous region or uncovering secrets hidden in a dense forest. The dynamic and diverse environments encourage players to immerse themselves deeply in exploration, enhancing the game's overall sense of adventure and discovery.

Mini-games and side quests provide a break from the main storyline.

One of the standout features of **Final Fantasy VII** is its array of mini-games and side quests that complement the main narrative. These elements offer players a chance to engage in diverse activities that break the monotony of the main storyline while providing a fun and often rewarding diversion.

From the excitement of the Chocobo races to the strategic intricacies of the Fort Condor battles, these mini-games allow players to explore different aspects of gameplay. Additionally, side quests such as the Gold Saucer events or the quest to unlock Vincent and Yuffie as party members offer not only added content but also rich backstories and character development. These elements enhance the game's depth and provide players with the opportunity to explore the world and its inhabitants from a fresh perspective.

Visuals and Soundtrack

The visuals and soundtrack of Final Fantasy VII were groundbreaking for its time.

The 3D graphics were state-of-the-art, setting new standards in gaming visuals.

When *Final Fantasy VII* was released, its 3D graphics were nothing short of revolutionary. For many players, this was the first RPG that brought characters and environments to life in three dimensions. The transition from 2D to 3D graphics in video games allowed developers to craft more detailed and engaging worlds.

This advancement in visual technology set a new standard for what could be achieved in gaming. Characters were more expressive, with dynamic animations that contributed greatly to the narrative experience. The polygonal models, though primitive by modern standards, provided players with a greater sense of immersion than pixel art could offer.

Pre-rendered backgrounds created a rich and immersive world.

One of the standout features of *Final Fantasy VII* was its use of pre-rendered backgrounds. These meticulously crafted scenes added a layer of depth and artistic detail that was both beautiful and functionally effective. Players traversed environments that were vibrant and intricately designed, creating a sense of realism and wonder.

The pre-rendered backgrounds complemented the 3D character models beautifully, allowing for an aesthetic that was both unique and captivating. Every location in the game felt distinct and contributed to the overarching atmosphere, from the bustling streets of Midgar to the serene landscapes of the overworld.

Nobuo Uematsu's soundtrack is iconic, enhancing the emotional depth of the game.

Nobuo Uematsu's work on the *Final Fantasy VII* soundtrack remains one of the most celebrated in the history of video game music. His compositions not only set the mood but also deepened the emotional connection players felt with the story and its characters.

From the hauntingly beautiful "Aerith's Theme" to the intense battle anthems, the music elevated every moment of the game. Uematsu's ability to convey a wide range of emotions through his compositions was pivotal in making *Final Fantasy VII* a landmark in storytelling.

The game's music resonates with players even decades after its release.

Decades after its release, the music of *Final Fantasy VII* continues to resonate with gamers worldwide. Fans often find themselves reminiscing about memorable scenes, with the soundtrack acting as an auditory bridge to the past. This continued relevance is a testament to the enduring quality and emotional depth of Nobuo Uematsu's work.

Concerts and symphonies still perform pieces from the game, introducing its music to new generations. Its lasting impact shows that music is not just an accompaniment in video games, but an integral part of the experience, capable of leaving an indelible mark on its audience.

Impact and Legacy

Final Fantasy VII's impact on the gaming industry and its enduring legacy are undeniable.

The game brought RPGs into mainstream popularity, expanding their audience.

Final Fantasy VII played a pivotal role in introducing role-playing games (RPGs) to a broader audience. Before its release, RPGs were primarily enjoyed by a niche group of dedicated fans. However, with its stunning 3D graphics, engaging storyline, and highly accessible gameplay, Final Fantasy VII shattered these boundaries. The game appealed to both seasoned players and newcomers alike, providing an entry point into the complex world of RPGs. Its success demonstrated the commercial viability of RPGs, encouraging other developers to invest in this genre.

Moreover, Square's innovative use of technological advancements allowed for authentic emotional storytelling, a draw for gamers seeking more than just action and adventure. As a result, RPGs began to gain prominence on the international stage, establishing a solid foundation for future titles in the genre. Final Fantasy VII's influence on popularizing RPGs can't be overstated, marking a significant shift in gaming history as it reached a level of mass appeal previously unseen in the genre.

It inspired numerous sequels, spin-offs, and a highly anticipated remake.

The legacy of Final Fantasy VII extends far beyond its initial success, manifesting in numerous sequels and spin-offs that have expanded its rich narrative universe. Titles such as “Final Fantasy VII: Advent Children,” a CGI film sequel, and games like “Dirge of Cerberus” and “Crisis Core” delve deeper into the backstories of beloved characters, further enriching the lore that fans cherish.

Moreover, the immense popularity of the original game led to the highly anticipated "Final Fantasy VII Remake" series, which revisits and reimagines the classic adventure with modern technology. This remake not only presented stunning graphics and reworked gameplay mechanics but also introduced new story elements, captivating both original fans and a new generation of players. Square Enix's dedication to evolving the universe of Final Fantasy VII underscores its lasting legacy and fans' continued enthusiasm for the series.

Final Fantasy VII set the stage for storytelling in video games.

Final Fantasy VII's intricate narrative and character development set a new benchmark for storytelling in video games. The depth of its plot, centered around themes of identity, loss, and environmentalism, showcased video games as a medium capable of delivering complex and moving narratives. Players were introduced to a diverse cast of characters, each with their own backstory and emotional journeys, allowing for a deeply immersive experience.

Notably, the game's dramatic moments, such as the unexpected demise of a central character, left a lasting emotional impression on its audience. This profound impact demonstrated that video games, much like movies and literature, could evoke strong emotional responses and tell stories with significant narrative depth. By doing so, Final Fantasy VII paved the way for future titles to explore sophisticated storytelling, influencing how narratives are crafted across the gaming industry.

The game is celebrated as a classic, influencing countless future titles.

Final Fantasy VII is celebrated as a classic within the gaming community, having influenced countless games that followed. Its groundbreaking use of cinematic cutscenes and intricate gameplay mechanics set a standard that many developers have since emulated. The game's blend of strategic combat, exploration, and narrative richness has served as a blueprint for numerous RPGs and other genres.

Furthermore, Final Fantasy VII's impact extends beyond direct gameplay and storytelling influences. It has inspired game designers to innovate in ways that elevate the gaming experience, such as crafting more immersive worlds and creating emotionally resonant characters. This classic's enduring legacy is reflected in its frequent appearance on "greatest games of all time" lists and its continued presence in discussions about gaming history, proving its status as a milestone in the evolution of gaming.

Chapter 21: Myst - A Journey into Mystery

With its stunning visuals and challenging puzzles, *Myst* captivated players and offered a fresh experience unlike any other. Released in 1993, it's still remembered for its beauty and immersive storytelling.

The Creation of Myst

Developed by brothers Robyn and Rand Miller, Myst was a groundbreaking game that set new standards for interactive storytelling in the gaming industry.

The brainchild of Cyan, a small American gaming studio led by Robyn and Rand Miller, Myst was a passion project born out of a desire to create a new genre of adventure games.

Founded in 1987 by brothers Robyn and Rand Miller, Cyan was a small startup driven by a shared enthusiasm for innovative storytelling through video games. Their flagship game, *Myst*, sprang from their ambition to craft an engaging adventure experience that defied conventional gaming norms. The Millers aimed to create a game that was not only visually compelling but also intellectually stimulating.

At the time, most games focused on fast-paced action, but *Myst* set itself apart by embracing exploration and puzzlesolving at its core. Its development was fueled by the Millers' belief in the potential of games to provide deeply immersive narratives. This bold vision propelled *Myst* to become a cornerstone in adventure gaming and established Cyan as a pioneering force in the industry.

The game was originally designed for the Macintosh computers and later ported to other platforms, broadening its audience.

Released in 1993, *Myst* was initially crafted for the Macintosh, a platform known for its graphical capabilities. The decision to start on Macintosh allowed Cyan to leverage its high-resolution screen and advanced audio technology, providing players with a rich visual and auditory experience.

As the game's popularity soared, *Myst* was successfully ported to various other platforms such as Windows, PlayStation, and Sega Saturn. These adaptations expanded its reach to a broader audience, enabling more gamers to partake in the unique journey it offered. The strategic cross-platform releases contributed significantly to its historical importance, helping it to become one of the best-selling PC games of its era.

Robyn Miller composed the iconic soundtrack, enhancing the immersive experience with ambient melodies.

The auditory landscape of *Myst* played a vital role in drawing players into its enigmatic world. Robyn Miller, one of the game's creators, was responsible for the composition of its hauntingly beautiful soundtrack. The music blended seamlessly with the game's atmospheric visuals, creating an environment ripe for exploration and discovery.

Through the use of ambient melodies and subtle sound effects, the soundtrack heightened the feeling of mystery and suspense. Robyn's compositions provided not just a background score, but an integral component of the game's narrative. This innovative approach to integrating music within gameplay set a new standard for how audio could enhance the video game experience, influencing countless future titles.

The innovative use of pre-rendered graphics provided a depth of visual realism previously unseen in games.

A major breakthrough for *Myst* was its implementation of pre-rendered graphics, which allowed for unparalleled visual realism. Utilizing high-detail rendering, each scene in the game was crafted meticulously, creating an illusion of a fully realized 3D world.

This method of developing static, high-resolution images for backgrounds permitted an extraordinary level of detail and depth. Players could explore richly textured environments that felt lived-in, despite the technological limitations of the early 90s. The painstaking attention to detail in the game's graphics played a substantial role in its ability to captivate audiences and raise the bar for visual storytelling in games.

Myst was created using HyperCard, a multimedia system developed by Apple, which was a significant technological advancement for its time.

At the core of *Myst*'s development was HyperCard, an advanced multimedia programming environment created by Apple. HyperCard enabled the Millers to piece together complex, interactive experiences and was instrumental in bringing their vision to life.

Through HyperCard, the designers could effortlessly combine static images, text, and clickable objects to form the game's immersive landscapes and puzzles. This technological tool was cutting-edge at the time and empowered *Myst* to deliver an intricate, seamless user experience. By pushing the boundaries of what was possible within a gaming framework, the use of HyperCard underscored *Myst*'s status as a pioneering work that inspired future multimedia and adventure game creations.

Gameplay and Mechanics

Myst was unique in how it encouraged exploration and problem-solving, challenging players with logically complex puzzles.

The game is played from a first-person perspective, immersing the player in the enigmatic island environment.

Myst introduced a groundbreaking first-person perspective that allowed players to deeply engage with its mysterious world. By placing the player directly in the shoes of the protagonist, the game heightened the sense of immersion in the enigmatic island setting.

This perspective was crucial for establishing a personal connection to the environment, urging players to explore every nook and cranny. The sense of being present in the game world was enhanced by the ability to inspect intricate details at one's own pace, creating a personal journey of discovery.

Players move through pre-rendered environments, clicking through static scenes that slowly reveal the story.

The gameplay of *Myst* relies on a series of pre-rendered scenes, each acting as a piece of the elaborate puzzle. Players navigate the island by clicking through these static images, experiencing the world in snapshots that slowly unfold the narrative.

This click-and-explore mechanic was innovative in the early '90s, creating a methodical pace that matched the game's mysterious and contemplative tone. Each scene transition invited players to scrutinize details, piecing together the story from visual and auditory clues scattered across the island.

The game relies on environmental cues and observations to solve its intricate puzzles, requiring players to think critically and methodically.

Myst is celebrated for its intricate puzzles, which require players to engage deeply with their surroundings. Solutions are thoughtfully woven into the environment, prompting players to make astute observations and interpret subtle cues found throughout the game.

This approach demands critical thinking, encouraging players to explore connections and deduce solutions from fragmented information. As players delve deeper into the island's mysteries, they discover that paying attention to detail and exercising patience are key to unraveling the game's complex challenges.

There are no user interfaces, health bars, or combat elements, which was revolutionary for its focus purely on exploration.

A pioneering aspect of *Myst* is its absence of conventional gaming elements like user interfaces, health bars, or combat mechanics. This design choice was revolutionary, emphasizing pure exploration and discovery rather than typical gaming conventions.

The lack of distractions meant players could immerse themselves entirely in the island's ambiance and narrative. By removing these elements, the game fostered a more contemplative and unhurried experience, setting a new standard for adventure games and influencing countless titles that followed.

Myst's Impact on Gaming

Myst's release marked a significant turning point in gaming history, influencing countless games and developers with its innovative approach.

Myst became the best-selling PC game until The Sims dethroned it in 2002, demonstrating the game's widespread appeal.

Upon its release in 1993, *Myst* quickly rose to prominence, becoming the best-selling PC game—a title it held for nearly a decade. The game's success was remarkable, given that it emerged during a time when the gaming industry was dominated by action and platformer titles.

The widespread appeal of *Myst* can be attributed to its unique blend of visuals, storytelling, and interactive puzzles. Players were immediately drawn to its stunning, pre-rendered graphics and the sense of wonder that came with exploring its mysterious islands. This immersive experience captivated a broad audience, including many who were new to computer gaming.

It paved the way for narrative-driven games, showing that a game could succeed without traditional action elements.

Myst broke the mold by proving that a compelling narrative and immersive environment could engage players just as effectively as traditional action or combat. This innovative approach resonated with those who sought more meaningful experiences in gaming.

The success of *Myst* highlighted the viability of storytelling as a core gaming component, inspiring developers to focus more on plots and character development. This laid the groundwork for future narrative-driven games, emphasizing exploration, choice, and story over fast-paced gameplay.

The success of Myst proved there's a market for games that offer intellectual challenges rather than reflex-based gameplay.

Prior to *Myst*, the gaming industry largely favored titles requiring quick reflexes and action-packed scenarios. *Myst* challenged this notion by offering a different kind of gaming experience—one based on exploration and puzzlesolving.

This shift highlighted a significant market demand for cerebral, contemplative games that encouraged players to immerse themselves in solving intricate puzzles. It opened the door for puzzle-centric games and underscored the potential success of games that provide intellectual stimulation alongside or instead of traditional gaming thrills.

It led to multiple sequels and spin-offs, cementing the Myst series as a staple in the adventure gaming genre.

The overwhelming success of *Myst* inevitably led to the development of sequels and spin-offs that expanded its universe. Games such as *Riven* and *Myst III: Exile* continued to captivate players with their intricate puzzles and rich storytelling.

These sequels not only built upon the original's legacy but also introduced new elements and mysteries, ensuring the series remained relevant and engaging. The longevity and evolution of the *Myst* series have solidified its place as a cornerstone of the adventure gaming genre, influencing numerous games and developers over the years.

Myst's Legacy and Longevity

Even decades after its initial release, Myst continues to be celebrated, revisited, and adapted for new technologies and audiences.

The game has been remastered and released on numerous platforms over the years, including VR, keeping it accessible to modern audiences.

Myst's journey from its original CD-ROM release to modern platforms is a testament to its lasting appeal. It has seen multiple remasters, each enhancing graphics and gameplay to suit contemporary expectations. From the early versions on Windows and Mac to later editions for iOS, Android, and consoles, *Myst* has remained accessible to new generations of gamers.

One significant update is the inclusion of Virtual Reality (VR), which offers an even more immersive experience. Players can now explore the enigmatic world of Myst with a sense of presence that was previously unimaginable. This commitment to keeping *Myst* relevant underscores its status as a classic that adapts to technological advances while maintaining the core experience that captivated its first players.

Myst's influence can be seen in modern adventure and puzzle games, which often strive to replicate its success in narrative and design.

The mark *Myst* has left on the gaming world is undeniable. Its pioneering use of environmental storytelling and openended exploration paved the way for modern adventure and puzzle games. Developers often draw inspiration from its seamless blend of narrative and gameplay, crafting experiences that encourage exploration and curiosity.

Games like *The Witness* and *Firewatch* are notable examples of titles that reflect *Myst*'s influence. They offer meticulously designed worlds and puzzles that require players to think critically and immerse themselves in the storyline. These elements have become cornerstones in the genre, proving that the legacy of Myst continues to shape gaming experiences today.

An active fan base and community continue to discuss and analyze the game, contributing to its enduring legacy.

Myst has cultivated a passionate fan base that remains engaged even decades after its release. Online forums, social media groups, and dedicated websites serve as vibrant hubs where enthusiasts discuss theories, share experiences, and debate aspects of the game. This active community thrives on the complexity and mystique of *Myst*, sustaining interest through continuous dialogue.

Fan-generated content, such as walkthroughs and mods, further enrich the Myst ecosystem. These contributions not only keep the game alive but also introduce it to new audiences. Such engagement underscores the profound impact *Myst* has had on its fans, ensuring that its mysteries and challenges remain part of gaming culture.

The title is frequently cited in academic discussions on video games as an art form, underlining its cultural significance.

Throughout its history, *Myst* has been a focal point in discussions about video games as a legitimate art form. Academics and critics consistently cite it in analyses of the medium's narrative potential and immersive qualities. *Myst* is often used as a case study in courses on game design and storytelling, illustrating how a game can evoke emotion and engage players intellectually and aesthetically.

The game's artistic and cultural resonance goes beyond entertainment, contributing to scholarly debates about interactivity and digital art. This recognition underscores *Myst*'s role not just as a game, but as a cultural artifact that continues to stimulate thought and inspire creativity in various fields.

Chapter 22: Pokémon Red and Blue - Gotta Catch 'Em All

The Pokémon series began with **Pokémon Red and Blue**, introducing millions to the joy of collecting and battling creatures. It became a cultural phenomenon and laid the foundation for a global franchise.

The Origins of Pokémon Red and Blue

Pokémon Red and Blue first arrived in Japan and later on international shores, shaping a new gaming era. Here's how it all started.

The games were first released in 1996 in Japan as Pokémon Red and Green, with Blue released later.

In February 1996, the Japanese gaming landscape witnessed the arrival of **Pokémon Red and Green**. These games marked the beginning of what would become a globally dominant franchise. Pokémon Red and Green captured players' imaginations by allowing them to step into the shoes of a young Pokémon Trainer on a quest to become a Champion.

Later in October 1996, *Pokémon Blue* was released, offering various bug fixes and slight graphical improvements over the originals. The staggering success and popularity of these versions laid a solid foundation for future international releases. This evolution of Pokémon catered not only to adventure seekers but also to strategists, ensuring its popularity across diverse player demographics in Japan.

The US versions debuted in 1998, unbelievably transforming Nintendo's Game Boy into a must-have device.

The international debut of **Pokémon Red and Blue** in 1998 marked a significant milestone in the gaming industry. When the games arrived in North America, they were met with unparalleled enthusiasm. Pokémon quickly became a household name, seizing the imagination of a generation and significantly boosting Game Boy sales.

This transformation turned the Game Boy into an essential device for gaming fans, who were captivated by the challenge of collecting 151 Pokémon creatures. The games facilitated a unique blend of exploration, strategy, and social interaction, which kept players engaged for hours on end. As a result, the Pokémon franchise expanded far beyond expectations, prompting a surge in Nintendo's popularity and presence worldwide.

The concept was created by Satoshi Tajiri at Game Freak, with a love for collecting insects inspiring the gameplay.

The brainchild of Satoshi Tajiri, **Pokémon** was conceived from his childhood fascination with collecting insects. Tajiri, working at the now-famous Game Freak studio, envisioned a game where players could experience the joy of discovery and collection, much like he did while exploring the outdoors.

Tajiri's unique concept transformed into a detailed virtual world filled with diverse creatures that players could capture, train, and battle. His innovative vision blended elements of collecting and strategy, which appealed to both children and adults alike. This foundation, rooted in personal passion, ensured that Pokémon resonated with audiences globally, cementing its status as a cultural phenomenon.

The games were developed by Game Freak and published by Nintendo and The Pokémon Company.

Game Freak, under the guidance of Satoshi Tajiri, played a crucial role in crafting the Pokémon universe. As the development studio behind the games, Game Freak meticulously designed a world where players could immerse themselves in the role of a Pokémon Trainer.

Meanwhile, **Nintendo** and **The Pokémon Company** worked hand-in-hand to publish the games, ensuring widespread distribution and marketing appeal. Their collaboration combined innovative game design with high-quality production and strategic outreach, ultimately captivating audiences worldwide. This partnership also laid the groundwork for the expansive Pokémon multimedia empire, extending into television, movies, and merchandise.

The unique trading aspect was revolutionary, allowing players to exchange Pokémon between different Game Boy systems.

One of the most groundbreaking features of **Pokémon Red and Blue** was the introduction of Pokémon trading. This feature encouraged players to connect their Game Boy systems via a link cable to exchange creatures. This innovation created a social gaming experience, prompting communication and collaboration between players as they aimed to complete their Pokédex.

The trading mechanic not only enhanced replayability but also fostered a community-driven culture among fans. This exchange system became a defining aspect of the Pokémon series, highlighting the importance of player interaction and cooperation, which was a rarity in a predominantly single-player gaming era.

The games became the highest-grossing video game franchise, leading to more titles and spin-offs.

With their widespread acclaim and commercial success, **Pokémon Red and Blue** paved the way for an unprecedented expansion of the franchise. Pokémon quickly became the highest-grossing video game series, a title it holds to this day, with an empire encompassing numerous games, anime series, movies, and merchandise.

This remarkable growth was fueled by the launch of subsequent titles that built upon the core concepts of collecting and battling Pokémon. The franchise's adaptability and commitment to innovation have allowed it to evolve continuously while staying true to its origins. Pokémon's enduring popularity continues to inspire new generations of players, making it a timeless cornerstone of the gaming world.

Game Mechanics and Features

Exploring the innovative mechanics that made Pokémon Red and Blue captivating for players of all ages.

The game follows a classic RPG format with turn-based combat and random encounters.

Pokémon Red and Blue are rooted in the traditions of role-playing games (RPGs), featuring a turn-based combat system that became iconic. Players take turns choosing moves from a set list, adding a strategic layer to battles. Each move has its own strengths and weaknesses, which means players must carefully plan their strategy to win.

Random encounters add another dimension. While traversing various terrains—from forests to caves—players face unexpected battles with wild Pokémon. This unpredictability keeps the game engaging, as players never know when they'll encounter a rare Pokémon or face a wild challenge. These mechanics helped set Pokémon apart and laid a foundation upon which future titles would build. The combination of strategy and chance delivers an experience that is both captivating and rewarding.

Players take on the role of a trainer, capturing and training Pokémon to battle other trainers.

In Pokémon Red and Blue, players embark on a journey as Pokémon trainers, with a mission to capture and train creatures known as Pokémon. This role-playing aspect forms the heart of the game's appeal, providing a sense of progression and accomplishment as players collect Pokémon and enhance their skills.

Training is crucial to success. Players must raise their Pokémon by gaining experience points in battle, allowing them to level up and become more powerful. This is supplemented by battling other trainers encountered throughout the game. These encounters offer players a chance to test their teams and refine their strategies. This dynamic—capturing, training, and battling—creates a cycle of engagement that keeps players immersed in the world of Pokémon.

Players choose a starter Pokémon from three options: Bulbasaur, Charmander, or Squirtle.

At the start of their adventure, players make a pivotal choice that influences their gameplay experience: selecting a starter Pokémon. The options—Bulbasaur, Charmander, or Squirtle—each represent a different element with unique strengths and weaknesses. Bulbasaur, a grass type, is known for its sturdy nature and healing capabilities.

Charmander, a fire type, offers offensive power with its flame-based attacks. Lastly, Squirtle, a water type, provides a balanced approach with its defensive skills.

This choice impacts the initial strategy players will employ, as each starter type has elemental advantages and disadvantages in battles throughout the game. This decision introduces players to the elemental rock-paper-scissors dynamic that is fundamental to Pokémon battling strategy, making it a thoughtful and replay-worthy part of the Pokémon experience.

The ultimate goal is to defeat the Elite Four and become the Pokémon Champion.

In Pokémon Red and Blue, the central narrative arc leads players to the challenge of the Elite Four. This group of powerful trainers represents the pinnacle of Pokémon mastery. Defeating them requires a well-balanced team, strategic planning, and a deep understanding of Pokémon types and tactics.

The journey to challenge the Elite Four involves collecting all eight gym badges, each requiring players to defeat a Gym Leader with their own specialized teams. This progression builds anticipation and hones the player's skills, culminating in a climactic showdown to become the Pokémon Champion. This structure not only provides a satisfying sense of progress but also encourages players to experiment with various strategies and team compositions, enhancing the game’s replayability.

Players must also complete their Pokédex by capturing all 151 Pokémon.

Beyond battling, Pokémon Red and Blue introduced the concept of the Pokédex—an encyclopedic device that tracks Pokémon as they are captured. Completing the Pokédex by capturing all 151 Pokémon is one of the game's core objectives, adding a layer of depth and challenge.

This task encourages exploration and interaction with other players for trading exclusive Pokémon. Some Pokémon are only available in one version of the game, making cooperation essential to complete the Pokédex. This not only fosters a sense of community among players but also adds a collectible component to the game, appealing to completionists and encouraging players to fully engage with the Pokémon world.

Pokémon can evolve into stronger forms, which adds depth to the strategy involved in the game.

Evolution is a key feature in Pokémon Red and Blue that significantly impacts gameplay strategy. As Pokémon gain experience and levels, they can evolve into more powerful forms. This evolution often results in stat boosts and the acquisition of new abilities, making them more effective in battle.

Players must decide whether to evolve Pokémon when they reach the appropriate level or wait to learn specific moves earlier. This decision-making process adds complexity and personalization to team-building, as players weigh the benefits and drawbacks of evolving at different times. Evolution enriches the strategic depth of the game, encouraging players to consider both short-term and long-term goals while managing their teams. This mechanic remains a beloved and integral part of the Pokémon series.

Cultural Impact and Legacy

Pokémon Red and Blue didn't just sell millions of copies; they ignited a global phenomenon. Here's a look at their lasting impact.

The games contributed significantly to the global Pokémon craze, influencing toys, collectibles, and an animated TV series.

The release of Pokémon Red and Blue in the late 1990s sparked an unprecedented Pokémon mania. These games introduced players to a captivating world of adventure, strategy, and discovery, but their impact extended far beyond the digital realm. The success of the games catalyzed a lucrative market for Pokémon-themed merchandise.

Toys and collectibles became must-have items for fans eager to continue their Pokémon journey outside the Game Boy screen. Action figures, plush toys, and a plethora of other collectibles quickly filled store shelves, embodying the characters players had come to adore.

Moreover, the animated TV series, which debuted shortly after the games, played a crucial role in enhancing the franchise's popularity. It provided a vibrant narrative that expanded on the games' storyline, allowing fans to engage with their favorite Pokémon in new ways. The show's catchy theme song and memorable characters helped anchor Pokémon as a fixture in popular culture.

Pokémon Red and Blue paved the way for numerous sequels, expanding lore and capturing new fans.

The success of Pokémon Red and Blue laid a strong foundation for an ever-expanding franchise. Since their release, countless sequels and spin-offs have been launched, each building upon the rich lore established by the original games. This allowed developers to explore new regions, introduce new Pokémon species, and create more intricate storylines.

The fresh installments continually innovate gameplay mechanics and enhance graphics and sound, attracting new generations of players. Each new game maintains the core elements of exploration and collection while adding novel features to keep the experience engaging and fresh.

This strategic approach not only builds on nostalgia but also ensures the franchise remains relevant. Pokémon's ability to adapt and evolve has kept older fans returning while drawing in curious newcomers, thus perpetuating its legacy across decades.

They introduced the concept of 'Gotta Catch 'Em All,' promoting exploration and collection.

Pokémon Red and Blue introduced an iconic tagline that encapsulates the series' core appeal: "Gotta Catch 'Em All." This phrase became a driving motivator for players, encouraging them to explore the game’s vast world in search of every Pokémon species.

The games rewarded meticulous exploration and the completion of the Pokédex, instilling a sense of achievement. Players traded Pokémon with friends, both in-person and later online, fostering a community of cooperation and competition.

This mantra of collecting them all was innovative, setting a precedent for future games that emphasize collecting as a significant gameplay element. The excitement of discovering and capturing rare Pokémon has become a timeless thrill, repeatedly drawing players back into the series to see what's new.

The Pokémon Trading Card Game arose from this solid foundation, further cementing its place in popular culture.

The Pokémon Trading Card Game (TCG) emerged as a natural extension of the Pokémon Red and Blue experience.

Released to capitalize on the games' success, the TCG offered fans another way to interact with their favorite Pokémon.

With strategic gameplay that mirrored the competitive elements of the video games, the Pokémon TCG quickly became a popular hobby in its own right. It encouraged social interaction as players met to trade cards and partake in competitive matches.

The trading card game not only helped sustain interest in the Pokémon brand but also expanded its reach into different entertainment sectors. Today, it remains a staple in the card gaming community, providing fans with a tangible connection to the franchise and contributing to its enduring popularity.

Pokémon remains a highly profitable franchise, influencing how games are marketed and franchised today.

Pokémon's journey from video game sensation to a globally recognized brand offers valuable lessons in franchise marketing and management. The success of Pokémon Red and Blue highlighted the importance of cross-media promotion, where games, anime, merchandise, and events complement each other to reinforce brand presence.

This approach has since been emulated by many in the gaming and entertainment industries, showcasing the potential of a cohesive, multifaceted marketing strategy. By continuously reinventing itself through new iterations and collaborations, Pokémon has maintained its relevance and profitability over decades.

The franchise's impact is visible in how it has set new standards for the business models of game merchandising and marketing, influencing brands to create ecosystems that extend brand longevity well beyond the virtual world.

They demonstrated the potential of handheld gaming as a dominant force in the gaming industry.

Pokémon Red and Blue were instrumental in proving the viability and allure of handheld gaming systems. Released for the Nintendo Game Boy, these titles showcased that deep, engaging game experiences weren't limited to home consoles.

The success of these games contributed significantly to the Game Boy system's popularity, demonstrating that players valued the ability to take their adventures on the go. This momentum encouraged developers to invest more in handheld game development, leading to a wealth of innovative titles across various platforms in subsequent years.

Today, handheld gaming continues to thrive through more sophisticated devices and mobile platforms. The groundwork laid by Pokémon Red and Blue has been crucial in shaping the portable gaming landscape, influencing how games are designed and played on mobile platforms.

Critical and Commercial Success

Analyzing the critical acclaim and commercial triumphs of Pokémon Red and Blue. They weren't just games; they were milestones.

The games received strong positive reviews for their depth, creativity, and replayability.

Upon release, **Pokémon Red and Blue** garnered widespread critical acclaim due to their innovative approach to role-playing games (RPGs). Reviewers noted the games' depth, with over 150 Pokémon to collect, each with unique abilities and evolutionary paths. This provided extensive opportunities for strategic gameplay and encouraged players to explore different combinations in battles.

Additionally, the creativity involved in designing a world filled with diverse creatures and engaging environments set these games apart from their contemporaries. The replayability factor was enhanced by the need to trade Pokémon with friends to complete the Pokédex, fostering a sense of community among players.

They sold over 31 million copies worldwide, making them some of the best-selling games of all time.

The commercial success of **Pokémon Red and Blue** was nothing short of phenomenal. With sales exceeding 31 million copies worldwide, these titles became one of the best-selling video games of all time. Their success can be attributed to their appeal across various age groups and cultural barriers. The allure of capturing and battling mythical creatures captivated players globally.

This commercial triumph laid the groundwork for the Pokémon franchise to become a global powerhouse. The games' massive sales figures were a testament not only to their quality but also to their ability to resonate with a vast audience, ensuring Pokémon's place in the annals of gaming history.

Reviewers praised the intuitive gameplay mechanics and the balance between simplicity and depth.

Pokémon Red and Blue stood out for their carefully crafted gameplay mechanics. Reviewers applauded the games for their intuitive design, which made them accessible to newcomers while offering depth for seasoned players. The basic mechanics of catching, training, and battling Pokémon were simple enough for anyone to grasp, making the experience enjoyable and addictive.

Yet, beneath this simplicity lay a layer of strategic depth. Players could optimize their teams, recognize type advantages, and devise strategies to defeat rival trainers and gym leaders. This balance between accessibility and depth was a core factor in the games' enduring appeal, allowing players to progressively master their skills. **Despite being released on an aging platform, they**

showcased the Game Boy's capabilities and revitalized handheld gaming markets.

Released on the original Game Boy, **Pokémon Red and Blue** demonstrated that the aging platform still had significant potential. The games maximized the hardware's capabilities, featuring detailed sprites and a richly interactive world. This technical achievement contributed significantly to their charm and appeal.

Their success revitalized the handheld gaming market, proving that compelling game design could extend the lifespan of older hardware. This led to renewed interest in the Game Boy and handheld gaming overall, paving the way for future innovations in the sector.

The success of Pokémon Red and Blue was a breakthrough for Nintendo, ensuring the Game Boy's continued popularity.

For Nintendo, the success of **Pokémon Red and Blue** marked a significant breakthrough. At a time when the Game Boy's popularity was waning, these games reinvigorated interest in the handheld console. They transformed the Game Boy into a must-have device once more, boosting its sales and prolonging its relevance in the market.

Moreover, the games established a secure platform for future Pokémon titles, creating a sustainable ecosystem for the franchise to grow. Their success underscored the importance of innovative game design in revitalizing hardware platforms, a lesson that continues to inform Nintendo's strategy.

The games' success paved the way for localization of further titles, bringing more Japanese games to Western audiences.

The international success of **Pokémon Red and Blue** set a new standard for localizing Japanese games for Western markets. Before Pokémon, many Japanese titles remained confined to their home country due to perceived cultural differences and market risks. The widespread popularity of these games demonstrated the global appeal of wellcrafted RPGs.

This paved the way for other Japanese developers to bring their titles to a broader audience, expanding the global gaming landscape. As a result, Western players gained access to a wealth of new experiences and genres previously unavailable, influencing game design and player expectations worldwide.

Chapter 23: Half-Life - A New Era of Storytelling

Valve's **Half-Life** was a landmark title in narrative-driven games. Released in 1998, it combined traditional gameplay elements with a compelling story, forever changing how developers approached storytelling in games. **The Birth of Half-Life**

Half-Life was developed by Valve, pushing the boundaries of how stories were told in games during the late 1990s.

Half-Life was released in 1998, developed by the then-newfound company Valve Corporation.

In 1998, **Half-Life** marked the debut of Valve Corporation, a new player in the gaming industry. The game's release was a significant event, showcasing the ambition and creativity of a team that would go on to shape the future of gaming. Valves entry into the market was filled with promise, as they sought to innovate within the boundaries of what was considered possible at the time.

This initial release was met with both critical and commercial success, establishing Valve as not just a capable developer but a pioneer in the field. Half-Life quickly gained a reputation for its rich storytelling and immersive gameplay, setting a high standard for the era. The impact of this release resonated throughout the gaming community, marking a pivotal moment for both Valve and the gaming landscape as a whole.

The game was built using a heavily modified version of the Quake engine, showcasing technical innovations.

Valve employed a considerably modified version of the Quake engine to construct Half-Life, highlighting their commitment to technical innovation. This allowed them to achieve groundbreaking visual effects and refined gameplay mechanics that were unprecedented at the time. By tweaking this engine, Valve was able to create more complex environments and realistic physics.

These engine modifications were crucial in delivering the seamless, narrative-driven experience that Half-Life is known for. Players could explore intricately designed levels that reacted dynamically to their actions, offering a level of immersion that had not been felt in first-person shooters before. This attention to detail in the technical aspects was instrumental in the game's critical acclaim and lasting legacy.

Half-Life introduced players to the character Gordon Freeman, an unlikely hero who became an iconic figure in gaming.

In Half-Life, gamers were introduced to **Gordon Freeman**, a scientist turned hero in the midst of chaos. Unlike the typical protagonists found in games of its time, Freeman was portrayed as an ordinary man thrust into extraordinary circumstances, making him a relatable and enduring character. His silent persona allowed players to project their own emotions and strategies onto him, enhancing the immersive experience.

Gordon Freeman's character design and backstory were integral in crafting a narrative that felt personal and engaging. As players guided Freeman through the Black Mesa Research Facility, they developed a connection to both the character and the storyline. This strong narrative connection helped cement Gordon Freeman's status as an iconic figure in the gaming community, influencing character development in future games.

The game's blend of action and storytelling set a new standard for first-person shooters.

Half-Life expertly combined fast-paced action with a compelling story, redefining what players could expect from firstperson shooters. Unlike earlier games that often prioritized action over narrative depth, Half-Life seamlessly integrated the two, delivering a cohesive and engaging experience. The game balanced tense combat scenarios with plot-driven exploration, ensuring that players were always immersed.

This blend of action and storytelling was a revelation for the genre, providing a template for how first-person shooters could evolve. Developers saw the possibilities of narrative focus without sacrificing gameplay intensity, pushing the medium towards more sophisticated and mature storytelling. Half-Life's success in this regard set a precedent that many future games would aspire to follow.

Valve's focus on a linear, story-driven experience was a departure from the norm, setting it apart from its predecessors.

Half-Life's linear narrative was a bold departure from the multiplayer-focused or level-based structure of contemporary shooters. Valve's deliberate choice to emphasize a story-driven experience allowed players to feel like active participants in an unfolding movie. This decision represented a significant shift in game design principles, moving away from the traditional fragmented level approach.

The cohesive storyline provided a sense of progression and engagement that was different from the episodic nature of previous games. This focus on storytelling allowed players to become deeply invested in the game's world and its characters, creating a memorable and impactful experience. Valve's approach set Half-Life apart from its predecessors and competitors, solidifying its place in gaming history.

Groundbreaking Gameplay Mechanics

Half-Life revolutionized gameplay mechanics in ways that influenced countless other games.

The game's use of scripted sequences allowed for a more immersive storytelling experience.

The introduction of scripted sequences in **Half-Life** was a pivotal innovation that set a new standard for storytelling in video games. Unlike traditional cutscenes that often detached the player from the action, scripted sequences unfolded dynamically within the game world. This meant that crucial story events, character interactions, and dramatic moments occurred in real-time, seamlessly integrating with the gameplay.

These sequences were carefully choreographed to maintain player immersion, ensuring that gamers remained an active participant rather than a passive observer. Such a design choice enhanced the overall narrative impact, providing an unparalleled level of engagement. By witnessing events firsthand through the protagonist's eyes, players experienced a deeper emotional connection to the unfolding story, paving the way for more sophisticated storytelling in gaming.

Half-Life minimized the use of cutscenes, giving players more control and a seamless narrative flow.

In a bold departure from established norms, **Half-Life** minimized the reliance on traditional cutscenes, which often disrupted gameplay flow and broke immersion. Instead, the game allowed players to remain in control for much of the narrative, ensuring a continuous and uninterrupted experience.

By allowing players to explore at their own pace and interact with the game world during critical plot points, Valve successfully crafted a more fluid storytelling approach. This method not only kept the player engaged but also offered a sense of agency seldom seen at the time. The ability to influence the pace of narrative exploration helped usher in a new era, where storytelling and player interaction could exist harmoniously without sacrificing the integrity of either.

Environmental storytelling was heavily utilized, with the game world itself conveying parts of the narrative.

Half-Life mastered the art of environmental storytelling, where the game world itself became a conduit for narrative exposition. This design philosophy allowed the setting and environments to tell stories through visual cues, background details, and interactive elements.

Pictured documents scattered across desks, cryptic messages scribbled on walls, and the eerie silence of abandoned facilities all contributed vital context and background to the main story. Through this immersive technique, players could piece together the narrative puzzle on their own, engaging them intellectually and emotionally. This approach deepened the player's connection to the game world, inviting exploration and curiosity **Innovative AI made enemy encounters feel dynamic and challenging.**

Half-Life excelled in creating a sense of realism and unpredictability through its groundbreaking AI systems. Enemies in the game were designed with sophisticated behavior patterns, allowing them to react dynamically to the player's actions.

For instance, soldiers could coordinate tactical maneuvers, take cover, and flank the player, while alien creatures showcased distinct attack patterns based on their nature. This level of AI responsiveness not only heightened the challenge but also suggested a greater intelligence and awareness within the game world. Players were prompted to devise strategic approaches and adapt to evolving scenarios, ensuring that each encounter felt fresh and stimulating.

Puzzle-solving elements integrated with combat kept the gameplay engaging and varied.

Incorporating puzzle-solving elements into the core gameplay of **Half-Life** added a layer of depth that distinguished it from purely action-oriented titles. These puzzles were intricately woven into the environment, seamlessly blending with the narrative and combat mechanics.

Players needed to employ both strategic thinking and reflexive skills to solve challenges, such as figuring out how to advance past blocked pathways or manipulating the environment to defeat enemies. This multifaceted gameplay approach prevented monotony, as players were constantly required to switch between thoughtful problem-solving and adrenaline-pumping combat. As a result, **Half-Life** delivered a richly varied experience, holding players' interest throughout the entire journey.

Storytelling and Atmosphere

The game's atmosphere and narrative approach created an unmatched sense of immersion.

Half-Life's narrative unfolded in real-time, allowing players to feel part of the unfolding story.

Unlike many games of its time, *Half-Life* eschewed traditional cutscenes in favor of a real-time narrative experience. This design choice allowed players to stay in control as the story unfolded around them, creating a seamless blend of gameplay and storytelling. Players assumed the role of Gordon Freeman, a scientist at the Black Mesa Research Facility, witnessing unexpected events in real time.

The immersive storytelling was enhanced by the decision to keep the player in first-person perspective at almost all times. By doing so, players felt an unprecedented level of immersion, as they were never pulled away from Freeman's viewpoint. This approach to real-time storytelling was revolutionary at the time, and it influenced countless games in the industry, setting a new standard for how stories could be told in an interactive medium.

The setting of the Black Mesa Research Facility was richly detailed and eerily believable.

The Black Mesa Research Facility was more than just a backdrop for *Half-Life*; it felt like a living, breathing place. The creators at Valve meticulously crafted this labyrinthine complex, filling it with detailed textures, functioning laboratories, and realistic machinery. This attention to detail made the facility feel both authentic and foreboding.

Each section of Black Mesa, from its underground rail network to its surface labs, was intricately designed to enhance the player's sense of exploration and curiosity. The level of detail contributed significantly to the game's atmosphere, making each corridor, lab, and office feel unique. The realistic setting grounded the fantastical elements of the game, allowing players to suspend disbelief and become fully immersed in this intricately constructed world.

Sound design played a critical role in building tension and maintaining an immersive environment.

Sound in *Half-Life* was not just an afterthought—it was a tool used carefully to enhance the game's mood and amplify its narrative. The subtle sounds of distant machinery, echoing footsteps, and ominous ambient noises all worked together to create a sense of isolation and tension. These elements kept players on edge, as they never knew what lurked around the next corner.

The game's music, composed by Kelly Bailey, complemented these ambient sounds with tracks that heightened moments of action and suspense. This well-executed sound design was crucial in maintaining the immersive environment of Black Mesa, drawing players deeper into the world of *Half-Life* and ensuring that every sound contributed to the storytelling and atmosphere.

Characters and interactions were woven seamlessly into the gameplay, enhancing realism.

In *Half-Life*, characters were not merely there to provide exposition through dialogue. Instead, they were active participants in the game's world, reacting to events, interacting with the environment, and contributing to the story's progression. The scientists and security guards at Black Mesa had their own personalities and agendas, making them feel like real people caught in extraordinary circumstances.

The interactions with these characters added to the game's realism. Players could witness and participate in NPC conversations, observe their behaviors, and even affect their fates, which made the player feel truly a part of the story. This seamless integration of characters into the gameplay was a significant departure from the static NPCs seen in earlier games.

The game's pacing was meticulously balanced to keep players engaged from start to finish.

Valve's attention to pacing in *Half-Life* ensured that players remained engaged throughout the entire experience. The game expertly balanced moments of high tension and intense action with periods of exploration and problem-solving, allowing for a dynamic and varied gameplay experience. Challenges were introduced in a way that felt organic, maintaining the flow of the narrative.

This careful balance prevented the game from becoming monotonous while still providing a coherent and evolving story. Players were constantly driven forward by their curiosity and the need to unravel the mystery of the Black Mesa incident. This balanced pacing was a key factor in the game's success, as it captured players' attention and guided them through the gripping narrative.

Technical Achievements

Half-Life was notable for its technical accomplishments, setting new benchmarks for video game production.

The modified Quake engine allowed for advanced graphics and physics for its time.

Half-Life's visual achievements were partly due to its modified Quake engine. This engine offered advanced graphics capabilities that were groundbreaking in the late 1990s. Valve took the existing engine and extensively reworked it, enhancing its capabilities to support more realistic environments and complex animations.

One of the standout features was the implementation of more sophisticated lighting effects, which added depth and realism to the game world. Additionally, the engine allowed for impressive physics, such as realistic object interactions and environmental effects. These innovations provided players with a more immersive experience, setting a new standard for graphical fidelity in games.

Innovative use of AI created lifelike behavior in non-player characters and enemies.

Half-Life was revolutionary in its use of artificial intelligence to enhance gameplay. The game's AI system enabled non-player characters (NPCs) and enemies to exhibit lifelike behaviors and adapt to players' actions. This was a significant leap from the predictable patterns seen in earlier games.

The AI was capable of forming tactical responses, such as flanking or retreating to cover, making encounters more challenging and dynamic. This intelligence made the game more engaging, as players had to strategically navigate through enemy encounters rather than just relying on brute force. Valve's approach to AI not only enriched the gameplay experience but also inspired future games to adopt more sophisticated AI systems.

Cinematics and environments were loaded in real-time, minimizing load screens and maintaining immersion.

A key technical advancement in Half-Life was its seamless loading of cinematics and environments. Rather than relying on frequent loading screens that could disrupt gaming immersion, Half-Life employed a real-time loading system. This allowed players to transition smoothly between different levels and scenes without noticeable interruptions.

This feature contributed significantly to maintaining the game's narrative flow and keeping players engaged. By ensuring that the game's pacing wasn't hindered by technical limitations, Valve enhanced the overall storytelling experience. This approach was a game-changer and influenced the design of future narrative-driven games.

Half-Life's modular design facilitated the creation of mods, fostering a robust modding community.

Valve's decision to implement a modular design in Half-Life was instrumental in building a strong modding community. The game's architecture allowed players and aspiring developers to create their own content, from simple tweaks to entirely new game scenarios.

This openness not only extended the game's longevity but also led to the development of many successful mods, such as Counter-Strike, which eventually became a standalone game. The ease of modding encouraged creativity and community engagement, establishing Half-Life as a pivotal title not just for its gameplay, but also for its impact on the gaming community as a whole.

Critical Reception and Legacy

Upon release, Half-Life was met with acclaim, cementing its place in gaming history.

Critics praised Half-Life for its innovation and groundbreaking approach to storytelling.

Upon its release, **Half-Life** was lauded for its innovative design, particularly its seamless integration of narrative and gameplay. Unlike many of its predecessors, the game minimized the use of cutscenes, instead immersing players through scripted sequences that unfolded in real time. This pioneering approach gave players a sense of agency and immersion that was unprecedented. Critics noted how this technique effectively maintained the game's momentum and tension, setting a new standard for storytelling in video games.

Moreover, the detailed environmental storytelling in Half-Life allowed players to piece together the narrative by exploring the game world. This approach invited players to engage with the story on a deeper level, analyzing clues and inferring plot details as they progressed. It was this attention to narrative depth and player engagement that earned Half-

Life critical acclaim and set it apart as a trailblazer in the genre.

The game won several "Game of the Year" awards and continues to top "best games of all time" lists.

The accolades for **Half-Life** were numerous and well-deserved. Its unique combination of immersive storytelling and engaging gameplay resulted in it being recognized with numerous "Game of the Year" awards from esteemed publications and gaming authorities. This critical success was echoed by its sustained presence on lists ranking the best video games of all time.

Years after its release, Half-Life maintains its reputation as a groundbreaking title. Its continued inclusion in "best of" lists is a testament to its enduring impact and the influence it had in defining a new era of gaming. By setting such high standards, Half-Life not only exemplified excellence in game design during its time but also remains a benchmark against which new titles are measured.

Its success led to the creation of expansions, sequels, and community-driven projects.

The phenomenal success of **Half-Life** spurred a wealth of expansions and sequels that expanded the original game's universe and further captivated its audience. Titles such as *Half-Life: Opposing Force* and *Half-Life: Blue Shift* offered fresh perspectives and new narratives, enhancing the original story and keeping players engaged.

Beyond official releases, Half-Life also inspired a vibrant modding community, leading to the creation of fan-driven projects and spinoffs, the most famous being *Counter-Strike*, which began as a mod and became a highly successful franchise in its own right. These expansions and community projects underscored the game's broad appeal and its capacity to incite creativity and continued engagement among players.

Half-Life's impact is seen in many modern games, influencing both design philosophy and narrative techniques.

Half-Life's groundbreaking approach to narrative integration and design philosophy had a lasting impact, influencing a generation of game developers. Modern games often incorporate techniques pioneered by Half-Life, such as environmental storytelling, dynamic scripted sequences, and minimal reliance on cutscenes, to enhance immersion and narrative flow.

Games like *Bioshock* and *Portal* demonstrate the lasting legacy of Half-Life's design innovations. Many developers openly cite the game as a major influence in their understanding of interactive storytelling. By reshaping how stories could be told in video games, Half-Life has left a mark on the industry that continues to inspire and challenge game creators to push the boundaries of the medium.

Chapter 24: The Sims - Life Simulation at Its Best

When *The Sims* launched in 2000, it introduced a new kind of gaming focused on life simulation. Players could create and control people in a virtual world, leading to endless possibilities and massive success.

The Beginnings of The Sims

The Sims was developed by Maxis and published by Electronic Arts. The idea came from Will Wright, who had a vision for a game where players could simulate everyday life.

Will Wright, creator of The Sims, drew inspiration from real life and architecture.

Will Wright, the visionary behind *The Sims*, found creative inspiration in his fascination with architecture and urban planning, as well as his own personal experiences. After losing his home in a fire, Wright reimagined the remnants of his life in terms of architectural layouts and urban designs. His passion for building and modifying life environments translated seamlessly into the game's concept, allowing players to craft and control their virtual universes.

Further melding real-world inspiration with playfulness, Wright explored the idea of life-simulation games through his earlier works, notably *SimCity*. With *The Sims*, he built upon these ideas, moving from city simulation to managing the minutiae of human life. Through this unique blend of realism and creativity, Wright provided players with the tools to construct and manage their own social experiments.

The concept of simulating regular life was revolutionary at the time, diverging from traditional gaming genres.

When *The Sims* was conceptualized, the idea of simulating daily life was a departure from the existing gaming norms that involved clear objectives or battles. Traditional games often focused on adventure, strategy, or action, rather than mundane activities like in-game cooking, cleaning, or building interpersonal relationships. However, this shift opened up a new horizon for gaming, embracing the essence of life's unpredictability and routine.

This innovation allowed players to dictate the direction of their gameplay, devoid of predefined goals, thus epitomizing 'sandbox' gameplay. It appealed to players' innate desire to create, control, and experience a myriad of life scenarios. Wright's revolutionary approach invited gamers to engage in a digital reflection of reality, mirroring the intricacies and outcomes of everyday decisions.

Released in 2000, The Sims quickly gained popularity for its unique gameplay and player-driven experiences.

Upon its release in 2000, *The Sims* captured the gaming world's attention with its groundbreaking gameplay and expansive player agency. Unlike many games of its era, *The Sims* was a refreshing experience that emphasized creativity over competition. Players were transported to a digital dollhouse, free to design unique life stories and manage their virtual families as they saw fit.

As word spread about its innovative approach, *The Sims* rapidly gained a devoted fan base, appealing to a broad spectrum of gamers. Its popularity was fueled by the endless possibilities of player-driven storytelling and the customization of characters and homes. The game's success led to an array of expansion packs that further fueled its growth, solidifying *The Sims* as a significant milestone in gaming history.

Maxis ensured the game was user-friendly, making it accessible to a wide audience.

Maxis, understanding the groundbreaking nature of *The Sims*, focused on creating an intuitive and accessible user experience. Their design philosophy was rooted in simplicity, catering to both seasoned gamers and newcomers alike.

This approach was crucial in demystifying complex simulations, making the game enjoyable for a diverse audience.

The user interface was developed to be straightforward, providing easy navigation through various menus and building tools. Maxis prioritized an approachable tutorial system within the game, helping players of varying skill levels understand and engage with gameplay mechanics.

Accessibility features and user-friendly controls ensured that *The Sims* resonated beyond the traditional gaming community, becoming a cultural phenomenon that invited everyone to participate in the virtual simulation of life.

Gameplay Mechanics

The Sims offered players the freedom to create characters and build their lives. Its gameplay mechanics were a major draw.

Players could design and build homes, a feature that encouraged creativity.

One of the most revolutionary aspects of *The Sims* was the ability to design and build homes from the ground up. This feature allowed players to unleash their creativity by constructing anything from a humble abode to a sprawling mansion. The intuitive building tools made it accessible for everyone, regardless of their experience in gaming or architecture.

Players could choose from an array of architectural styles, interior furnishings, and decorations that allowed for personal expressions of style and flair. The customization options offered multiple possibilities, from traditional to modern designs.

The character creation tool allowed players to customize their Sims' appearances and personalities.

The character creation tool in *The Sims* was another standout feature. Players had the ability to tailor their Sims' physical appearances, from hairstyles and facial features to clothing choices. This level of customization connected players to their digital avatars like never before. But it was not just about looks—the personality sliders let players assign traits that would impact how Sims interacted and reacted within the game.

These traits influenced the Sims' aspirations, shaping what made them happy or sad. This depth of personalization added layers to gameplay and encouraged players to experiment with different character dynamics.

Day-to-day activities simulate real life, from eating and sleeping to forming relationships.

The gameplay of *The Sims* was rooted in its realistic simulation of daily life. Players guided their Sims through mundane tasks and significant life events, such as eating meals, maintaining personal hygiene, and managing sleep. This attention to detail created an immersive experience that resonated with players who could relate to these everyday activities.

Moreover, forming relationships was a pivotal part of the game. Sims could develop friendships, fall in love, and even get married. The complex social interactions required players to navigate conversations, emotions, and social skills, making the game both challenging and engaging.

The game's open-ended nature meant there were no strict win conditions, offering endless playability.

Unlike many games at the time, *The Sims* did not impose rigid goals or win conditions. This open-ended nature was groundbreaking, giving players freedom to define their own objectives. Whether players pursued career success, personal happiness, or creative endeavors, the game allowed them to forge their own paths.

This flexibility fostered a sense of exploration and replayability—each new game could unfold differently, based solely on player choices. The absence of a definitive end game provided an invitation to continue playing indefinitely, appealing to those who enjoyed charting life's unpredictable journey.

The Social Aspect

The Sims was more than just a building and simulation game; it was about social interaction.

Sims could form relationships, ranging from friendships to romantic connections.

One of the core elements that made *The Sims* groundbreaking was its sophisticated relationship mechanics. Players could steer their Sims into a wide range of relationships, from casual friendships to deep romantic entanglements. By interacting through conversations, shared activities, and even gestures, Sims could develop bonds that influenced their behavior and emotions.

These relationships were not merely for decoration; they had tangible effects on gameplay. Friends could offer emotional support, while romantic partners could enhance the life satisfaction of a Sim. This complexity in relationship dynamics allowed players to explore different social paths and outcomes, adding layers of realism and engagement to the virtual world. The depth of relationship-building in *The Sims* was one of its most compelling features, making it an enduring classic.

Social interactions could influence Sims' moods and progress in the game.

In *The Sims*, social interactions played a pivotal role in determining a Sim's mood and overall progress. A well-curated social network could open doors to career advancement, faster skill development, and enhanced life satisfaction. Conversely, negative interactions, such as arguments or breakups, could lead to mood declines and stifled progression.

Moods in *The Sims* were a critical game mechanic, dictating a Sim's willingness and efficiency in tackling daily tasks and reaching personal goals. By placing such a strong emphasis on interpersonal relationships, the game mirrored real-life consequences where social success is tightly knit with individual fulfillment. This feature resonated well with players, encouraging them to meticulously manage their Sims' social circles and ensuring their virtual lives are wellbalanced and fruitful.

Players often found joy in creating drama and stories within their Sims' lives.

One of the most cherished aspects of *The Sims* is the storytelling potential it offers players. Many found joy in orchestrating dramatic scenarios and weaving intricate narratives within their Sims' lives. Whether it was crafting a tumultuous love triangle or engineering a rivalry between neighbors, the sandbox nature of the game provided endless creative outlets.

This ability to create drama wasn't merely for entertainment; it became a form of self-expression for many players. As drama unfolded, players could observe the repercussions and alter the course of events, effectively becoming the writers and directors of their private soap operas. This freedom to manipulate the narrative not only heightened player engagement but also fostered a vibrant community that shared experiences and stories, further enriching the game's legacy.

The game's AI allowed for natural interactions, adding depth to the social dynamics.

The AI system in *The Sims* was revolutionary for its time, allowing for interactions that felt organic and nuanced. Sims would autonomously react to the environment and each other, generating unexpected yet believable social dynamics. This sophisticated AI brought a layer of unpredictability and authenticity to the game, as Sims would initiate conversations, conflict, or friendships without direct player intervention.

This autonomy helped simulate a living world, where players could witness genuine social interactions unfold before their eyes. It added a strategic element to the game as well, where players needed to anticipate and influence their Sims' social behavior strategically. The natural interactions fostered by the AI created a rich tapestry of social possibilities, making each playthrough unique and deeply immersive.

Cultural Impact and Legacy

The Sims made a significant impact on the gaming world and popular culture, leaving a lasting legacy.

The game appealed to a broad, diverse audience, including many who didn't consider themselves gamers.

When *The Sims* was released, it quickly resonated with a diverse demographic that extended beyond the traditional gaming community. Its intuitive gameplay and relatable themes of everyday life drew in people who often considered themselves non-gamers. The game offered the ability to express creativity through designing and managing sims' lives, homes, and careers, attracting players who had interests in storytelling, interior design, and social dynamics.

Moreover, the absence of overt violence or complex skill requirements made it accessible to people of varying ages and backgrounds. *The Sims* became a social phenomenon, bridging the gap between hardcore gamers and casual players. It allowed individuals to explore fictitious lives, actions, and outcomes, which had a cathartic and often humorous appeal, thereby broadening its appeal across different segments of society.

The Sims influenced other life simulation games and contributed to new genres in gaming.

The Sims not only revolutionized life simulation games but also paved the way for future titles by setting a new standard. Its success inspired a multitude of similar games that adopted its core mechanics—creating and managing virtual lives. Additionally, it had an influential role in the development of sandbox and open-world genres, as the freedom it offered to players defined a new approach to interactive storytelling.

Developers across the globe took notice, leading to the emergence of games like *Animal Crossing* and *Second Life*, each integrating life simulation aspects that *The Sims* showcased. This ripple effect expanded beyond traditional gaming, influencing mobile games and virtual reality spaces, ultimately demonstrating the versatile and far-reaching impact of life simulation concepts introduced by *The Sims*.

Its success led to numerous expansion packs and sequels, expanding on the original concept.

Following its groundbreaking success, *The Sims* saw the release of numerous expansion packs and sequels, each adding new dimensions to the original game. Expansion packs introduced fresh elements such as pets, new career paths, and additional customizable in-game items, enhancing the depth and replayability of the game.

This iterative approach kept the player base engaged and continuously attracted new players. Each sequel integrated updated graphics, expanded customization options, and more sophisticated life simulations, adhering to the franchise's evolving innovation standard. By consistently expanding and refining the core gameplay, *The Sims* maintained its relevance and adaptiveness, cementing its legacy as an ever-evolving digital life simulation that captivated millions.

The Sims remains a benchmark for life simulation games, beloved by fans worldwide.

Today, *The Sims* stands as a quintessential life simulation benchmark, renowned for its ability to engage players with endless creativity possibilities. It has built a profound community, thriving with enthusiastic fans who actively engage in modding, sharing stories, and creating gameplay content, further extending the game's life cycle beyond official releases.

The franchise's influence is global, its localizations adapting to diverse cultures while maintaining universal appeal. It serves as an enduring cultural touchstone noted for its narrative flexibility and open-ended style, offering limitless ways to play. Even two decades after its initial release, *The Sims* continues to evoke fond nostalgia and remains a pivotal reference point within the genre, capturing the essence of everyday life in a way few other games have achieved.

Chapter 25: World of Warcraft - MMORPG Giant

World of Warcraft took the MMORPG genre to new heights after its release in 2004. With a rich world, extensive lore, and social gameplay, it attracted millions of players and defined online gaming for a generation.

The Birth of a Giant

When Blizzard Entertainment released World of Warcraft (WoW) in 2004, it transformed the MMORPG landscape with its innovative gameplay and immersive world.

WoW launched on November 23, 2004, and quickly became a massive success.

Released by Blizzard Entertainment on November 23, 2004, **World of Warcraft** (WoW) immediately captured the gaming world's attention. Within weeks, it had amassed a staggering number of players, solidifying *WoW* as not just a game but a cultural phenomenon. The seamless integration of expansive worlds and rich narrative content set it apart from previous MMORPGs.

WoW's early success was driven by its appeal to both hardcore gamers and a broader audience. Blizzard's reputation for quality also contributed to the trust and interest surrounding the game. As players embarked on quests and formed alliances, the game offered a blend of adventure and community-driven interaction that resonated with many.

In just a few months, *WoW* had over a million subscribers, setting records and ensuring its place in gaming history.

The game was built on the success and lore of the Warcraft series.

World of Warcraft drew from the rich tapestry of the established *Warcraft* series, leveraging its extensive lore and beloved characters. This deep narrative foundation gave WoW a unique advantage, as fans were already invested in the game's universe. The intricate stories of the WarCraft world provided a compelling backdrop for the game's gameplay mechanics.

The familiar environment, combined with an entirely new way to experience it, attracted longtime followers of the series. Players explored iconic locations and encountered famous characters like Thrall and Illidan. This seamless transition from the real-time strategy format to a massive multiplayer online experience was a masterstroke in game development, allowing players to feel at home while discovering new aspects of the *Warcraft* lore.

WoW offered a vast online universe that connected millions of players.

One of **World of Warcraft's** distinguishing features was its ability to create a living, breathing universe that players inhabited together. Its innovative server technology allowed millions of players worldwide to explore, quest, and collaborate in a continual online environment. Each player could personalize their journey by selecting a race and class, providing a unique gaming experience.

The communal aspect of WoW was enhanced by guilds and raids that encouraged player cooperation. These features fostered long-term friendships and alliances within the game, bringing players closer regardless of geographical differences. This profound interconnectivity was instrumental in the sustained success of WoW, as it transformed gaming into a shared experience.

The game's subscription model changed how players engaged with games.

Blizzard's decision to adopt a subscription-based model for **World of Warcraft** marked a significant shift in the gaming industry. It established a steady revenue stream and allowed the developers to fund continuous updates and expansion of the game. This model redefined how players interacted with the game, encouraging a deeper commitment to the *WoW* universe.

By requiring a monthly fee, the game cultivated a dedicated player base willing to invest in an ever-evolving experience. This investment was reciprocated with frequent content updates and robust customer support, creating a sense of value in the subscription. As a result, WoW not only set the standard for future MMORPGs but also influenced the broader gaming industry's approach to monetization and player engagement.

With continuous updates, Blizzard kept the game fresh and engaging.

Continuous updates and expansions were crucial in maintaining **World of Warcraft's** allure. Blizzard's commitment to evolving the game world kept players engaged and returning for more. Landmark expansions such as *The Burning Crusade* and *Wrath of the Lich King* introduced new areas, quests, and gameplay mechanics, enhancing and expanding the game's universe.

Besides expansions, regular patches addressed gameplay balance and introduced new events, keeping the world dynamic and challenging. This proactive approach to development ensured that even the most seasoned players always found something new to explore or achieve.

Blizzard's strategy of constant innovation and modification was a key factor in WoW's long-lasting appeal, illustrating the potential of online games to grow and change over time.

Core Gameplay Mechanics

World of Warcraft's gameplay mechanics set a new standard for MMORPGs, providing a rich and accessible player experience.

The game featured a class-based system, allowing for diverse playstyles.

World of Warcraft introduced a robust class system that provided players with a wide array of playstyles, each tailored to different gaming preferences. From the arcane magic of Mages to the brute force of Warriors, the game offered a class for everyone. Each class had unique abilities and roles within the game world, encouraging players to specialize and master their chosen paths.

This system promoted both individuality and collaboration. Players could make strategic choices about their characters, encouraging a deep connection with their avatars. Additionally, it supported diverse team dynamics, as parties often required a mix of classes to excel in challenging content such as dungeons and raids. This diversity not only enhanced the gameplay experience but also fostered a vibrant community.

Players could choose from multiple races, each with unique abilities.

World of Warcraft offered players the chance to customize their characters further by choosing from a variety of races. Each race, ranging from stalwart Humans to exotic Night Elves, came with its own unique set of racial abilities, adding an extra layer of strategy and personalization.

The choice of race influenced gameplay style, with abilities that provided distinct advantages, such as increased agility or bonus professions skills. This variety within the game enabled players to craft characters that aligned not only with their gameplay goals but also their narrative preferences, creating a uniquely personalized journey through the immersive world of Azeroth.

Quest-driven progression encouraged exploration and adventure.

In **World of Warcraft**, quests served as the primary method of character progression. This design encouraged players to delve into every corner of Azeroth, uncovering its mysteries and lore in the process. Quests ranged from simple tasks to epic storylines, each contributing to the world's deep narrative and the player's growth.

This quest-driven approach ensured that players had a sense of purpose and direction, reducing aimlessness often found in early MMORPGs. It also fostered a spirit of adventure and discovery, as uncovering new areas and completing quests often led to significant rewards, be it powerful gear, experience points, or new allies. Players found themselves immersed in a living, breathing world full of stories waiting to be revealed.

Innovative raid and dungeon mechanics promoted group play.

Dungeons and raids were cornerstones of the **World of Warcraft** experience, providing challenging content that required teamwork and strategy. The game introduced innovative mechanics that defined the standard for collaborative gameplay in MMORPGs, establishing roles such as tank, healer, and damage dealer as essential.

Players needed to communicate and coordinate effectively, overcoming complex encounters with meticulously planned actions. These group-oriented activities not only rewarded players with powerful equipment and prestigious titles but also strengthened social bonds and fostered a sense of community, as friends and strangers alike could rally together to conquer Azeroth's most formidable foes.

WoW's user-friendly interface was accessible to new and veteran players alike.

A major factor in **World of Warcraft's** widespread appeal was its user interface, designed to be both powerful and accessible. The game's interface allowed players to easily manage their characters, update equipment, and track quests, making it intuitive for newcomers while offering depth for seasoned gamers.

WoW also supported customization, enabling players to tailor the interface to their specific needs, enhancing both gameplay efficiency and aesthetic preference. This adaptability made WoW's interface not just a tool for gameplay but a part of the immersive experience, ensuring players of all skill levels could enjoy its rich content without unnecessary complexity.

Social Dynamics in Azeroth

WoW wasn't just a game; it was a community that brought people together from around the world.

Guilds provided a way for players to organize and collaborate.

Guilds in **World of Warcraft** became foundational to the game's social structure. These player-organized groups allowed individuals with common goals to work together, creating a sense of camaraderie and belonging. Guilds offered players a structured environment to communicate, share resources, and strategize for complex game challenges like raids and dungeon runs.

The collaborative nature of guilds extended beyond gameplay. They fostered a sense of responsibility, with roles such as guild leaders and officers who would manage events and mediate conflicts. For many, guild participation mirrored real-world social dynamics, teaching valuable leadership and teamwork skills.

The game's economy involved complex player-driven trade networks.

The *World of Warcraft* economy was largely player-driven, featuring bustling trade networks that mirrored real-world markets. Players could engage in professions such as blacksmithing and herbalism to gather resources and craft goods, which were then sold through an auction house system.

This economy added another layer of interaction, where entrepreneurial players became virtual merchants, capitalizing on supply and demand. It encouraged players to explore market trends and develop negotiation skills while fostering a robust economic community within the game.

In-game events and holidays created a living world feeling.

WoW's developers introduced in-game events and seasonal holidays, immersing players in a dynamic virtual world. Celebrations like **Hallow's End** and the **Lunar Festival** provided unique quests, rewards, and themed items that captivated the player base.

These events made Azeroth feel alive, as players eagerly anticipated each occurrence, often planning their gameplay around them. The events also offered opportunities for players to engage in cooperative and competitive activities, further enhancing the sense of community within the game.

WoW forums and external websites fostered a rich community culture.

A vibrant culture emerged around **World of Warcraft**, sustained by forums and external websites. These platforms became hotspots for players to share strategies, participate in heated discussions, and exchange fan art and stories inspired by their in-game experiences.

Such resources not only helped deepen the community's engagement with the game but also allowed players to form connections beyond the virtual world. This expansive and active external network solidified WoW's standing as more than just a game, building it into a cultural phenomenon.

Real-life friendships and even marriages emerged from in-game interactions.

The social environment of *World of Warcraft* extended beyond the screen, facilitating real-life friendships and even marriages. Players often reported meeting some of their closest friends through their in-game interactions.

These relationships grew from shared experiences, collaborative gameplay, and persistent communication. It’s not uncommon for guild mates to organize real-world meetups, transforming virtual acquaintances into lifelong friends and partners. This highlights the profound impact online gaming can have on personal relationships, bridging geographical and cultural divides.

Expansions and Evolution

Blizzard continually expanded World of Warcraft, keeping the game relevant with new content and features.

The Burning Crusade was the first major expansion, introduced in 2007.

The release of **The Burning Crusade** in 2007 marked a pivotal moment for *World of Warcraft*. This expansion introduced the shattered world of Outland, which added new zones, dungeons, and raids, enhancing the game's depth. Players could explore alien landscapes filled with new challenges and opportunities, pushing the boundaries of the MMORPG genre.

Moreover, **The Burning Crusade** increased the level cap from 60 to 70, allowing players to further develop their characters. The introduction of the new races, the Blood Elves for the Horde and the Draenei for the Alliance, expanded the game's lore and provided fresh gameplay experiences. The expansion set new standards for content quality and player engagement in the MMORPG industry.

Wrath of the Lich King expanded on the game's lore and increased the level cap.

Wrath of the Lich King, released in 2008, delved deeper into the rich lore of Azeroth, focusing on the iconic antagonist, the Lich King. Set in the frozen continent of Northrend, this expansion captivated players with its intricate storytelling and immersive environments, breathing new life into the *World of Warcraft* universe.

In addition to a gripping narrative, the expansion raised the level cap to 80, offering players new skills and abilities to master. The introduction of the Death Knight, the game's first hero class, provided a unique gameplay experience and strategic depth. *Wrath of the Lich King* cemented the game's status as a legend in the gaming world.

Cataclysm redesigned the game world with massive changes.

Released in 2010, **Cataclysm** dramatically reshaped the *World of Warcraft* landscape by fundamentally altering the game's original zones. The cataclysmic event led by the devastating dragon Deathwing transformed familiar areas, adding new quests, stories, and challenges, offering a fresh perspective to veteran players.

This expansion introduced two new races: the Worgen for the Alliance and the Goblins for the Horde. Additionally, the level cap was raised to 85, continuing the tradition of extending player engagement through progression. **Cataclysm** not only revitalized the game for existing players but also invited newcomers to experience a redesigned world.

Each expansion introduced new races, classes, and regions to explore.

Over time, each expansion of *World of Warcraft* has systematically introduced new elements that enrich player experience. This includes unveiling new playable races and classes, fostering diverse playstyles and characters. Each expansion invites players to explore newly uncovered regions of Azeroth, complete with their distinct cultures, stories, and challenges.

The addition of new races allows for novel interactions and storylines, while new classes expand strategic gameplay and engagement. By consistently integrating fresh content, Blizzard has kept the world of Azeroth vibrant, providing players countless hours of exploration and adventure.

Regular updates addressed player feedback and game balance.

Blizzard's dedication to refining *World of Warcraft* is evident in their commitment to regular updates and patches. These updates are crucial for addressing player feedback, ensuring a balanced and fair gaming environment. By tweaking game mechanics, updating quests, and addressing bugs, Blizzard demonstrates a proactive approach to maintaining player satisfaction.

Such attention to detail not only enhances gameplay but also fosters a strong community spirit amongst players. Updates and adjustments based on user input allow the community to feel heard and valued, contributing to the enduring success of *World of Warcraft* as a hallmark in the MMORPG genre.

Cultural Impact

World of Warcraft influenced not just gaming, but broader popular culture as well.

WoW became a cultural phenomenon, referenced in TV shows and movies.

World of Warcraft, often referred to as WoW, quickly became a cultural icon following its release. Its pervasive influence was evident through frequent references in television shows such as *South Park*, which dedicated an entire episode to the game. This episode, titled "Make Love, Not Warcraft," highlighted the game's impact on social culture and humorously showcased how its virtual universe had become intertwined with everyday life. Furthermore, movies like *Detective Pikachu* and *Ready Player One* have incorporated nods to the MMORPG, signifying WoW's recognition as a staple in the gaming lexicon.

These references underscore WoW's role as a unifying cultural touchpoint, bridging diverse entertainment mediums. They demonstrate how WoW transcended the gaming world, entering mainstream consciousness and solidifying its place in popular culture. Its influence remains immeasurable, aiding in the blurring of lines between gaming and other entertainment forms.

Its impact led to documentaries and books about the game's legacy.

World of Warcraft's massive impact extended beyond active gameplay, sparking interest in its rich history and cultural significance. This interest led to a variety of documentaries and books examining its long-lasting legacy. Films like *World of Warcraft: Looking For Group* narrated the journey of WoW and its development, delving into the community's growth and the game's broader cultural implications.

Numerous authors and researchers have also penned books exploring various facets of WoW. These works dissect player experiences, the creation of virtual identities, and the intricate lore that captivated millions. The scholarly attention and resources devoted to understanding WoW highlight not only its stature as a groundbreaking game but also its enduring influence on digital culture.

WoW's large player base held in-game protests and events.

One of the fascinating aspects of World of Warcraft is its dynamic player base, which has used the game as a platform for various in-game protests and social events. Historically, players have organized virtual demonstrations to voice their opinions on game changes or highlight real-world issues. For example, when Blizzard Entertainment announced modifications that upset certain gameplay balances, players congregated en masse to express their dissent, showcasing the power of community action within cyber spaces.

Moreover, WoW has been the site of joyful and communal gatherings, such as digital weddings and festivals. These player-created events demonstrate the game's rich social fabric, emphasizing how WoW offered more than just gameplay—it created a virtual society capable of mirroring real-world interactions and communities.

Gamers often cited WoW as their introduction to online communities.

For many players, World of Warcraft served as a gateway into the realm of online communities. Before the advent of WoW, online gaming was relatively niche, but WoW's multiplayer functionality and rich narrative encouraged players to immerse themselves in its vast virtual landscape. It fostered a sense of belonging and camaraderie among its diverse player base.

Players from around the globe connected, forming friendships and alliances that often transcended the game. The social structures within WoW, such as guilds and raid groups, provided a strong framework for interaction, allowing players to experience true online community dynamics. As a result, WoW played an instrumental role in acclimating millions to the vitality and complexity of online social environments.

The game inspired countless other MMORPGs and gaming innovations.

World of Warcraft's success paved the way for numerous MMORPGs, influencing game design and development practices. Its ecosystem of progressively challenging content, expansive lore, and player-versus-player combat set new industry standards for genre excellence. Developers of subsequent MMORPGs often tried to emulate WoW's formula, seeking to replicate its commercial success and player engagement.

Additionally, WoW sparked technological advancements, particularly in server technology and network infrastructure, facilitating large-scale coordinated gaming experiences. By blending storytelling with strategic gameplay, WoW inspired innovations that have been integrated into various gaming genres, further cementing its role as a cornerstone of modern gaming culture.

Chapter 26: Minecraft - Infinite Creativity

Minecraft allows players to build and explore infinite worlds. Since its release, it has become a sandbox phenomenon, inspiring countless creative projects and captivating players of all ages.

The Genesis of Minecraft

Discover the origins of Minecraft, a game that started as a small project and grew into a global sensation. Learn about its early development stages and the vision behind its creation.

Markus Persson, also known as Notch, developed Minecraft in 2009 as an indie project, drawing inspiration from games like Dwarf Fortress and Infiniminer.

Markus Persson, affectionately known by his alias 'Notch,' embarked on the journey of creating Minecraft as a personal project in 2009. A Swedish programmer with a passion for game development, Persson was inspired by titles such as *Dwarf Fortress* and *Infiniminer*. These games, known for their complex mechanics and open-ended nature, laid the groundwork for his vision of an expansive sandbox game.

Notch sought to merge the intricate simulation aspects of *Dwarf Fortress* with the block-placing creativity found in *Infiniminer*. His goal was to allow players to explore randomly generated worlds filled with opportunities for creativity.
Despite initial constraints, Notch's ingenuity set the stage for what would become a cultural phenomenon.

The game was officially released to the public in 2011, quickly gaining popularity due to its open-ended nature and creative freedom.

After two years of development and community testing, *Minecraft* officially launched to the public on November 18, 2011. The game's immediate appeal lay in its revolutionary open-ended gameplay, allowing players to create anything their imagination conjured. Whether it was building elaborate castles or surviving the harsh environments, *Minecraft* catered to all play styles.

This freedom struck a chord with gamers worldwide, propelling *Minecraft* into the spotlight. Its sandbox style offered unparalleled creative expression and exploration, factors that were relatively new at the time and contributed to its rapid rise in popularity.

Minecraft's simple graphics and blocky style were initially a limitation, but they became iconic features that encouraged creativity and innovation.

From the outset, *Minecraft*'s graphics were simple and blocky, a byproduct of technical limitations. However, what began as a constraint soon became the game's distinctive style. The iconic pixelated graphics allowed players to view the world as a canvas of building blocks.

Instead of detailed textures, *Minecraft* provided a minimalistic aesthetic which did not detract from gameplay. This approach allowed the player's imagination to fill in the gaps, fostering an environment where creativity and innovation flourished. The simplicity extended to its accessibility, making it easy for people of all ages to engage and contribute to its growing community.

The game's early days were marked by community feedback and iterative updates, fostering a strong relationship between the developer and its players.

The early evolution of *Minecraft* was deeply intertwined with its community. Markus Persson and his team at Mojang were highly receptive to player feedback, using it to guide the development process. This iterative approach ensured the game evolved organically, with frequent updates responding to community desires and suggestions.

This relationship cultivated a loyal player base, as the community felt their voices were truly heard and valued. Such engagement helped Mojang nurture Minecraft into a living, breathing entity, continuously enriched by both the developers' innovations and the boundless creativity of its players.

Gameplay Mechanics

Explore Minecraft's core mechanics, which provide a foundation for endless creativity and exploration. Understand the game's primary elements that make it unique.

Minecraft features a procedurally generated 3D world consisting of cubes representing different materials, such as dirt, stone, and wood.

Minecraft's world is distinguished by its blocky, three-dimensional environment, crafted primarily from cubes. Each cube symbolizes a different material type, such as dirt, stone, wood, or even precious ores like diamond and gold. These blocks form the building "atoms" of Minecraft's universe, shaping sprawling landscapes and endless terrain variations.

This procedural generation ensures that every new world is unique, providing players with an unending assortment of potential environments to discover and modify. Players mine these cubes to gather resources, a core activity within the game that intertwines seamlessly with its open-ended exploration and building ethos.

The game modes vary, including Survival, where players gather resources to build and maintain health, and Creative, which allows unlimited access to all materials.

Minecraft offers several distinct game modes that significantly influence the player's experience. In **Survival** mode, players must strategically gather resources to build shelter, craft necessary tools, and maintain health in the face of diverse challenges and hostile mobs that appear at night. Survival mode introduces a level of tension and complexity that appeals to players seeking a test of resource management and survival skills.

Conversely, **Creative** mode liberates players from the constraints of resource acquisition. It grants unlimited access to all materials, enabling uninhibited architectural achievement and artistic expression. This mode is particularly attractive to those who enjoy experimenting with boundless construction possibilities and indulging in pure creativity.

Crafting is a fundamental aspect, enabling players to combine resources to create tools, weapons, and other items essential for progress.

The crafting system in Minecraft underpins much of the game's appeal. Players use a grid interface to combine items, transforming raw materials into useful tools, weapons, or alternative products critical to their survival and progress. Learning the myriad recipes is a rite of passage, guiding players on a journey of experimentation and discovery.

This mechanic adds layers of strategy and engagement as players determine optimal crafting paths and resource allocations to meet game objectives. Crafting is also instrumental for survival, enabling players to create items that protect against enemies or ensure efficient resource gathering.

Beyond building, players encounter various creatures, explore vast landscapes, and interact with villages and non-player characters.

Minecraft offers more than mere construction; it presents a dynamic world filled with diverse creatures known as 'mobs.' These include friendly entities like sheep and cows as well as hostile adversaries such as creepers and zombies. These creatures enrich the environment and present ongoing challenges or opportunities for resource gathering.

Players can explore the vast landscapes encompassing different biomes, leading to the discovery of hidden areas and fortuitous adventures. Furthermore, interactions with villages and non-player characters (NPCs) provide unique trading opportunities and quests, adding depth to the interactive and exploratory aspects of the game.

Redstone, an in-game resource, allows players to create complex contraptions and circuitry, adding depth to creative possibilities.

Redstone in Minecraft functions akin to electrical circuitry, enabling players to craft a myriad of mechanical devices and complex logic systems. By utilizing redstone, players can ingeniously construct anything from simple automated doors to intricate computing devices, pushing the boundaries of conventional gameplay.

This element not only magnifies creative potential but also encourages players to engage in problem-solving and innovative thinking. The redstone system has become an entire area of mastery within Minecraft, with a dedicated community sharing their creations and offering inspiration for new players eager to delve into digital engineering.

Cultural Impact

Minecraft has influenced culture and education, reaching beyond traditional gaming circles. Examine its impact and legacy in various fields.

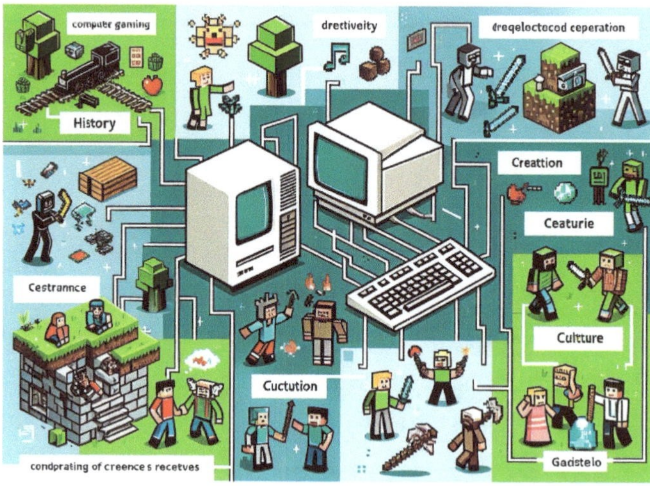

Minecraft has become a tool for educators, used to teach subjects like mathematics, history, and even programming.

Over the years, *Minecraft* has evolved from a popular video game into an innovative educational tool. Its block-based environment offers myriad possibilities for interactive learning. Educators around the world have harnessed *Minecraft's* versatility to teach a variety of subjects. In mathematics, for example, teachers use the game to illustrate concepts like geometry, measurement, and spatial awareness.

In history classes, *Minecraft* allows students to recreate historical landmarks, providing a tangible way to explore and understand ancient civilizations. Moreover, its open-ended nature supports the integration of complex programming lessons. Students can learn the basics of coding through *Minecraft's* redstone mechanics or modding tutorials, making programming more approachable and engaging. This seamless blend of fun and education has transformed *Minecraft* into a respected and useful tool in modern classrooms.

It has spawned a vibrant community on platforms like YouTube and Twitch, where players share tutorials, gameplay experiences, and creative projects.

The *Minecraft* community is a testament to the game's extensive cultural reach. Enthusiastic players routinely turn to platforms such as YouTube and Twitch to share their creations and strategies. These platforms serve as rich repositories of knowledge, where users upload thousands of hours of content ranging from beginner tutorials to advanced gigaprojects.

On YouTube, particular channels have amassed millions of subscribers, thanks to their detailed walkthroughs and innovative ideas. Meanwhile, streamers on Twitch engage audiences by broadcasting live gameplay and hosting interactive sessions with viewers. This dynamic exchange of ideas fosters creativity and innovation within the community, ensuring that *Minecraft* remains a staple in the gaming universe.

The game’s sandbox nature has inspired countless fan-made mods and maps, extending its replayability and versatility.

Minecraft's endless sandbox possibilities have sparked an explosion of player creativity, evident in the vast array of mods and custom maps developed by its community. Mods, short for modifications, allow players to alter various aspects of the game, from introducing new items and creatures to revamping the gameplay mechanics.

These modifications, often available for free, substantially enhance *Minecraft's* original content, providing fresh experiences and enabling imaginative exploration. Additionally, player-created maps offer novel adventures, puzzles, and survival challenges, ensuring players always have new content to explore. This user-generated content keeps the game vibrant and continually breathing new life into the beloved cubic landscapes.

As a cultural phenomenon, Minecraft has featured in popular media, including books, merchandise, and even collaborations with artists and musicians.

Minecraft has transcended its origins as a simple sandbox game to become a cultural icon. This is reflected in its widespread presence across various media. It has inspired a series of books, ranging from strategy guides to fictional tales set within its pixelated universe. These publications extend the game's storytelling potential and keep fans engaged beyond the digital realm.

Moreover, *Minecraft* merchandise, such as toys and apparel, has become ubiquitous, appealing to a diverse demographic.

Collaborations with artists and musicians have further expanded its cultural footprint, resulting in delightful fusions of art and gaming. These multifaceted engagements have cemented *Minecraft's* status as not just a game but a robust cultural entity resonating with millions worldwide.

Commercial Success and Legacy

Understand Minecraft's journey into being a commercial triumph and its lasting influence on the gaming industry.

In 2014, Microsoft acquired Mojang, the studio behind Minecraft, for $2.5 billion, marking one of the largest deals in gaming history.

This pivotal moment in gaming history highlighted the immense value of *Minecraft* and its potential for long-term growth. The acquisition by Microsoft was not just about securing a popular game; it was a strategic move to harness the burgeoning community and the infinite creative possibilities offered by the game. The mammoth $2.5 billion deal underscored the significant role *Minecraft* played in the industry, one that went beyond simple gameplay and delved into education and social connectivity. With Microsoft's resources, *Minecraft* continued to expand its platforms and offerings, maintaining its relevance years after its initial release.

The game has been ported to numerous platforms, from consoles to mobile, increasing its accessibility and fanbase.

Minecraft's adaptability is evident in its seamless integration across diverse gaming platforms. Initially launched for PC, the game quickly expanded to consoles, mobile devices, and eventually, even VR headsets. This widespread availability enabled *Minecraft* to reach a broader audience, with each port optimizing controls and graphics for the respective platform. This cross-platform presence not only expanded its player base but also fostered a global community that could collaborate and share experiences irrespective of the device they used. This accessibility was a crucial factor in cementing *Minecraft*'s standing as a cultural phenomenon.

Minecraft's consistent updates and large community support have maintained its position as a topselling game for over a decade.

Continuous innovation has been at the heart of *Minecraft*'s enduring success. Regular updates introduce new features, biomes, and items, ensuring the game remains fresh and engaging for veterans and newcomers alike. The robust community has played an indispensable role in this cycle, providing feedback and creating vast amounts of user-generated content, from mods to custom maps. This symbiotic relationship between developers and players has kept *Minecraft* at the forefront of gaming discussions worldwide, allowing it to remain a best-seller long after its original release.

The game's ability to engage multiple generations of players speaks to its timeless appeal and adaptability.

Minecraft captivates both young children exploring their first digital landscapes and adults reliving nostalgic pixelated adventures. Its simplistic graphics belie a deep, intricate world that allows players of all ages to interpret and engage with its environment uniquely. The game's mechanics encourage creativity and problem-solving, making it a favorite educational tool in schools globally. Its universal appeal stems from its ability to offer new adventures with every play session, ensuring that regardless of age, players find something relatable and enjoyable in its blocky universe.

Minecraft's success paved the way for other sandbox and indie games, demonstrating that innovative gameplay can triumph over high-end graphics.

By prioritizing gameplay innovation over graphical fidelity, *Minecraft* redefined what success looked like in the gaming industry. It proved that players value freedom, creativity, and community interaction. This shift inspired a wave of sandbox and indie games, like *Terraria* and *Stardew Valley*, which embraced similar principles. These games emphasized player agency and creativity, leading to a renaissance in game design that validated the efforts of indie developers worldwide. *Minecraft* demonstrated that with the right ideas, a game doesn't need cutting-edge technology to captivate millions.

The Origins of Minecraft

Minecraft was created by Markus Persson in 2009 and quickly grew from a humble independent project to a global gaming phenomenon.

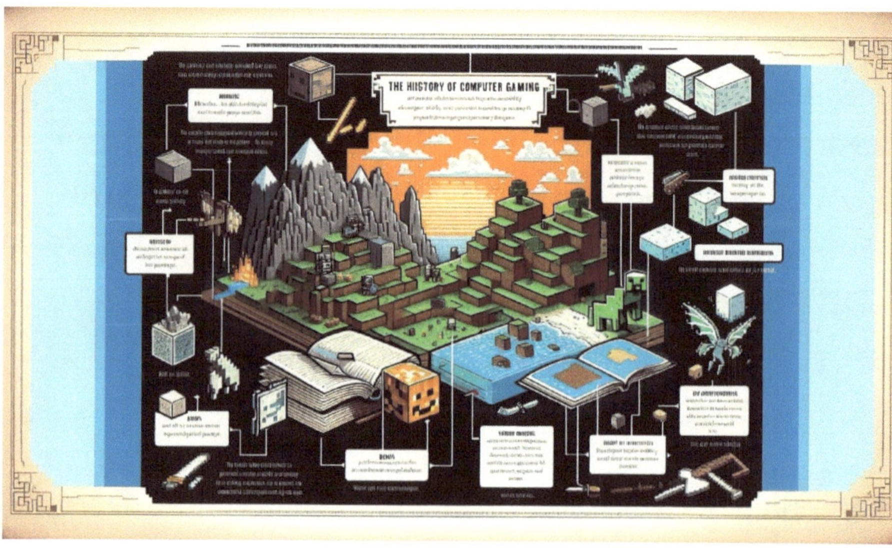

Initial Release: Minecraft first appeared to the public as a developmental release on May 17, 2009, offering basic gameplay.

Minecraft made its first public appearance on May 17, 2009, in a developmental release that intrigued early adopters with its simplistic yet innovative approach. This initial version, often referred to as "Minecraft Classic," offered basic gameplay mechanics centered around block placement and destruction. Players could explore a limitless, procedurally generated world, where creativity was only bounded by their imagination.

Despite its rudimentary graphics and limited features, the game allowed players to manipulate a world composed of blocks, which laid the foundation for the complex structures and elaborate projects we see today. The core concept of exploration, building, and creativity captured the attention of the gaming community, highlighting the potential for transformation and growth in the independent gaming scene.

Markus 'Notch' Persson: The brain behind Minecraft, Notch developed it as an indie game with emphasis on creativity and survival.

Markus "Notch" Persson, a Swedish programmer and designer, is the mastermind behind Minecraft. His vision was to create a game that emphasized creative freedom and survival, unshackled by the constraints commonly seen in mainstream titles. Drawing inspiration from games such as *Infiniminer* and *Dwarf Fortress*, Notch crafted Minecraft as a sandbox experience that would encourage players to explore and experiment.

By focusing on the core mechanics of mining, crafting, and building, Persson laid the groundwork for a game that appealed to individual creativity while providing a survival aspect that added an extra layer of engagement. This unique combination of elements positioned Minecraft as a standout indie title, earning critical acclaim and a dedicated player base. Notch's work not only revolutionized indie game development but also highlighted the importance of player-driven content in gaming.

Rapid Popularity: By word of mouth and online communities, the game blossomed quickly, gaining a dedicated following.

By harnessing the power of online communities and word of mouth, Minecraft rapidly rose from an indie curiosity to a gaming juggernaut. Players quickly took to social media and forums, sharing their creations and experiences, which fueled its viral growth. YouTube played a pivotal role, with countless hours of gameplay videos, tutorials, and inspired builds highlighting the game's endless possibilities.

The grassroots popularity was bolstered by its active and enthusiastic community, which embraced the game's openended nature and started forming a collaborative culture around it. Dedicated servers ran unique mods and hosted vast multiplayer worlds, further enriching the gaming experience. This passionate community helped drive the game's success, marking Minecraft as a defining moment in gaming history.

Official Launch: After various updates and beta versions, Minecraft officially launched on November 18, 2011.

Following a series of updates and extensive player feedback during its beta phase, Minecraft officially launched on November 18, 2011. This milestone version marked the culmination of years of development and the incorporation of a myriad of features that enriched the original concept.

The official release included new game modes, such as Creative and Survival, each offering unique experiences to cater to different playstyles. The grand scale of the game's world was complemented by the introduction of new blocks, mobs, and complex systems like Redstone circuits, which further expanded the creative and tactical possibilities for players.

The game's official release was celebrated by an enthusiastic global audience, affirming Minecraft's status as a pivotal and beloved entry in the annals of gaming history. Its continued evolution showcases an enduring legacy of innovation and community-driven content.

Gameplay Mechanics and Modes

Minecraft stands out because of its unique gameplay mechanics and multiple modes that cater to different types of players.

Survival Mode: Players must gather resources, manage health, and fend off enemies to survive in a procedurally generated world.

Survival Mode is arguably the most iconic way to experience *Minecraft*. Players are thrust into a vast, randomly generated world filled with diverse biomes, each with its own challenges and resources. The core objective is simple: survive.

Players must balance the collection of essentials like wood, stone, and food, while they navigate the landscape. As daylight fades, the world transitions into a more dangerous environment, where hostile mobs such as zombies and skeletons emerge. This necessitates the construction of shelters or crafting of weapons for protection.

The thrill of *Survival Mode* lies in its unpredictability; every new world spawns countless possibilities and challenges. This mode perfectly encapsulates the game's essence — a mix of exploration, creativity, and strategy.

Creative Mode: This mode provides unlimited resources, allowing players to build and create freely without the threat of danger.

In stark contrast to Survival, *Creative Mode* offers an entirely different appeal. Here, players are liberated from threats, health bars, and resource limitations, granting them full access to an extensive inventory of building materials. This creative playground allows for the unbridled expression of imagination.

From constructing intricate architectures to crafting pixel art mosaics, Creative Mode thrives on the principles of freedom and creativity. It empowers players to experiment with complex structures and designs without constraint.

The lack of constraints in Creative Mode has also made it an ideal platform for educators and those looking to implement learning through play, showcasing the game's versatility beyond traditional gaming experiences.

Adventure Mode: Designed for custom maps and adventures, this mode restricts certain blocks from being broken.

Adventure Mode brings another layer of depth to *Minecraft* by enabling custom map creation and exploration. Developed specifically with creators in mind, this mode restricts players from breaking most blocks, ensuring they adhere to an intended path or challenge designed by the map creator.

This mode is perfect for story-driven adventures, puzzles, and role-playing games where players follow a narrative or complete specific quests. Map designers can create immersive experiences with these restrictions, encouraging players to strategize and think creatively.

The mode accentuates gameplay diversity in *Minecraft*, offering players new stories and experiences crafted by an engaged and talented community.

Importance of Redstone: Redstone circuits in the game mimic electrical circuits and add layers of complexity and creativity.

Redstone in *Minecraft* functions much like electricity in the real world. It is integral to creating intricate mechanisms and devices within the game. Redstone wire can be used to build various contraptions ranging from simple door mechanisms to complex automated farms and binary computer systems.

Incorporating Redstone into gameplay adds a whole new dimension, appealing especially to players interested in engineering and problem-solving. It encourages learning through experimentation, allowing users to simulate basic and advanced electronic principles practically.

The technologies players have invented using Redstone have become a testament to its importance and versatility, further solidifying *Minecraft*'s standing as more than just a game, but a sandbox for creativity and innovation.

The Impact on Gaming Culture

Minecraft has had a profound influence on gaming culture and has spawned a wide range of community-driven projects and educational uses.

Community Creations: Players have built everything from simple houses to entire cities and replicas of famous landmarks.

Minecraft's creative platform has empowered players to stretch their imagination to its limits. From modest cottages to sprawling metropolises, each creation tells a unique story.

Players have gone beyond simple structures, replicating iconic landmarks such as the Eiffel Tower or recreating fantastical worlds from popular media. The scale and fidelity of these builds not only showcase talent but have also elevated Minecraft to a respected artistic medium.

Moreover, community servers often host collaborative projects, where players from around the globe contribute to constructing vast, intricate environments, exemplifying collective creativity and teamwork.

Educational Tool: Used in schools, Minecraft helps teach coding, mathematics, and creative problemsolving.

As an educational tool, Minecraft transcends traditional gaming to become an integral part of modern classrooms. Its sandbox nature makes it the perfect environment for teaching valuable skills such as coding and mathematics.

Through *Minecraft: Education Edition*, students tackle math problems by calculating resources needed for projects or construct complex circuits to teach basics in computational thinking. This hands-on approach aids in engaging students with varied learning styles.

The game also encourages creative problem-solving. Educators design challenges within the game that require students to apply logic and creativity to overcome obstacles, cultivating critical thinking skills essential for the 21st century.

Modding Community: Mods have enriched the game, adding new dimensions, creatures, and even entirely new gameplay experiences.

The vibrant modding community surrounding Minecraft is a testament to the game's open-ended nature. Thanks to its flexible code base, modders have introduced a plethora of modifications that vastly expand the game's capabilities.

Mods range from simple additions like new creatures or items to more ambitious undertakings such as entire new dimensions or game modes, enriching the core experience substantially. These modifications often enhance visuals, gameplay mechanics, or even incorporate elements from other game genres.

This vibrant scene not only keeps the game fresh and exciting for players but also fosters an inclusive space for budding developers to hone their skills and share inventions with the community.

Streaming and Let's Plays: Minecraft is among the most streamed games, with many players sharing their experiences on platforms like YouTube and Twitch.

The rise of digital platforms like YouTube and Twitch has propelled Minecraft into a global entertainment phenomenon. With a massive audience base, it remains one of the most streamed and viewed games online.

From **Let’s Plays** and tutorials to elaborate story-driven content, creators have found countless ways to engage audiences. These videos not only entertain but also build communities of fans who bond over shared interests and experiences.

Additionally, streaming has democratized content creation, allowing players of all ages to broadcast their adventures, showcasing the game's versatility and appeal. This dynamic interaction between creators and viewers plays a significant role in sustaining Minecraft's cultural relevance.

The Business Success of Minecraft

From its indie roots, Minecraft evolved into a major business success story that culminated in its acquisition by Microsoft.

Sales Milestones: Minecraft has sold over 200 million copies across all platforms globally, making it one of the best-selling games of all time.

Upon its release, *Minecraft* tapped into the creative spirit of millions, quickly becoming a commercial juggernaut.

Its blocky, open-ended design attracted audiences of all ages, leading to an explosive growth in popularity. The game achieved its first sales milestone when it sold one million copies within months.

Over the years, **Minecraft** consistently expanded its player base by releasing on diverse platforms, from desktops to mobile devices, and consoles. By 2020, *Minecraft* boasted over 200 million copies sold worldwide, cementing its place as one of the best-selling games ever. Its persistent popularity has been credited to continuous updates, playergenerated content, and an active online community.

Mojang Acquisition: In 2014, Microsoft purchased Mojang, the studio behind Minecraft, for $2.5 billion.

The acquisition of Mojang by Microsoft was a watershed moment in gaming history. In 2014, when Microsoft purchased Mojang for a staggering $2.5 billion, it underscored the immense value and potential Microsoft saw in *Minecraft*.

At the time, **Minecraft** had already captivated the imaginations of players, bolstering a vibrant community dedicated to building, collaborating, and sharing. The purchase allowed Microsoft to integrate their advanced technologies and resources into *Minecraft* while preserving the game's core appeal. The move also ensured a stable future for Mojang with access to Microsoft's vast array of development tools.

Brand Expansion: The game's brand now includes merchandise, spin-off games, and even educational versions like Minecraft: Education Edition.

Minecraft is not just a game; it's a cultural phenomenon. Its brand has diversified significantly over the years. Besides the core game, fans can explore various spin-offs, like **Minecraft: Story Mode** and **Minecraft Dungeons**, offering new narratives and adventures.

Moreover, *Minecraft* has permeated other markets through merchandise, including toys, clothing, and books. The educational sector also embraced *Minecraft* with the introduction of **Minecraft: Education Edition**. This version empowers teachers to create engaging learning experiences, enhancing subjects like math, history, and even chemistry. The brand's expansion showcases its versatility and widespread appeal.

Cross-Platform Play: Microsoft's involvement has increased Minecraft's accessibility and cross-platform integration, broadening its reach.

With Microsoft's acquisition came a renewed focus on accessibility and cross-platform play for *Minecraft*. Before, the game's fragmented ecosystem limited players on different platforms from interacting. Microsoft resolved this by developing the **Bedrock Edition**, which unified those systems.

The introduction of cross-platform play allowed players on consoles, PCs, and mobile devices to share worlds and adventures seamlessly. This feature significantly expanded *Minecraft*'s reach, bringing together a vast, global community and ensuring the game remains a favorite among diverse gaming demographics.

Chapter 27: Fortnite - The Battle Royale Craze

With its unique mix of battle royale gameplay and building mechanics, **Fortnite** captured the attention of the world. Known for its vibrant art style and frequent content updates, it remains a staple of modern gaming culture.

The Birth of Fortnite

Fortnite began as a unique twist on the burgeoning battle royale genre, resonating with players worldwide. Its inception traces back to 2017, quickly gaining popularity for its innovative concepts.

Fortnite was developed by Epic Games and released in 2017.

Epic Games, known for its innovation and industry leadership, developed **Fortnite**, launching it to the public in July 2017. Initially released as a paid early-access title, it quickly drew attention thanks to its unique game mechanics and engaging design. The game offered an unprecedented blend of cooperative gameplay and strategic depth, setting it apart from its contemporaries.

The development process was collaborative, involving a mix of veteran and creative developers who envisioned a new kind of gameplay experience. The decision to pivot towards the battle royale genre was a calculated risk that paid off massively, skyrocketing the game's popularity. It was strategically released as a free-to-play game alongside the success of other titles, a move that greatly expanded its user base.

The game is distinctive for its combination of shooting and building mechanics.

One of the most distinguishing features of **Fortnite** is its pioneering combination of shooting and building mechanics. Players can gather resources and construct structures on the fly, adding layers of strategy and creativity to the fastpaced combat typical of battle royale games.

This dynamic allows for a variety of playstyles, from aggressive attacks to strategic defenses, giving players the freedom to approach confrontations uniquely. The building element also introduces a tactical dimension, enabling players to gain high ground or fortify positions quickly. This innovation has set *Fortnite* apart, making it a trendsetter in the gaming industry.

Originally conceived as a cooperative survival game, it evolved into a leading battle royale title.

Fortnite's initial concept was far different from what it has become today. Originally designed as a player-versusenvironment (PvE) game titled **Fortnite: Save the World**, it focused on cooperative survival against waves of zombie-like creatures. The spontaneous development of the battle royale mode was a transformative pivot for the franchise.

This shift leveraged the emerging popularity of the battle royale genre, a decision that proved wise as it catapulted **Epic Games** into new heights of success. The extensive feedback loop between developers and the community enabled continuous improvements, solidifying its status as a leading title in the genre.

The game quickly gained traction due to its colorful graphics and engaging gameplay.

One of the many reasons for **Fortnite**'s rapid success is its vibrant, cartoonish art style, which appeals to a broad audience. This graphic identity makes the game accessible to players of all ages, removing the gritty realism that characterizes many other shooters.

The engaging gameplay mechanics, combined with its frequent updates and seasonal events, keep the experience fresh and captivating. Frequent interaction with its community has allowed *Fortnite* to remain at the forefront of gaming, maintaining a culturally relevant status through collaborations and in-game events.

Gameplay and Mechanics

A unique mix of mechanics sets Fortnite apart in the crowded battle royale market. With building as a core feature, it offers a different strategic layer.

Players can gather resources to build structures for defense and navigation.

In Fortnite, gathering resources is an essential aspect of gameplay that adds a unique strategic layer to the battle royale genre. Players can use a harvesting tool to collect materials such as wood, stone, and metal, which are used to build defensive structures. These structures provide cover during firefights and create tactical advantages when engaging opponents.

Not limited to defense, the building mechanics allow for creative navigation across the map. Players can construct ramps to scale cliffs, bridges to cross ravines, or platforms to reach otherwise inaccessible areas. Mastery of building can be a determining factor in winning matches, as it allows quick defensive maneuvers and high ground advantage.

The map is constantly changing with new features and locations every season.

Fortnite's map is dynamic and continually evolving, offering fresh challenges and experiences with each new season. Epic Games periodically introduces new points of interest or alters existing areas, ensuring that players encounter diverse environments and strategic opportunities. Major events often dramatically reshape the landscape, keeping the gameplay experience feeling fresh and unpredictable.

This constant evolution helps maintain player interest, as strategies must be adapted to new terrain and opportunities learned through exploration. The frequent updates also reflect real-world influences and seasonal themes, which keeps the game culturally relevant and engaging for its global audience.

Fortnite's weapon variety and aiming systems cater to various playstyles.

Fortnite boasts a diverse arsenal of weapons that cater to different playstyles and strategies. Players can choose from an array of weapon types, including shotguns for close combat, sniper rifles for long-range engagements, and assault rifles for versatile combat scenarios. Each weapon class offers unique attributes, demanding players adapt their strategies accordingly.

The aiming system in Fortnite further complements this diversity, allowing for precise hits even with the game's whimsical physics and construction mechanics. Players can fine-tune their approach to combat, deciding between aggressive rush tactics or strategic engagements, thereby accommodating both seasoned veterans and casual players alike.

Engaging progression systems and challenges keep players invested over time.

Fortnite incorporates a robust progression system that includes a variety of challenges and milestones. Players can unlock new skins, emotes, and other cosmetic rewards through the Battle Pass—an optional subscription model featuring both free and premium tiers. Daily and weekly challenges provide objectives beyond simply winning matches, encouraging continued play and skill development.

This system rewards consistent engagement and complements the core competitive nature of the game. The sense of achievement from completing challenges and leveling up in the Battle Pass keeps players motivated and ensures that the gaming experience remains rewarding over the long term, even after hundreds of matches.

Cultural Impact and Popularity

Fortnite didn't just influence the gaming industry; it became a cultural phenomenon, impacting entertainment and beyond.

The game's dances and emotes have become viral trends on social media.

Fortnite's introduction of dances and emotes significantly influenced pop culture, turning these in-game actions into real-world trends. Players celebrate their victories with iconic moves like the "Floss" and "Orange Justice," which rapidly gained popularity beyond the game itself. These emotes are not only fun in-game expressions but also a bridge to real-world interactions. They have been featured in music videos, TV shows, and by celebrities on various platforms.

Social media platforms, especially TikTok and Instagram, have seen countless users replicating these dance moves, often leading to viral challenges. The integration of these emotes reflects Fortnite's ability to adapt gaming culture into mainstream entertainment, enhancing both player engagement and brand visibility. Thus, Fortnite's influence extends beyond gaming, tapping into broader cultural trends and highlighting its role as a phenomenon in the digital age.

Fortnite has hosted virtual concerts and events, showcasing its versatility as a platform.

One of Fortnite's groundbreaking achievements is its successful transformation into an entertainment hub by hosting virtual concerts and live events. The game has seen epic performances by artists like Travis Scott, Marshmello, and Ariana Grande, attracting millions of viewers worldwide. These events are not mere concerts; they are interactive experiences where players can engage with the environment in novel ways.

Such events showcase Fortnite's robust platform versatility, allowing it to transcend traditional gaming boundaries. They provide a new way for artists to reach global audiences, especially during times when physical gatherings might be limited. This strategic move positions Fortnite not only as a leading game but also as a pioneer in virtual event hosting, redefining how entertainment is consumed in the digital era.

The game collaborated with numerous franchises, enhancing its appeal.

Fortnite's collaborations with popular franchises have significantly amplified its appeal, drawing in fans from various interests. Epic Games has integrated elements from franchises like Marvel, Star Wars, and DC Comics, offering exclusive in-game content such as special skins, weapons, and themed events. These partnerships have not only captivated fans of the original properties but also expanded Fortnite's player base.

Collaborations have proven mutually beneficial, providing unique marketing opportunities for both Fortnite and the partnered franchises. This cross-promotion approach keeps the game fresh and exciting, ensuring continuous player engagement. By aligning itself with well-loved cultural icons, Fortnite remains relevant in a fast-paced digital landscape, proving that strategic alliances are key to sustaining its appeal and cultural resonance.

It has a significant presence in eSports, with numerous tournaments worldwide.

Fortnite's robust presence in the eSports arena has been monumental in establishing its competitive reputation. Hosting numerous tournaments internationally, like the Fortnite World Cup, the game has attracted professional gamers and aspiring players alike. These events offer substantial prize pools, making competitive Fortnite a lucrative pursuit for skilled players.

Such tournaments have further legitimized Fortnite as an eSports staple, garnering sponsorships, media coverage, and sustaining viewer interest. This competitive aspect contributes to the game's longevity, providing new challenges and goals for players to strive for. As a result, Fortnite has not only changed the casual gaming landscape but has also cemented its place in the professional gaming echelon, influencing the eSports industry's evolution.

Monetization and Business Model

One of Fortnite's revolutionary aspects is its monetization strategy, setting a benchmark in the industry.

The game is free-to-play, with revenue coming from cosmetic items and battle passes.

Fortnite revolutionized the gaming industry with its free-to-play model, attracting millions of players globally. This strategy lowered the barrier to entry, allowing players to download and experience the game without any upfront cost. The game's primary revenue stream comes from *cosmetic items* and *battle passes*.

Cosmetic items encompass skins, emotes, and other visual enhancements that players can purchase to personalize their gaming experience. These items are purely aesthetic, which maintains the game's fair play standards while generating substantial income for the developer, Epic Games.

Battle passes, another key component, offer a structured system of progressive rewards. By purchasing a battle pass, players are encouraged to engage more deeply with the game to unlock exclusive content, thereby enhancing both player retention and monetization.

Cosmetic items do not affect gameplay, balancing fairness with profit.

A cornerstone of **Fortnite's** success is its commitment to ensuring that cosmetic items do not impact gameplay. This approach creates a balanced playing field where skill, rather than purchased advantages, defines success. Players can choose from various skins and emotes, allowing them to express their unique style and personality.

By separating aesthetics from gameplay mechanics, Epic Games effectively combined fairness with profitability. This model maintains player trust while still encouraging microtransactions, turning cosmetics into a lucrative source of revenue without compromising the competitive integrity of the game.

This philosophy has set a precedent in the industry, proving that a game can be both financially successful and fair for its entire community.

Seasonal battle passes offer players progression through exclusive rewards.

The introduction of *seasonal battle passes* was a pivotal move in the game's monetization strategy. With each new season, a battle pass offers players a progression system filled with exclusive rewards such as unique skins, emotes, and other in-game items.

Players are motivated to complete challenges and earn experience points, advancing through tiers to unlock these rewards. This system not only enhances engagement by encouraging continuous play but also fosters a sense of accomplishment as players progress through the tiers.

Additionally, the seasonal nature of these battle passes keeps the game dynamic and exciting, with regular updates and new content that refresh the game's universe and player interest, ensuring long-term engagement and retention.

Fortnite's in-game currency, V-Bucks, enhances the virtual economy.

V-Bucks, Fortnite's in-game currency, play a crucial role in its virtual economy. Players purchase V-Bucks with real money, which can then be used to buy cosmetic items, battle passes, and more within the game. This system allows for a fluid and user-friendly transaction process, encouraging players to spend.

The inclusion of V-Bucks adds an additional layer to the monetization model, providing both a tangible and convenient way for players to make purchases and manage their in-game finances. It strategically ties into the game's broader economic framework, enhancing player retention through regular spending opportunities.

Furthermore, the ability to earn V-Bucks through gameplay as rewards from the battle pass enriches the player's experience, blending in-game success with economic capability, and deepening player engagement in the game's ecosystem.

Evolution and Updates

A hallmark of Fortnite's success is its frequent and engaging updates, keeping the game fresh for players.

Epic Games releases major updates that introduce new seasons, themes, and gameplay changes.

Fortnite stands out in the gaming industry due to its structured seasonal updates, which have become a pervasive gameplay element. Every few months, Epic Games launches a new season that typically introduces innovative themes, such as the space-themed "Galactic Battle" or the primal-era "Wild Heart" season. These seasons not only enhance visual aesthetics but also integrate unique gameplay mechanics, reflecting Epic Games' commitment to keeping the game exhilarating.

Moreover, each season is accompanied by a battle pass that offers a plethora of rewards, incentivizing players to engage consistently. This system is effectively a game in itself, as players strive to unlock numerous unlockable items and skins. By frequently rotating these themes and rewards, Fortnite ensures that no two gaming experiences are identical, fostering a sense of novelty and adventure.

The game has undergone significant map changes, maintaining player interest.

Map changes in Fortnite are a core component of its ongoing appeal. Unlike many games that rely on static environments, Fortnite frequently transforms its map to not only refresh the gameplay experience but also push narrative boundaries. Landmark events, such as the eruption of the volcano or the mammoth overhaul that introduced Chapter 2's new landscape, keep the players guessing.

This evolving map serves both to surprise players with novel visual elements and to strategize gameplay. Players continuously adapt to new terrains, ensuring that strategies remain fresh and engaging. By upending player expectations with each significant map change, Fortnite solidifies its position as a dynamic and innovative game.

Collaboration events introduce new, exciting content regularly.

Fortnite's collaboration events represent a fusion of gaming culture with broader entertainment sectors. These events have introduced a myriad of popular franchises, from Marvel superheroes to Star Wars, transforming Fortnite into an entertainment crossover hub. Such collaborations not only attract fans of these franchises but also enrich the game's universe with exclusive skins, weapons, and themed game modes.

By tapping into global phenomena, Fortnite extends its reach beyond traditional gaming audiences. These events often coincide with live in-game events, attracting millions of viewers and active participants. Such strategic partnerships fuel excitement, engage both new and veteran players, and bolster the game's cultural relevancy.

Dynamic updates allow Fortnite to remain relevant and continually entertaining.

Fortnite's capacity to stay relevant hinges on its well-timed dynamic updates. These updates range from minor tweaks and bug fixes to expansive gameplay overhauls. The responsiveness of Epic Games to player feedback ensures that the game ecosystem remains balanced and exciting.

Frequent updates reflect a deliberate strategy to enhance player experience, address emergent issues, and align with burgeoning trends. Regular additions of new game modes, weapons, and features prevent the experience from becoming stagnant. By seamlessly adapting to the rapidly changing landscape of player interests and technological developments, Fortnite maintains its position at the forefront of the gaming world.

The Launch of Fortnite

Fortnite was released in 2017 and quickly gained popularity with its unique features and engaging gameplay. Let's explore how it first entered the gaming scene.

Fortnite was initially launched as a co-op survival game called Fortnite: Save the World.

When **Fortnite** first hit the gaming world, it was not the battle royale sensation we know today. It originally debuted as *Fortnite: Save the World*, a co-op survival game that tasked players with defending against waves of zombie-like creatures. While this mode encouraged strategic teamwork and player collaboration, it didn't achieve the same level of success as its later iteration.

The concept was fresh, blending third-person shooter mechanics with resource gathering and fort-building. Although popular among a niche group, *Save the World* struggled to capture a broader audience. This early version laid the groundwork for what was to come, hinting at Epic Games' potential in creating a unique gaming experience, one that would revolutionize the industry with the addition of the now-famous battle royale mode.

The game introduced a battle royale mode in September 2017, inspired by popular games like PUBG.

September 2017 saw the release of **Fortnite Battle Royale**, a mode inspired by the runaway success of titles like *PlayerUnknown's Battlegrounds (PUBG)*. By adopting the 100-player fight-to-the-death concept and offering it for free, Epic Games captured the interest of both seasoned and casual gamers alike.

The mode was unique for its integration of building mechanics, allowing players to construct defenses and strategic structures on the fly. This blend of action and creativity set Fortnite apart from its contemporaries, propelling it to the forefront of gaming culture. Within months, its player base skyrocketed, with millions logging on to experience the new phenomenon.

Its colorful graphics and casual, accessible gameplay helped it stand out from other shooters.

Fortnite's vibrant, cartoonish art style distinctly separates it from other titles that embrace more photorealistic visuals. This choice not only appealed to a younger demographic but also encouraged a light-hearted, fun atmosphere. The accessibility factor was significant—players from all backgrounds and skill levels could dive into the action without feeling overwhelmed.

The mechanics were straightforward, yet the strategic depth offered through building added layers of complexity that seasoned gamers could master. This balance between simplicity and depth made Fortnite's battle royale mode inviting for newcomers while providing enough intrigue to keep veterans engaged. It marked a contrast to the more gritty, intense atmosphere of other shooters on the market, helping it secure a broad audience.

Epic Games leveraged their in-house resources, including Unreal Engine expertise, to create a polished experience.

Epic Games efficiently utilized its in-house resources to craft a finely-tuned gaming experience for **Fortnite**. With extensive expertise in the development of the *Unreal Engine*, they ensured the game ran smoothly across various platforms, providing players with a consistently polished experience. Their technical prowess facilitated the seamless execution of novel gameplay elements, particularly the real-time building mechanics.

This sophistication was not limited to performance but extended to regular content creation, ensuring new in-game events and items kept the experience fresh. Such adept handling of technology and content development played a pivotal role in fortifying Fortnite's position in the competitive gaming landscape, emphasizing the studio's capability to evolve and innovate rapidly.

Regular updates and events kept players engaged, allowing Fortnite to cement its place in the gaming world quickly.

A cornerstone of **Fortnite's** success was its dynamic approach to game development and community engagement. Weekly updates introduced exciting new content, ranging from outfits and weapons to time-limited game modes. By continuously refreshing the gameplay experience, Epic Games maintained players' interest and anticipation for what might come next.

In addition, events like the *Fortnite World Cup* and virtual concerts, featuring high-profile artists, transformed the game from a mere pastime to a multifaceted entertainment platform. These innovations not only captivated the existing fanbase but also drew new players in, establishing Fortnite as a groundbreaking title in the chronicles of gaming.

Cross-platform play was a revolutionary feature that contributed to Fortnite's growing player base.

One of the most revolutionary aspects of **Fortnite** was its commitment to cross-platform play. It bridged the traditional gaps between console, PC, and mobile gamers, allowing friends to join matches together irrespective of their device preferences. This inclusivity was unprecedented and garnished substantial attention from the gaming community.

Cross-platform interoperability enhanced the game's appeal by expanding its potential audience and simplifying matchmaking. It emphasized Epic Games' forward-thinking approach and commitment to inclusivity, contributing extensively to Fortnite's reputation as a groundbreaking example of modern gaming. This feature not only enriched the gaming experience but also set a new standard for future titles across the industry.

Gameplay Mechanics

Fortnite's gameplay is a combination of traditional battle royale elements and unique building mechanics. Here's what makes it special:

Players start with 100 people in a single match, and the last player or team standing wins.

Fortnite's battle royale mode sets the stage for intense and competitive gameplay. Each match begins with 100 players who skydive onto a massive map from a flying bus. The objective is to be the last person or team remaining, which introduces a thrilling survival element. Players engage in combat using a wide array of weapons and items, employing both strategic stealth and all-out combat to eliminate opponents. Compared with other games, Fortnite encourages both individual skill and teamwork, making it crucial for players to adapt and strategize in real time. This high-stakes mode has been a major factor in maintaining Fortnite's popularity and competitive edge in the gaming community.

The game features a 'storm' mechanic that shrinks the playable area, forcing players to encounter each other.

In Fortnite, the looming threat of an encroaching storm adds urgency and dynamism to gameplay. The storm gradually reduces the playable area, known as the safe zone, compelling players to move towards its shrinking circle. This mechanic ensures that players cannot simply hide throughout the match – they must continuously reposition themselves, often leading to unexpected encounters and dynamic battles. As the game progresses, the storm intensifies in speed and damage, heightening the stakes and accelerating the pace of the game. This feature transforms each match into a fast-paced, thrilling experience, encouraging strategic planning and quick reflexes.

Building structures for defense or mobility adds a strategic layer not found in other games.

One of Fortnite's defining features is its building system, which adds a unique tactical layer to the gameplay. Players can construct structures using materials gathered throughout the match, creating walls, ramps, and towers on-the-fly. This mechanic allows players to quickly build fortifications for defense, gaining a strategic advantage over their opponents. Additionally, building is essential for mobility and accessibility, providing new routes and vantage points. The system demands skill and creativity, as adept building can quickly turn the tide of a battle. This innovative feature distinguishes Fortnite from other battle royale games and fosters a deeply engaging and evolving combat environment.

Resource gathering is essential for survival, as players need materials to build and protect themselves.

In Fortnite, effective resource gathering is crucial for success. Players harvest materials—wood, stone, and metal—from the environment by using their trusty pickaxes on objects like trees, rocks, and structures. These materials are essential for building, with each type offering different strengths and weaknesses in terms of durability. Skilled players must balance the need for quick, accessible resources with the strategic acquisition of stronger materials. This constant gathering not only supports the building mechanics but also adds a layer of depth to the gameplay, requiring players to manage resources efficiently in the heat of battle.

Frequent updates introduce new weapons, items, and themes, keeping the experience fresh.

Fortnite is renowned for its regular updates that continually breathe new life into the game. Epic Games, the developer, frequently introduces new weapons, items, and seasonal themes that transform the gameplay experience. These updates often coincide with global events or holidays, generating excitement and anticipation within the community. New content can significantly alter strategies, encouraging players to experiment and adapt. The variety and frequency of these updates have been key in sustaining player interest and ensuring Fortnite remains a dynamic and entertaining experience.

Its creative mode allows players to build their own worlds, fostering innovation and creativity.

Fortnite's Creative Mode is a playground for innovation and expression, allowing players to construct and explore their unique virtual worlds. This mode grants access to a vast toolkit of in-game assets, enabling players to design custom maps, mini-games, and aesthetic experiences. Since its introduction, Creative Mode has nurtured a vibrant community of creators who showcase their impressive designs and ideas. This feature not only extends the game's longevity but also empowers players to push the boundaries of what is possible within Fortnite. In doing so, Creative Mode has evolved into a platform for creativity and social interaction.

Cultural Impact and Popularity

Fortnite's influence extends beyond gaming, touching various aspects of popular culture and social media.

The game's dances and emotes became viral sensations, known even to those who don't play games.

Fortnite's dances and emotes are iconic, transcending their origins as in-game expressions to become cultural phenomena. The "Floss" and "Orange Justice" are examples of dances that rocketed to internet fame, often seen across social media platforms and in countless YouTube videos. These moves have been reproduced from schoolyards to professional sports arenas, where athletes incorporate them into their celebrations.

The appeal lies in their accessibility and fun nature. These emotes became a form of communication within the game, allowing players to express themselves without words. Their popularity is such that even non-gamers recognize Fortnite dances, cementing their place as part of modern pop culture. This viral appeal widened Fortnite's audience, drawing attention from mainstream media and creating a bridge between gaming culture and everyday life.

Many celebrities and athletes have appeared in the game or streamed it live, increasing its reach.

Fortnite's influence is evident in its ability to attract a wide array of celebrities and athletes into its virtual world. Highprofile stars like rapper Travis Scott and athlete Neymar have not only appeared in the game but also contributed to its content and appeal. These collaborations often bring new skins and events, enticing fans across different domains to engage with the game.

Additionally, live streaming platforms have served as a conduit for celebrity engagement with Fortnite. Well-known figures, such as Drake, have teamed up with popular streamers to play live. These events draw massive audiences, as fans are eager to watch their favorite celebrities navigate the game. This symbiotic relationship has helped to boost Fortnite's presence, making it not just a game but a bustling hub of entertainment and interaction.

Fortnite's esports scene attracted a large audience, with big tournaments like the World Cup showcasing top talent.

From its inception, Fortnite carved out a significant niche in the esports industry, encapsulated by the monumental Fortnite World Cup. This event, held in 2019, boasted a $30 million prize pool, capturing the attention of the global gaming community. Young talents like Kyle 'Bugha' Giersdorf gained fame and fortune, as he emerged victorious from the intense competition.

The spectacle of competitive Fortnite is designed to thrill, featuring fast-paced action and strategic gameplay. These elements not only engage seasoned players but also attract viewers who are new to esports. The tournaments are meticulously broadcasted, with high production values that enhance the spectator experience. The result is a dynamic esports scene that continues to grow, leveraging a diverse audience base who appreciate the skill and excitement that Fortnite's competitive landscape provides.

The game became a social hub, with players gathering not just to compete, but also to interact and socialize.

Fortnite redefined what it means to be a social platform within gaming. Unlike traditional multiplayer modes that focus purely on competitive play, Fortnite offers a space where players worldwide can interact and bond. Its battle royale format inherently supports large groups, leading to spontaneous collaborations and friendships.

This aspect is particularly appealing to younger audiences, who often log in as much for social interactions as for the gameplay. Fortnite encourages creativity through its building mechanics and distinct modes like "Creative," fostering a sense of community among players. This social dynamic is crucial to the game's ongoing popularity, resonating with a generation that values connectivity and shared experiences alongside gaming prowess.

Its live concerts and in-game events set a new standard for entertainment experiences in gaming.

Epic Games has seamlessly integrated live events into Fortnite, significantly raising the bar for in-game entertainment. These events, such as the Marshmello and

Travis Scott concerts, transformed the game into a virtual venue that can host millions of players simultaneously. These performances are choreographed with dynamic visuals and interactivity, offering players an experience that transcends typical gaming boundaries.

In-game events are often tied to storylines or updates, keeping the community engaged and eagerly anticipating what's next. These spectacles not only provide entertainment but also highlight what is possible when technology and creativity intersect. Fortnite's live events capture the imagination of gamers and non-gamers alike, setting a precedent for how digital spaces can be creatively leveraged for large-scale engagement.

The game's cultural references and collaborations with other brands keep it in the public eye consistently.

Fortnite's lasting presence in the limelight is partly due to its adept use of cultural references and strategic collaborations. Epic Games continuously integrates recognizable characters from movies, comics, and other video games, such as Spider-Man and Kratos from God of War. These collaborations create a sense of novelty and excitement, constantly refreshing the game's content and maintaining player interest.

Moreover, seasonal updates often align with cultural events, be it Halloween, Christmas, or movie premiers, allowing players to engage with the game in a contextually relevant manner. These constant infusions of fresh content and familiar themes ensure that Fortnite remains a topic of conversation, both within and outside the gaming community. This savvy integration of pop culture with gameplay secures Fortnite's position as a significant cultural touchstone in the modern entertainment landscape.

Economic Impact

Fortnite's business model and revenue generation strategies have had significant effects on the gaming industry.

Fortnite popularized the free-to-play model with in-game purchases, leading to massive profits.

Fortnite's success largely stems from its innovative approach to monetization through the free-to-play model. By eliminating upfront costs, Epic Games made Fortnite accessible to a vast audience. This strategy was coupled with ingame purchases, allowing players to buy cosmetic items like skins, emotes, and weapons. These microtransactions generated significant revenue, contributing to Fortnite's financial success.

The decision to focus on cosmetics rather than gameplay advantages ensured a fair experience for all players, maintaining engagement across the player base. This model not only maximized profits but also encouraged similar business strategies in other games across the industry.

It introduced the Battle Pass system, which encourages players to engage with game content over a season.

Fortnite revolutionized player engagement with the introduction of the Battle Pass system. This incentive-based feature offered tiers of rewards that players could unlock by completing challenges and earning experience points. By structuring it over a defined season, players were encouraged to spend more time in the game to unlock exclusive cosmetics, ensuring regular gameplay participation.

The strategic design of the Battle Pass not only extended gameplay longevity but also fostered community interaction as players shared their progress and sought to complete challenges together. Many games have since adopted similar systems, recognizing the blend of player reward and content longevity Fortnite perfected.

Epic Games' aggressive marketing and partnerships led to successful brand collaborations and merchandise.

Epic Games adeptly used its marketing prowess to elevate Fortnite's presence beyond the digital realm. Through partnerships with brands like Marvel, DC, and numerous musicians, Fortnite seamlessly integrated pop culture elements into the game. These collaborations resulted in unique in-game events and sought-after cosmetic items that fueled community excitement.

Additionally, Epic capitalized on Fortnite's popularity by expanding into physical merchandise, offering branded apparel, toys, and collectibles. These initiatives broadened Fortnite's reach and established a diversified revenue stream, strengthening its position in the entertainment industry.

Fortnite's success led Epic Games to pursue legal changes in app store policies, challenging industry norms.

Fortnite's ambition extended beyond gaming, as Epic Games embarked on a mission to reform app store policies. In August 2020, Epic strategically challenged Apple and Google by introducing a direct payment system in Fortnite, circumventing the standard app store revenue cut. This led to legal battles aimed at altering how platform holders charge developers.

The dispute spotlighted the contentious topic of revenue sharing in digital marketplaces, pushing for favorable terms for developers. Epic's stand against industry norms highlighted the significant influence and financial clout Fortnite provided, which many developers viewed as a potential catalyst for change.

The game's revenue enabled significant investment into Unreal Engine advancements, benefiting other developers.

Fortnite's financial triumph allowed Epic Games to reinvest in its versatile Unreal Engine, a cornerstone in game development technology. These investments meant significant advancements in engine capabilities, including improved graphics, physics, and rendering techniques.

Such enhancements benefitted developers worldwide, as Unreal Engine remained a popular choice for creating visually stunning and efficient games. Beyond gaming, sectors like film and virtual reality also leveraged these developments, showing Fortnite's wider impact on technological innovation.

Fortnite paved the way for other games to follow the free-to-play model with optional cosmetics and battle passes.

Fortnite’s success story served as a blueprint for numerous games seeking to tap into the lucrative free-to-play market. The model of providing a free base game, supplemented by optional purchases for cosmetics and seasonal battle passes, became widely adopted.

This structure altered the industry landscape, as developers discovered financial viability without relying on initial game sales. Fortnite illustrated that engaging content and community-driven progression could sustain a title economically over time, influencing a generation of game designers to prioritize player engagement and monetization compatibility.

Criticisms and Controversies

Despite its popularity, Fortnite has faced its share of criticisms and controversies. Let's look at some of them.

The game has been criticized for its addictive nature, especially among younger players.

Fortnite's captivating gameplay loop has proven particularly alluring to younger audiences, raising concerns among parents and educators. The game's addictive mechanisms, such as the constant rewards and in-game incentives, often keep players engaged for extended periods. These elements can lead to excessive screen time, affecting social interactions and academic performance.

Moreover, the introduction of competitive elements and frequent events that encourage players to return daily exacerbates this issue. Mental health professionals and researchers have debated the long-term consequences of such engagement, noting potential impacts on attention spans and lifestyle habits. While Fortnite is hardly the first game to employ these tactics, its global popularity has amplified these concerns.

Microtransactions and their impact on players with addictive tendencies have raised concerns.

Microtransactions in Fortnite, primarily through the purchase of V-Bucks (the in-game currency), have sparked significant debate. While the game is free-to-play, its business model capitalizes on in-app purchases, which can be particularly enticing for players with addictive tendencies. The allure of limited-time skins, emotes, and other cosmetic items often creates a sense of urgency to buy.

This monetization strategy can lead to excessive spending, especially among younger players who might use their parents' credit cards. Critics argue that these practices undermine the gaming experience by prioritizing revenue over player welfare, highlighting the need for greater control and transparency regarding in-game purchases to protect susceptible users.

Some players and critics have pointed to a lack of innovation in more recent updates.

While Fortnite began with groundbreaking mechanics combining battle royale elements with building, some players and critics have noted stagnation in innovation over time. Initial updates introduced diverse elements and new gameplay experiences, yet recent iterations appear to recycle existing concepts with minimal groundbreaking changes.

This perceived lack of creativity could risk alienating its dedicated player base, eager for fresh content and challenges. As competing games explore new mechanics and genres, Fortnite faces pressure to innovate continually to maintain its relevance and prevent players from seeking alternative experiences. Epic Games must balance meeting player expectations with innovative development to sustain its leading position.

Epic Games has faced legal battles over dance emotes, accused of appropriating artists' works without credit.

Fortnite's dance emotes, enjoyed by millions, have also placed Epic Games in legal hot water. Various artists and creators have accused the company of replicating their choreography without acknowledgment or proper compensation. Lawsuits filed by celebrities such as Alfonso Ribeiro, known for "The Carlton," and rapper 2 Milly highlight the challenges regarding intellectual property and artistic rights in gaming.

These legal disputes underscore the ongoing tension between gaming companies and original content creators. As gaming continues integrating real-world cultural elements, ethical considerations will play an increasing role in how game developers design content, emphasizing respect for artistry and creativity.

The competitive environment has sparked debate over balance issues and the game's casual appeal.

Fortnite's competitive scene has grown exponentially, yet it has sparked discussions about balance and accessibility. Epic Games consistently updates the game, striving to maintain fairness while introducing new items and mechanics. However, these updates can disrupt the balance, creating advantages for certain players and leading to frustration within the community.

The dichotomy between catering to skilled, competitive players and maintaining a laid-back, enjoyable experience for casual gamers is a difficult line to tread. As tournaments and esports gain traction, the importance of balance becomes ever more crucial, requiring meticulous consideration by developers to ensure both competitive integrity and broad appeal.

Fortnite's immense popularity has sometimes overshadowed smaller games, impacting indie developers.

Fortnite's colossal success has inadvertently impacted the indie gaming community, overshadowing smaller titles that often struggle for exposure. The game's prominence draws significant player attention and media coverage, potentially limiting the visibility of innovative indie games that might otherwise benefit from a broader audience.

This phenomenon exacerbates the challenge indie developers face in a competitive market dominated by blockbuster titles. While some indie games have thrived despite this environment, the industry struggles to adapt, highlighting the need for platforms that champion diverse gaming experiences and celebrate smaller-scale successes alongside major gaming milestones.

The Legacy of Fortnite

Fortnite's legacy is assured in gaming history, having influenced both the industry and culture.

The game set new standards for live service games with its continuous updates and events.

Fortnite revolutionized the live service game model by delivering consistent, novel updates and in-game events that kept the player base engaged. Epic Games, the developer, understood the necessity of keeping content fresh and exciting. The incorporation of seasonal events, interactive storylines, and surprise crossovers with popular media franchises like Marvel and Star Wars set new expectations for live game operations.

This approach not only retained existing players but also attracted new audiences. The live events, such as the iconic "The End" event during Chapter 2's launch, became major online spectacles, drawing millions of concurrent viewers. By setting such a high bar for engagement and content delivery, Fortnite redefined how games as a service could be executed, influencing countless other games in the industry.

Its success demonstrated the viability of the free-to-play model without sacrificing quality or engagement.

Fortnite's overwhelming success showcased the potential of the free-to-play (F2P) model when executed with finesse. Unlike many earlier F2P games, which were often criticized for being "pay-to-win," Fortnite offered a genuinely balanced experience. It generated revenue through optional cosmetic items, emotes, and seasonal battle passes, allowing players to enhance their avatars without affecting gameplay fairness.

This model proved incredibly lucrative, propelling Fortnite to become a financial powerhouse. It demonstrated to developers and publishers that quality and extensive player engagement could coexist with a free-to-play structure. As a result, numerous titles have adopted similar monetization strategies, reshaping the financial landscape of the gaming industry.

Fortnite has paved the way for further innovation in multiplayer and social gaming experiences.

Fortnite broke new ground in multiplayer gaming by seamlessly integrating social experiences into its core gameplay. Players weren't just engaging in battle royale matches; they were participating in in-game concerts, movie screenings, and cultural phenomena. Events like the Travis Scott concert and the screening of Christopher Nolan films turned Fortnite into a social platform, not just a game.

This innovative blend of gameplay and social interaction laid the groundwork for subsequent innovations in multiplayer experiences. Developers have since explored similar avenues, creating environments where players can interact socially as part of the gaming experience. Fortnite's success has underscored the importance of building communities within games, influencing the design of games to promote social interaction and connection.

Its impact is evident in how other games have adopted similar models and strategies to engage players.

Many games that emerged in the wake of Fortnite's rise have adopted its successful strategies. Titles in various genres have replicated Fortnite's model of frequent updates, seasonal events, and cultural tie-ins to maintain interest and engagement. This approach to player retention has become a staple industry practice, deeply influencing game development strategies across the board.

Moreover, Fortnite's monetization model — where revenue is primarily driven by cosmetics and battle passes — has been widely adopted. Games like Apex Legends and Call of Duty: Warzone have utilized these strategies to similar success. This trend highlights Fortnite’s vast influence and the profound shifts it has triggered within the industry, particularly regarding player engagement and monetization practices.

Fortnite's innovation in cross-platform play has become an industry standard, benefiting players worldwide.

One of Fortnite's most lauded innovations was its emphasis on cross-platform play. By bridging gaps between consoles, PCs, and mobile devices, Fortnite ensured that players could engage with one another regardless of the hardware they owned. This became a significant selling point and a competitive advantage, fostering a more unified player community.

This breakthrough in cross-platform capability has since set new expectations within the industry. More games now offer similar experiences, allowing players from various platforms to interact seamlessly. Fortnite's leadership in championing cross-platform play has, therefore, led to a more inclusive gaming environment, benefiting millions of players worldwide by removing traditional barriers to online interaction.

As of today, Fortnite continues to evolve, maintaining its position as a leading game in the industry.

Even after several years post-launch, Fortnite continues to be at the forefront of innovation in the gaming industry. Epic Games' commitment to evolving the game is evident in their persistent content updates, constant improvements, and attention to community feedback. Each new season brings a wave of excitement, with new mechanics, maps, and collaborations with popular IPs introduced regularly.

The game remains a cultural touchstone, frequently appearing in discussions around game design, marketing, and entertainment integration. Its ongoing adaptation and resilience showcase its ability to stay relevant amidst evolving gaming landscapes, affirming Fortnite's status as a seminal title in modern gaming history. The game’s continuous evolution ensures its legacy is not only cemented but thriving.